Geopolitics and the Decline of Empire

For

Marlene Anne

In a world that seems like oatmeal,
a chocolate-chip cookie.

Geopolitics and the Decline of Empire

Implications for United States Defense Policy

by
George M. Hall

McFarland & Company, Inc., Publishers
Jefferson, North Carolina, and London

Grateful acknowledgment is made to the following sources for permission to reprint excerpts.

Council of Foreign Relations: "Camp David—The Unfinished Business," by Abba Eban. Copyright 1978 by the Council of Foreign Relations, Inc. Reprinted by permission of *Foreign Affairs* (Winter 1978).

Doubleday & Company, Inc.: *Gettysburg,* copyright 1974 by Bruce Catton. *Never Call Retreat,* copyright 1965 by Bruce Catton. *Mandate for Change 1953–1956,* copyright 1963 by Dwight D. Eisenhower. *Seven Pillars of Wisdom,* by T.E. Lawrence; copyright 1926 by Doubleday & Company, Inc.

Encyclopaedia Britannica, Inc.: *1989 Britannica Book of the Year, World Data Section.* Copyright 1989 by Encyclopaedia Britannica, Inc. Reprinted by permission.

J.M. Dent & Everyman's Library, London, England, and Encyclopaedia Britannica, Inc.: *Thucydides: The History of the Peloponnesian War,* translated by Richard Crawley, revised by R. Feetham. Copyright 1952 by Encyclopaedia Britannica.

Merriam-Webster, Inc.: From *Webster's Ninth New Collegiate Dictionary.* Copyright 1988 by Merriam Webster Inc. Reprinted by permission.

Newsweek, Inc.: From George F. Will's column, January 16, 1989, and from "Sticker Shock: The Stealth Is a Bomb," by Gregg Easterbrook, January 23, 1989. Copyright 1989 by Newsweek, Inc.

Princeton University Press: Carl Von Clausewitz, *On War,* edited and translated by Michael Howard and Peter Paret. Copyright 1976 by Princeton University Press. Reprinted by permission.

Simon & Schuster, Inc.: *New World Dictionary of the American Language.* Copyright 1988 by Simon & Schuster, Inc.

William Heinemann, Ltd., London: *The Brothers Karamazov* by Fyodor M. Dostoevsky, translated by Constance Garnett. Copyright 1952 by Encyclopaedia Britannica, Inc.

W.W. Norton and Company, Inc.: *Present at the Creation.* Copyright 1969 by Dean Acheson. Reprinted by permission.

British Library Cataloguing-in-Publication data are available

Library of Congress Cataloguing-in-Publication Data

Hall, George M. (George Morgan), 1935–
    Geopolitics and the decline of empire : implications for United States defense policy / by George M. Hall.
        p.   cm.
    Includes bibliographical references and index.
    ISBN 0-89950-538-4 (50# alkaline paper : lib. bdg.) ∞
    1. United States—Military policy.   2. Geopolitics.   3. Balance of power.   4. United States—Foreign relations—1945–   5. World politics—1945–   I. Title.
UA23.H33   1990
355'.033073—dc20   90-52638
                                                                    CIP

Manufactured in the United States of America

McFarland & Company, Inc., Publishers
    Box 611, Jefferson, North Carolina 28640

Table of Contents

Preface

Like many books, this one started out as an article, expanded into a monograph and eventually grew into full length. The underlying argument — that the more powerful nations have evolved into a kind of geopolitical checkmate, a situation which has major implications for defense policy — developed from pursuing the courses of study at the three senior colleges: the Air War College, the Army War College, and the Naval War College, and also the short course offered by the National Defense University. For the most part, this study was accomplished courtesy of the U.S. Postal Service over an eight-year period. Fortunately, these programs had little overlap and thus offered a wide range of perspectives into the subjects of national power and war. Unfortunately, only the Naval War College seemed to approach the crux of the relationship and none of them paid much attention to geopolitics.

The impetus for the argument goes back 12 years when I was teaching the U.S. Army Command and General Staff College course to a class of active-duty officers at Fort Leonard Wood, Missouri. At the time, the course included a subcourse on national security. Among the materials was a major excerpt from Frederick Hartmann's *Relations of Nations* on the elements of national power. The bottom line, according to Hartmann, was that military power should be considered the proverbial tip of the national power iceberg. When a nation invests too many of its resources in military power, it overtaxes the supporting base of its national power. Bruce Catton, referring in *Never Call Retreat* to the plight of the Confederacy, captured the essence of that problem in one sentence: "One thing that made it impossible to enlarge the armies was the number of men exempt and on detail; one thing that made it impossible to feed and clothe the armies properly was the fact that not enough men were exempt and on detail, so that railroads and wagon lines and processing plants and mills operated badly; and one thing that caused desertions was the fact that the armies were poorly fed and clothed." (p. 404)

Some years later, I was discussing World War II with an old friend who had escaped from the Nazi occupation of his native Czechoslovakia, only to be forced to repeat the escape from the Soviet occupation less than ten years later. He said he initially doubted any kind of freedom would remain in Europe, until the day Germany attacked Russia. At that point, he recognized that Germany's reach had exceeded her grasp and that she would eventually be defeated. That is, while the Soviet military forces were in disarray at the time, the elements of Russia's raw national power were massive compared to Germany's. In time those resources could be brought to bear, and, of course, they were. His observation crystallized my thinking.

A few problems arose in writing this book. One was interpreting the significance of current events in light of the argument. These events were often dramatic and command attention, but most of them either fade in the presence of the structured mass of geopolitics or only serve to strengthen the argument, particularly the growing independence of the countries that until recently were considered firmly entrenched in the Soviet bloc. On the other hand, while the coming of the geopolitical spring in Europe is a welcome event and warrants further discounting of Communism as an ideological force, those discounts do not apply to Soviet military force. To disregard that force is to risk Soviet hegemony in Europe without their firing a shot.

A second problem was the subtitle of the book, "Implications for United States *Defense* Policy." By all rights it should have been "Implications for *Foreign* Policy," but two reasons prevent it. First, I am not qualified by education or experience to write in that field. Second, most significant foreign policy initiatives seem to arise ultimately from balance-of-power considerations, which boil down to defense policy.

Lastly, the problem of remaining completely objective, and letting the facts speak for themselves, proved difficult. No matter how hard a writer tries to reach this goal, a personal outlook will often work its way into the analysis. However, the reader of this work is likely to feel more inundated with data than badgered with opinion. At any rate, the mass of facts makes it difficult to avoid concluding that if geography—in the largest sense of that word—does not equate with the destiny of nations, it is certainly the most dominant gene. For this reason, it is imperative that geopolitics play a larger role in the formulation of defense policy.

A Note on Terminology

As far as possible obscure terms are either avoided or, when used, defined. However, several common terms are confusing in their own right, especially those relating to the Department of Defense. The term *Department of Defense* (DOD), or alternately *Defense* (capitalized), means the largely civilian-staffed superstructure imposed over the separate services.

The *Joint Chiefs of Staff* (JCS), per se, comprise the Chief of Staff of the Army, the Chief of Staff of the Air Force, the Chief of Naval Operations, and the Commandant of the Marine Corps, and are superintended, when serving in their joint capacity, by the Chairman and Vice Chairman of the JCS. The Chairman and the Vice Chairman also command the *Organization of the Joint Chiefs of Staff* (OJCS). The OJCS is a 1,600-member organization with its own full-time senior-general-officer staff.

The *separate services* are the Departments of the Army, the Navy and the Air Force. The expression *defense establishment* (not capitalized) combines DOD and the separate services but refers primarily to those elements located in the Washington, D.C., area and is synonymous with "the Pentagon," though the defense establishment now occupies all or part of more than 50 buildings (as can be inferred from the Department of Defense telephone directory). The word *defense,* when not capitalized, is used when referring to the entire structure of the armed forces worldwide. However, this word is also used in a military context. The term *secretariat* refers to that of Defense except when specified as the secretariat of a particular service.

The working relationships among all these components is not precise and is vaguely analogous to the dynamics of tides, with the separate services being gradually pushed into tidal estuary status. This complexity arises from unique historical roots. In 1947, the cabinet-level Departments of the Army and of the Navy, and the concurrently created Department of the Air Force, were subordinated to the newly created Department of Defense. However, the real decision-making power remained with the separate services. Accordingly, the civilian bosses of each service retained the title "Secretary" (and remained in the cabinet until 1958). During the succeeding 43 years, a series of defense establishment reorganizations and other measures gradually strengthened DOD and OJCS at the expense of the separate services, yet to this day the services retain their own secretariats and their own military chains of command for those functions not explicitly exercised by DOD and OJCS via various unified and specified commands. All things considered, this ambiguity may be unavoidable and thus the confusion remains.

Another set of difficult terms are *strategy, strategic,* and *strategist.* They are ubiquitous in the defense literature, but the usage lacks consistency and hints at abuse. Virtually every locale on earth, with the possible exception of Pitcairn Island, has been identified at one time or another as being of "strategic" importance to the United States. This situation is unfortunate because good definitions are readily available. For example, *Webster's Ninth New Collegiate Dictionary* defines strategy with great clarity: (1) "the science and art of employing the political, economic, psychological, and military forces of a nation or group of nations to afford the maximum support to adopted policies in peace or war" and (2) "the science and art of military command exercised to meet the enemy in combat under advantageous conditions." (p. 1165).

Because these terms are used inconsistently, the text excludes them except in reference to a document or system name, e.g. *Strategic Defense Initiative, strategic missiles,* and *strategic lift.* Instead, terms like *national defense policy* and *operational principles* are used. The definitions of these terms match the dictionary definitions quoted above with one subtle difference. The dictionary uses the word "employing" for the national perspective, implying a form of geopolitical offensive, whereas this book argues that many defense objectives can be attained by maintaining the equilibrium.

For similar reasons, the expression *national security* is avoided, except for a few references to the *National Security Council* and the President's *National Security Advisor.*

Another term that is often misunderstood is *casualties.* This term commonly equates with *fatalities,* but in the Defense literature the former includes the wounded. Accordingly, the Defense definition is maintained.

The final term is *parameters,* which capitalized is the name of the Journal of the U.S. Army War College, and is often inferred to mean "limits." The more accurate meaning is closer to a set of properties or factors which determine the dynamics or behavior of a system or paradigm. This book relies heavily on that connotation. By way of analogy, only a few of the many rules governing every competitive sport account for the degree of offense or defense in the respective game or match. In baseball, these parametric rules would be the three-strike/four-balls rule, the three-outs rule, the distance between the bases, and the more-or-less minimum distance to the outfield wall. True, such rules are inherently "limits," but these limits set the tone of the sport. And so it is with geopolitics, wherein a relative handful of parameters set the tone for how much offense and how much defense the international scene will likely witness.

An Overview

The complexity of the subject matter of this book compelled its subdivision into five major parts, some of which are supported by appendixes. Unfortunately but of necessity, the first two parts do not logically flow from one to the other.

Part I concentrates on the science and art of geopolitics and the eight elements of national power. The common theme is that geography, in the broadest sense of that word and notwithstanding the always underestimated force of ideology and the proliferation of thermonuclear power, means that a relative handful of nations will eventually gain the upper hand in terms of international clout. The analysis is supported by extensive statistical data, suggesting that "eventually" is "now."

Part II of necessity breaks from this chain of thought and instead focuses on the nature of war, beginning with its anatomy and growing into the principal sub-thesis of this book, namely that the use of military force is subject to reaching a culminating point, beyond which it begs defeat. Moreover, that point seems to be moving ever closer to practitioners of aggrandizement, as well as those with a penchant for coming to the rescue of distressed lesser nations. The critical argument here is that the United States has never understood how small a battlefield role she played in World War II (though her logistical contributions to the war effort were enormous), and as a result developed an exaggerated perception on the efficacy of war as an instrument of policy.

Part III picks up on this theme of the culminating point, which combined with many other considerations, suggests that with the exception of a few potential contingencies, the global equilibrium resulting from the interaction of geopolitics and national power is likely to remain permanent. However, those "few potential contingencies" are not to be underestimated.

Part IV then applies this logic to defense concerns, first by reviewing the bidding on parameters and policy and then applying those didactics to a subdivision of defense concerns into five areas: nuclear deterrence; NATO, Korea and Japan; the Middle East; the balance of the world, and finally terrorism. This subdivision is somewhat arbitrary, but it does reflect the way defense policy is managed in practice, and somewhat brackets the consequences of policy failure.

Part V finishes the book with a look at two longer-range, subjective issues that pertain to all defense considerations. The first is that the large standing forces essential to maintain the equilibrium by way of deterrence comes packaged with the slow rot of idleness and an inappropriate itch for war. The second reconsiders the elusive pursuit of "peace," concluding that precedence should be given to the concept of international justice rather than peace itself.

The book is supported by five appendixes. Appendix A suggests that military technology follows an evolutionary cycle that increasingly favors the defense, thus enhancing the global equilibrium. Appendix B then looks at the differences between military operations and tactics, suggesting the judgment and persistence rather than battlefield heroism is what counts in the larger perspective. Next, Appendix C takes a more detailed look as at using mobilization as an instrument of deterrence rather than an after-thought, and Appendix D covers an automated decision support system for long-term defense funding and planning. Lastly, Appendix E provides some comparative chronological data on some of the elements of national power.

Part I
Empire, National Power and Geopolitics

Power more often than not is thought of in the pejorative sense, perhaps because it is so often abused or at least because it becomes more readily apparent when abused. In geopolitical terms, this abuse usually takes one of two forms — outright military invasion or economic aggrandizement backed up by military force. Both forms are encompassed by the term empire, and there have been many empires in the course of history. Yet all of those empires have collapsed, including the former military grip the Soviet Union held over six European nations. The ghost of empire appears only in China's suzerainty over isolated Tibet and in the handful of dependencies and territories — mostly small islands — still maintained by various salient powers. This is strange stuff in an era where enormous military power is concentrated in the hands of a few nations. Clearly, global conditions have changed to the point where military power has met its match, and that match is national power.

Unquestionably, military power remains a major facet of national power, but the study of the latter must go beyond armaments to the national fountainhead that sustains military force. This fountainhead includes the elements of geography and demographics, of economic prowess and technology, of national ethos and infrastructure, and of alliances among nations with common interests. Thus the absence of global wars during the past 45 years, and the unlikelihood of such wars in the future, can only be explained by the salient powers having become too powerful in the national sense to rely on war as a means of resolving conflicts among themselves. That is, war has become too expensive, not just in military terms, but in terms of what it would do to the reservoirs of national power.

Yet this still doesn't explain the absence of empires. Obviously, many of the third-world states lack the ability to deter or prevent aggrandizement, notwithstanding the *mujahedin,* who kept a sizable slice of Soviet military power at bay and eventually caused the Soviet Union to withdraw from Afghanistan. The explanation lies in part in the fact there isn't much territory left to colonize

1

without risking a major and largely futile war among the salient powers and their principal allies, the cost of which would far exceed the political and economic gains of the attempt at empire. Elsewhere — that is, where aggrandizement might be practiced without much risk of major war — the political and economic gains would be of questionable value, or what Francis Fukuyama, deputy director of policy and planning at the State Department, recently called "The End of History," meaning the end of geopolitical struggles.

Restating the case in more theoretical terms, a nation may attempt to apply what could be thought of as the art of geopolitics to rearrange or reconfigure the elements of national power, but those elements pose inherent limitations, which might be called the science of geopolitics. When art attempts to go beyond the ability of science to support it, the results usually prove ephemeral. This part of the book develops an understanding of the relationship between geopolitical art and science, which in turn becomes the basis for the subsequent parts. It is a difficult subject, of course, due to the wide range of the elements of national power and the even more complex spectrum of interactions and dynamics among those elements. Yet it must be undertaken if the favorable aspects of geopolitics are ever to be harnessed to the end of developing an effective defense policy at the least possible cost.

Chapter 1. The Argument

The true strength of a prince does not consist so much in
his ability to conquer his neighbors as in the difficulty they
find in attacking him.
— Montesquieu

The term *power* means the ability to make or resist change. In terms of
national power, resisting change includes the ability to successfully deter or
resist invasion or other forms of aggrandizement. That form of power is increasing for the preponderance of nations, at least for those with the lion's
share of natural assets. The significance is that the world may be experiencing
a more-or-less permanent balance of power. Military conflict has been rele-
gated, for the most part, to the relatively weaker nations outside this evolving
pattern of global stability or equilibrium. If this argument is correct it has major implications for the defense policy of the United States.

The argument is supported by the record of global conflict over the last
92 years. During the 47-year period 1898–1945, the United States engaged in
two world wars and numerous lesser conflicts, starting with the Spanish-
American war. In almost every case, she was victorious or successful as the case
may be. In the nearly equal 45-year period since that era, there have been no
world wars, and nothing on the horizon evinces a future war of that magnitude. Moreover, of the lesser conflicts in this period, the United States has compiled something short of a sterling record of accomplishment. This radical
change warrants a comprehensive analysis with sufficient leverage to extend the
reasoning into the foreseeable future. This analysis must address the elements
of national power, how those elements interact in international relations, and
why these complex relationships are evolving towards equilibrium.

Some elements of national power are better understood than others. The
elements of military strength, comprising both nuclear and conventional force,
are perhaps the most obvious, but others are of equal if not greater significance, including political infrastructure, economic vitality, geographical position and size, population, and technology. At times, the nonmilitary elements
may contribute the lion's share to an effective national defense. For example,
the insularity of the United States, combined with peaceful neighbors north
and south, was arguably a more dominant factor in national defense prior to

3

1941 than actual armed force. To this day, this insularity remains a major element of strength to resist any land invasion of the conterminous states.

National power, then, is an amorphous mixture of many elements. Those elements combine in different ways to enhance or weaken the pursuit or protection of national interests. A nation that has substantial economic leverage may at the same time be weak if not defenseless militarily. Further, in the past the national power of most nations has changed with the course of history. Many nations and empires have withered if not disappeared, supplanted by new nations or other nations grown strong. Many of these "new" powers have in turn succumbed to still other nations. Today, however, the rate of such change is slowing. Most of the larger and more powerful nations have reached a form of geopolitical maturity, at least in terms of their ability to deter aggrandizement. That failing, the price of war against them would inevitably prove too expensive.

For the sake of analysis this situation permits dividing all nations into two groups: the *salient powers* and the *minor states.* Salient powers are those who possess the bulk of the available geopolitical clout but for whom war as an instrument of policy has become too expensive and self-destructive, some more so than others. The "more so's," of course, are the *superpowers* – the United States and the Soviet Union. The others, which can be thought of as *major powers,* comprise China, Canada, Australia, Brazil, the European core of the North Atlantic Treaty Organization (NATO), and as a theoretical limit, India.

China's inclusion needs no further comment. Canada and Australia each possess land mass roughly equal to the United States and to China, are formally allied with the United States, have good geographical position, and evince very stable governments. Brazil is the dominant regional power in South America and has sufficient insularity to ward off invasion by any eastern hemispheric nation. India, though lacking alliances and favorable position, nevertheless has the world's second largest population and intractable poverty. Only a salient power could consider an invasion of India, ostensibly the Soviet Union or possibly China. But where is the profit of "investing" in that much destitution?

The inclusion of the European core of NATO as a composite power bears more comment. Five reasons apply. First, while the central NATO states may not unify politically, they are strongly interlocked by both military treaty and the Common Market, and if they did unify it would only serve to strengthen the argument. Second, the Common Market will become a single trading unit by 1992. Third, the probability of further war among these states is nil. Fourth, the residual threat posed by the Soviet Union will likely remain sufficient motivation to maintain NATO, at least for the near future. Fifth, the argument here focuses on the ability to deter aggrandizement. This does not detract from the unique ethnicities among the members, but in the event of an external attack, this divergence would quickly yield to the problem at hand.

The minor states — which outnumber the salient powers almost 20-to-1 — share what's left of the geopolitical clout. Moreover, these states can be sub-divided into two subgroups — the *buffer states* and the *remainder states.* Buffer states may not exert the same influence as the salient powers, but their semi-permanent alliance with one or more of the latter, or long-standing neutrality, or geographical isolation, significantly reduces the potential for becoming in-volved in a major or global war. Buffer states include the balance of the NATO membership, the former Warsaw Pact nations, all but one of the European neutrals, the balance of South America, about half of the Asian nations, and most of the island states strongly linked to salient powers.

By contrast, the remainder states — which comprise the numerical ma-jority of all nations and are so named because they must share the small remainder of global resources — lack the clout, alliances, or position to success-fully deter invasion, and some of them tend to be bent on regional aggrandize-ment. They include all of Central America, Africa, and the Middle East; the balance of the Asian nations; and most independent island states.

A Statistical Overview

Table 1 offers a statistical summary of the magnitude of some of the elements of national power among nations. The data strongly suggest why the global equilibrium is evolving. For starters, the salient powers and the buffer states combined encompass 70 percent of the earth's land surface (exclusive of Antarctica), include 77 percent of the world's population, command 88 per-cent of the military power as gauged by annual military expenditures, and con-trol 93 percent of the gross national product (GNP) and more than 95 percent of the discretionary resources, which are arbitrarily defined as a country's GNP minus $500 per person. This figure equates roughly with those resources not required to provide or trade for the means of bare subsistence.[1] To restate the case, as illustrated in figure 1:

- The superpowers, controlling 42 percent of the world's GNP and 61 percent of the world's military power, stand in virtual checkmate with respect to each other.
- The salient powers, which add six major powers to the superpowers, control 67 percent of the world's GNP and 77 percent of the military power. Thus for all practical purposes the superpower checkmate extends to all salient powers.
- When the assets of the buffer states are added to the salient powers, the resulting totals are as cited above, of which the 93 percent share of GNP and the 88 percent share of military power are overwhelming. War be-tween any salient power and any buffer state entails an unacceptable risk of global war with another salient power, and so is likely to be avoided.

MEASURES→ COUNTRIES	AREA [Sq Miles]	POPULATION [nearest1000]	GROSS NATIONAL PRODUCT Total Discretionary [All data in millions of $ U.S.]		MILITARY BUDGET
SUPERPOWERS					
United States	3,679,192	246,113,000	$4,221,750	$4,098,694	$265,800
Soviet Union	8,649,500	285,796,000	2,356,700	2,213,802	275,000
Subtotal	12,328,692	531,909,000	$6,578,450	$6,312,496	$540,800
Percentage	23.5%	10.4%	41.9%	45.8%	61.4%
MAJOR POWERS					
Australia	2,966,200	16,470,000	$190,470	$182,235	$5,105
Brazil	3,286,488	144,262,000	245,520	173,389	2,307
Canada	3,849,675	25,880,000	361,720	348,780	7,902
China	3,696,100	1,088,200,000	314,800	none	24,870
India	1,222,559	801,806,000	213,440	none	7,493
Central NATO	687,260	265,359,000	2,697,940	2,565,262	85,436
Subtotal	15,708,282	2,341,977,000	$4,023,890	$3,269,666	$133,113
Percentage	29.9%	45.9%	25.6%	23.7%	15.1%
SALIENT POWERS (Superpowers + Major Powers)					
Cumulative Total	28,036,974	2,873,886,000	$10,602,340	$9,582,162	$673,914
Percentage	53.4%	56.4%	67.5%	69.6%	76.6%
BUFFER STATES					
Mexico&Caribbean	761,558	87,104,000	$172,310	$128,765	$1,052
South America	3,589,541	142,103,000	229,620	158,569	6,471
Other NATO	622,236	113,824,000	307,980	251,069	9,074
Warsaw Pact	382,409	112,639,000	871,595	815,276	47,470
Other Europe	1,331,001	58,685,000	533,013	503,694	8,949
Hong Kong	403	5,683,000	37,360	34,519	[UK]
Indonesia	741,101	175,904,000	82,110	none	2,181
Japan	145,875	122,620,000	1,559,720	1,498,410	13,080
Malaysia	127,581	16,965,000	29,500	21,018	1,227
Mongolia	604,800	2,041,000	1,911	891	unknown
Nepal	56,827	18,004,000	2,640	none	32
North Korea	47,250	21,903,000	17,400	6,449	5,400
Pakistan	339,697	109,434,000	34,690	none	2,378
Singapore	240	2,641,000	19,160	17,840	1,196
South Korea	38,291	42,593,000	98,370	77,074	4,891
Pacific/Oceania	113,416	4,095,000	26,984	24,940	451
Subtotal	8,902,226	1,036,238,000	$4,024,363	$3,538,476	$103,852
Percentage	17.0%	20.3%	25.6%	25.7%	11.8%
SALIENT POWERS + BUFFER STATES					
Cumulative Total	36,939,200	3,910,124,000	$14,626,703	$13,120,638	$777,765
Percentage	70.4%	76.7%	93.1%	95.3%	88.4%
REMAINDER STATES					
CenAmer&Caribbean	288,830	53,560,000	$66,200	$40,162	$3,198
Africa & Cyprus	11,669,808	618,686,000	382,329	159,526	21,658
Middle East	2,409,638	135,291,000	429,442	365,661	68,266
Balance of Asia	861,795	316,555,000	166,445	78,373	8,684
Pacific/Oceania	321,186	64,069,000	39,794	7,774	759
Subtotal	15,551,257	1,188,161,000	$1,084,210	$651,496	$102,565
Percentage	29.6%	23.3%	6.9%	4.7%	11.7%
World Total	52,490,457	5,098,285,000	$15,710,913	$13,772,134	$880,330

Table 1. Summary Statistical Data on Comparative National Power. Source: *1989 Britannica Book of the Year, World Data Section,* pp. 746–751, 770–775, and 860–865. See also Table 2 in Chapter 2.

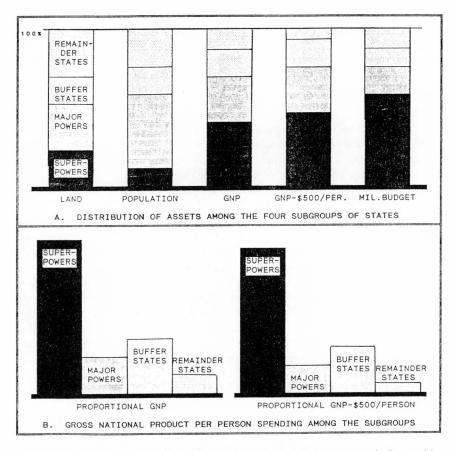

Figure 1. **Distribution of National Power.** Source: Data for the graphs is from tables in the *1989 Britannica Book of the Year, World Data Section,* pp. 746–751, 770–775, and 860–865.

- This leaves the remainder states, controlling less than 7 percent of the world's GNP and 12 percent of the military power. Over these economic gnomes do the giants squabble. About half of the remainder-state GNP and the bulk of its military power is concentrated in the Middle East, most nations of which avoid entangling alliances with either superpower. The superpower per capita GNP, which is about 12 times greater than the corresponding measure among the remainder states, is nearly 18 times greater if the Middle East is excluded.

Additionally, many of the remainder states are too weak to sustain much war among themselves, civil conflict excepted. When such wars do occur, the consequences seldom threaten the vital interests of the salient powers and buffer states, though the Middle East in particular offers some contingencies which might conflagrate into a major war under "worst case" conditions.

Implications and Significance

The implications of this paradigm are significant. They may not include a reduction of the competitive antagonism between the United States and the Soviet Union, but the equilibrium serves to deter escalation of that antagonism to outright war. The same may be said for the relationships among all the salient powers and buffer states. In fine, and aside from maintaining decisive deterrent postures, the military pickings for the superpowers are slim, confined essentially to the remainder states. Moreover, these pickings appear even slimmer when the sad record on the use of military force by the United States—and the Soviet Union for that matter—since the end of World War II is considered, a point discussed at some length in Chapter 8.

On the positive side of significance, the two superpowers have avoided nuclear conflict, while conventional war between them or with another salient power or buffer state has been essentially nil since 1953 and limited in the 1945–1953 period. The exceptions of the Soviet suppressions of the 1956 Hungarian Revolution and the 1968 Czechoslovakian "Prague Spring" were civil wars between a parent country and her then de facto satellites. The Cuban missile crisis in 1962 may have come close to war, but not a shot was fired.

Continuing, the Soviet invasion of Afghanistan in late 1979 may have been an outright case of aggrandizement, but Afghanistan should be considered a remainder state, and in any event the Soviet Union completely withdrew its military forces after eight years of futility. Further, while the United States openly supported the Afghan resistance fighters, the superpowers did not come to blows over the situation. Nor has the long-standing antagonism between the USSR and America's ally Japan, over the disposition of the Kuril Islands, led to any superpower conflict more serious than the trading of a few barbs.

On the negative side, armed conflict involving primarily the remainder states shows little sign of abatement. Wars and conflicts since World War II have caused 20,000,000 fatalities, most of which occurred in these states, especially from 1953 forward.[2] Moreover, the relative few that accrued to the other nation groups since that year did so almost entirely in civil conflicts, and those largely restricted to China, India, Indonesia, and Colombia, with most of the fatalities occurring more than 30 years ago.[3] Poverty, not ambition, now seems to be the paramount cause of war.

Another startling fact of armed conflict in this era is that nearly half of the fatalities have resulted from genocide, be it by direct means or by indirect means, e.g. by way of policies that exacerbate famine and other fatal environmental conditions.[4] This means that a much higher percentage of the total fatalities compared to previous eras are noncombatants. Returning to the analysis, then, the reasons which explain the historical evidence of the evolving equilibrium, at least among those nations which control the bulk of the world's available clout, virtually demand a hearing.

Chapter 2. Geopolitics as Science and Art

Geopolitics—1: the study of the influence of such factors as geography, economics, and demography on the politics and especially the foreign policy of a state. 2: a governmental policy guided by geopolitics.
—Webster's Ninth New Collegiate Dictionary

As implied by the dictionary definition, geopolitics can be divided into the study of the contributing elements (science) and what governments elect to do with those elements (art). Science focuses on magnitudes, configurations, and arrangements. The magnitudes—resources—of geopolitics comprise such items as land mass, population, and gross national product. Configurations would include the shape of a country, the density and distribution of its population, and the homogeneity or dispersion of its ethnicity. Arrangements would encompass the geographical position of a nation with respect to other nations, oceans, and waterways; alliances and treaties; international and domestic economic relationships; and the degree of cultural or ideological affinity within a state.

The art of geopolitics attempts to reconfigure or rearrange those resources to achieve some aim or purpose that would not occur by the natural course of events. Rearranging one's geography is a tall order, but it can and has been done by purchase or swapping of land, by outright aggrandizement, and by digging canals in the absence of waterways. Ideologies have been modified by revolutions, including attempts to foment revolutions in other nations. But there is a practical limit to how far a nation can push or modify its resources to attain international objectives. This is the stuff of "rise and fall" books, the latest installment of which is Paul Kennedy's *The Rise and Fall of the Great Powers*. Kennedy's thesis is that history demonstrates all great powers have declined and that many if not most accelerated the decline by an overextension of military and international economic involvement beyond the capacity of national resources to sustain such commitment.[1] He coined the expression *imperial overstretch*.

If Kennedy's thesis is on the mark for the future, the thesis of this book is moot. On the otherhand, history does not always repeat itself.[2] The concentration of national power in a handful of physically large and for the most part highly populated nations on a fixed globe augers against a new slate of empires. This does not mean the salient powers are immune to the consequences of bad judgment on a geopolitical scale. Any of them could somehow fatally weaken the magnitude or efficient arrangement of their resoures. Yet because the sheer size and scope of those resources enhances their internal resiliency, it would take a quantum leap in bad judgment for most salient powers to do themselves in. As will be developed later in this text, the Middle East offers a few opportunities to do just this.

Our analysis should begin with a closer look at the science of geopolitics. This science must confront three major hurdles. First, the relative or proportional influence among the resources—the elements of national power—depends on the aim or purpose to which they are applied. This is analogous to the periodic table of elements in chemistry. As fundamental and indispensable as that table is, it does not hint at the rich and varied number of compounds and the uses to which the compounds can be put. For the purpose of this analysis, however, the criterion of national power is straightforward—the ability of a nation to deter or resist military invasion or other form of forcible aggrandizement. To this end, the elements of national power, and their "compounds," are clear enough to support the categorization of nations as salient powers, buffer states, or remainder states, as the case may be.

The second hurdle is the difficulty of assessing the synergistic influence or its lack arising from the interactions among the elements. Some of these elements readily lend themselves to quantification, for example, population density and GNP per individual. But the effect of ideology or infrastructure, for example, can only be gauged by some rough indicator at best.

The third hurdle is the problem of projecting accurate trend lines for changes to the distribution of the elements of national power among various nations, for if the present distribution changes radically, then it follows the equilibrium might also undergo a radical weakening.

Perhaps a future scholar will develop a model that confronts and overcomes these hurdles and in the process create a field of study that might be called *powermetrics,* analogous to *econometrics.* The state of the art in computer technology, data base management software and expert systems would facilitate the work, as would the ability to test the model on historical data and events (paralleling the computer work now being done in econometrics). However, for the present the best that can be done is to perform a rudimentary qualitative analysis, comparing the degree or advantage existing for each element among different states, supported by a comparative analysis of statistical data.

Such an analysis would not be all that inaccurate. When a nation possesses all or nearly all of the elements of power in spades, fine tuning the analysis with tomes of data would not likely change a nation's status in the geopolitical order of things. Conversely, when a state evinces major deficiencies for most of the elements, it would be naive to consider it a nation to reckon with. Thus the analysis begins with a closer look at those elements which readily lend themselves to quantification: land mass, population, GNP, and military budgets.

World Statistical Data

Obtaining uncontestable, current worldwide statistical data is impossible except for land areas. There is no shortage of statistical compendiums, but few agree with each other to within a tenth of a percentage point. In terms of thoroughness, however, the *World Data Section* of the Encyclopaedia Britannica yearbooks appears to be the best and it was this source that was used. Data from the 1985 through 1989 editions were extracted, compiled, and compared in the text.* The worldwide percentage shares of land mass, among the subgroups, did not change by more than one-tenth of a percentage point among the five years; the population, by less than 1 percent. The GNP and military expenditure data changed by only 2 percent (in favor of the salient powers), and that due primarily to the method of calculating the GNP in Soviet bloc countries.

These data were also compared with similar data in the *World Fact Book,* compiled and issued annually by the Central Intelligence Agency.[3] For example, differences between the 1987 edition of that book and the 1987 Britannica yearbook were the rule more than the exception, but most of those differences were minor and the proportionality of the totals among the four subgroups was remarkably close. Unfortunately, the CIA reference does not list its sources, whereas the *Britannica* is scrupulous on this matter.

Table 2 presents the *Britannica* data on area, population, gross national product (GNP), discretionary GNP (GNP minus $500 U.S. equivalent per person), and annual military expenditure. In a few cases the GNP is really the gross domestic product. Negative discretionary GNPs were changed to "none." The table omits islands that are integral possessions of other states, e.g. the Azores (Portugal) and Canary Islands (Spain). It also omits the Vatican City and Pitcairn Island, which ironically represent the epitome of geopolitical establishment and anti-establishment thinking respectively. The GNP data lag the land mass and population data by two years; the military budget data, by three years. The lags are due the fact that authoritative compendiums from which the data are drawn are themselves two or three years in arrears. However,

---

*Appendix E includes 1990 data and makes comparisons for the six-year period.

MEASURES→ COUNTRIES	AREA [Sq Miles] 1988 Data	POPULATION [nearest 1000] 1988 Data	GROSS NATIONAL PRODUCT Total / Discretionary 1986/85 data in millions		MILITARY BUDGET of $ U.S.
SUPERPOWERS					
United States	3,679,192	246,113,000	$4,221,750	$4,098,694	$265,800
Soviet Union	8,649,500	285,796,000	2,356,700	2,213,802	275,000
Subtotal:	12,328,692	531,909,000	$6,578,450	$6,312,496	$540,800
World Percentage:	23.48%	10.43%	41.87%	45.84%	61.43%
MAJOR POWERS					
Australia	2,966,200	16,470,000	$190,470	$182,235	$5,105
Brazil	3,286,488	144,262,000	245,520	173,389	2,307
Canada	3,849,675	25,880,000	361,720	348,780	7,902
China	3,696,100	1,088,200,000	314,800	none	24,870
India	1,222,559	801,806,000	213,440	none	7,493
Central NATO	687,260	265,359,000	2,697,940	2,565,262	85,436
[Belgium]	11,783	9,865,000	91,010	86,078	2,414
[Denmark]	16,638	5,130,000	64,610	62,045	1,269
[France]	210,026	55,860,000	595,180	567,250	20,800
[Germany(FRG)]	96,026	60,782,000	735,940	705,549	20,800
[Italy]	116,324	57,401,000	489,880	461,180	10,010
[Luxembourg]	999	372,000	5,830	5,644	39
[TheNetherlands]	16,163	14,741,000	146,200	138,830	4,051
[Norway]	125,050	4,202,000	64,440	62,339	1,853
[United Kingdom]	94,251	57,006,000	504,850	476,347	24,200
MAJOR POWERS					
Subtotal:	15,708,282	2,341,977,000	$4,023,890	$3,269,666	$133,113
World Percentage:	29.93%	45.93%	25.61%	23.74%	15.12%
SALIENT POWERS					
Subtotal:	28,036,974	2,873,886,000	$10,602,340	$9,582,162	$673,913
World Percentage:	53.41%	56.36%	67.48%	69.58%	76.55%
BUFFER STATES NORTH AMERICA					
Bermuda	21	58,000	$1,140	$1,111	[UK]
Mexico	756,066	82,659,000	149,110	107,781	$1,052
StPierre&Miquelon	93	6,000	[Fr]	[Fr]	[Fr]
CARIBBEAN					
Anguilla	35	7,000	[UK]	[UK]	[UK]
Aruba, N.Antilles	383	243,000	860	739	[Neth]
British Virgin Is	59	12,000	98	92	[UK]
Cayman Islands	102	23,000	297	286	[UK]
Guadeloupe	687	340,000	1,110	940	[Fr]
Martinique	421	336,000	1,400	1,232	[Fr]
Montserrat	40	12,000	30	24	[UK]
Puerto Rico	3,515	3,301,000	17,190	15,540	[US]
VirginIslands(US)	136	107,000	1,075	1,022	[US]
SOUTH AMERICA					
Argentina	1,073,399	31,963,000	$72,920	$56,939	$2,368
Bolivia	424,164	6,993,000	3,540	none	171
Chile	292,135	12,750,000	16,200	9,825	760
Colombia	440,831	30,661,000	35,530	20,200	447
Ecuador	103,930	10,203,000	11,200	6,099	193
French Guiana	33,399	92,000	180	134	[Fr]
Guyana	83,000	757,000	400	22	34
Paraguay	157,048	4,007,000	3,360	1,357	65
Peru	496,225	21,256,000	21,540	10,912	1,388
Suriname	63,251	425,000	1,010	798	25
Trinidad & Tobago	1,978	1,258,000	6,170	5,541	204
Uruguay	68,037	2,981,000	5,630	4,140	134
Venezuela	352,144	18,757,000	51,940	42,562	682

Table 2. World Statistical Data. Sources: *1989 Britannica Book of the Year, World Data Section,* pp. 746–751, 770–775 and 860–865, which used the *World Bank Atlas 1988* (International Bank for Reconstruction and Development) for GNP data and *World Military Expenditures and Arms Transfers 1987* (U.S. Arms Control and Disarmament Agency) for military data.

MEASURES→ COUNTRIES	AREA [Sq Miles] 1988 Data	POPULATION [nearest1000] 1988 Data	GROSS NATIONAL PRODUCT 1986/85 data in millions Total	Discretionary	MILITARY BUDGET of $ U.S.
EUROPE					
Other NATO	622,236	113,824,000	307,980	251,069	9,074
[Greece]	50,949	10,055,000	36,690	31,663	2,506
[Iceland]	39,769	248,000	3,260	3,136	negligible
[Portugal]	35,672	10,349,000	22,880	17,706	650
[Spain]	194,898	38,996,000	188,030	168,532	3,502
[Turkey]	300,948	54,176,000	57,120	30,032	2,416
Warsaw Pact	382,409	112,639,000	871,595	815,276	47,470
[Bulgaria]	42,855	8,978,000	60,618	56,129	4,638
[Czechoslovakia]	49,382	15,604,000	142,550	134,748	7,923
[Germany (GDR)]	41,827	16,588,000	187,751	179,457	11,290
[Hungary]	35,919	10,591,000	83,806	78,511	3,536
[Poland]	120,727	37,864,000	259,524	240,592	14,610
[Romania]	91,699	23,014,000	137,346	125,839	5,473
Albania	11,100	3,149,000	2,800	1,226	143
Andorra	181	51,000	360	335	[Sp&Fr]
Austria	32,377	7,577,000	75,540	71,752	849
British Islands*	455	212,000	2,920	2,818	[UK]
Faeroe Islands	540	47,000	550	527	[Den]
Finland	130,559	4,952,000	60,040	57,564	772
Gibraltar	2	30,000	130	115	[UK]
Greenland	840,000	55,000	470	443	[Den]
Ireland	27,137	3,553,000	18,190	16,414	308
Liechtenstein	62	28,000	450	436	[Swtz]
Malta	122	347,000	1,240	1,067	11
Monaco	1	29,000	unknown	unknown	[Fr]
San Marino	24	23,000	188	177	negligible
Sweden	173,732	8,415,000	109,950	105,743	2,932
Switzerland	15,943	6,626,000	115,360	112,047	2,244
Yugoslavia	98,766	23,591,000	144,825	133,030	1,690
ASIA					
Hong Kong	403	5,683,000	$37,360	$34,519	[UK]
Indonesia	741,101	175,904,000	82,110	none	$2,181
Japan	145,875	122,620,000	1,559,720	1,498,410	13,080
Malaysia	127,581	16,965,000	29,500	21,018	1,227
Mongolia	604,800	2,041,000	1,911	891	unknown
Nepal	56,827	18,004,000	2,640	none	32
North Korea	47,250	21,903,000	17,400	6,449	5,400
Pakistan	339,697	109,434,000	34,690	none	2,378
Singapore	240	2,641,000	19,160	17,840	1,196
South Korea	38,291	42,593,000	98,370	77,074	4,891
PAC./INDIAN OCEANS					
American Somoa	77	38,000	190	171	[US]
BritIndianOcnTerr	31	none	none	none	[US/UK]
Christmas Island	52	2,000	[Aust]	[Aust]	[Aust]
Cocos Islands	6	1,000	[Aust]	[Aust]	[Aust]
Cook Islands	91	17,000	20	12	[NZ]
French Polynesia	1,359	188,000	1,370	1,276	[Fr]
Guam	209	126,000	670	607	[US]
New Caledonia	7,172	156,000	1,210	1,132	[Fr]
New Zealand	103,288	3,354,000	23,300	21,623	451
Niue	100	3,000	4	3	[NZ]
Norfolk Island	14	2,000	[Aust]	[Aust]	[Aust]
Pac.Is.Trust Terr	713	180,000	160	70	[US]
Tokelau	5	2,000	1	none	[NZ]
Turks & Caicos Is	193	11,000	49	44	[UK]
Wallis & Fortuna	106	16,000	10	2	[Fr]
BUFFER STATES					
Subtotal:	8,902,226	1,036,238,000	$4,024,363	$3,538,476	$103,852
World Percentage:	16.96%	20.33%	25.62%	25.69%	11.80%

*Guernsey, Isle of Man, Jersey, and St. Helena

Table 2. (continued)

MEASURES→ COUNTRIES	AREA [Sq Miles] 1988 Data	POPULATION [nearest1000] 1988 Data	GROSS NATIONAL PRODUCT Total Discretionary 1986/85 data in millions		MILITARY BUDGET of $ U.S.
SALIENT POWERS & BUFFER STATES					
Subtotal:	36,939,200	3,910,124,000	$14,626,703	$13,120,638	$777,765
World Percentage:	70.37%	76.69%	93.10%	95.27%	88.35%
REMAINDER STATES					
CENTRAL AMERICA					
Belize	8,867	178,000	$200	$111	$4
Costa Rica	19,730	2,672,000	3,790	2,454	33
El Salvador	8,124	5,083,000	4,000	1,459	254
Guatamala	42,042	8,681,000	7,640	3,300	174
Honduras	43,277	4,803,000	3,360	959	120
Nicaragua	49,363	3,622,000	2,670	859	702
Panama	29,762	2,322,000	5,190	4,029	102
CARIBBEAN&ATLANTIC					
Antigua & Barbuda	171	83,000	$190	$149	negligible
Bahamas,The	5,382	245,000	1,700	1,578	$9
Barbados	166	254,000	1,310	1,183	10
Cuba	42,804	10,421,000	26,920	21,710	1,600
Dominica	290	79,000	100	61	none
DominicanRepublic	18,704	6,850,000	4,680	1,255	142
Falkland Islands	4,700	2,000	[UK]	[UK]	[UK]
Grenada	133	106,000	120	67	negligible
Haiti	10,579	5,451,000	1,990	none	30
Jamaica	4,244	2,407,000	1,980	777	18
St Kitts	104	43,000	70	49	negligible
St Lucia	238	145,000	180	108	negligible
St Vincent & Gren	150	113,000	110	54	negligible
EUROPE					
Cyprus	3,572	720,000	2,920	2,560	31
AFRICA					
Algeria	919,595	23,849,000	58,040	46,116	1,364
Angola	481,350	9,386,000	6,930	2,237	690
Benin	43,450	4,443,000	1,140	none	24
Botswana	224,607	1,211,000	930	325	25
Burkina Faso	105,869	8,530,000	1,240	none	27
Burundi	10,747	5,131,000	1,140	none	33
Cameroon	179,714	11,206,000	9,580	3,977	156
Cape Verde	1,557	359,000	150	none	12
CentralAfricanRep	240,324	2,843,000	770	none	11
Chad	495,755	5,395,000	560	none	12
Comoros	719	433,000	130	none	[Fr]
Congo	132,047	2,266,000	2,020	887	69
Djibouti	8,950	484,000	302	60	27
Egypt	385,229	50,273,000	37,700	12,564	6,294
Equitorial Guinea	10,831	335,000	107	none	2
Ethiopia	472,400	47,501,000	5,400	none	411
Gabon	103,347	1,219,000	3,150	2,541	67
Gambia,The	4,127	811,000	180	none	2
Ghana	92,098	13,754,000	5,130	none	76
Guinea	94,926	6,540,000	1,950	none	60
Guinea-Bissau	13,948	931,000	150	none	6
Ivory Coast	123,847	11,634,000	7,730	1,913	76
Kenya	224,961	22,919,000	6,470	none	223
Lesotho	11,720	1,671,000	660	none	47
Liberia	38,250	2,427,000	1,030	none	28
Libya	685,524	4,316,000	26,980	24,822	5,225
Madagascar	226,658	10,917,000	2,390	none	56
Malawi	45,747	8,211,000	1,180	none	19
Mali	478,841	7,778,000	1,330	none	21
Mauritania	398,000	1,894,000	760	none	47
Mauritius	788	1,049,000	$1,240	$716	$2
Mayotte	144	78,000	[Fr]	[Fr]	[Fr]

Table 2. (continued)

MEASURES→ / COUNTRIES	AREA [Sq Miles] 1988 Data	POPULATION [nearest 1000] 1988 Data	GROSS NATIONAL PRODUCT 1986/85 data in millions	MILITARY BUDGET of $ U.S.	
			Total	Discretionary	
Morocco	177,117	23,809,000	13,160	1,256	780
Mozambique	308,642	14,890,000	3,030	none	164
Namibia/SoWestAfr	317,818	1,228,000	1,150	536	[S.Africa]
Niger	458,075	6,937,000	1,690	none	12
Nigeria	356,669	112,258,000	66,210	10,081	1,088
Reunion	982	575,000	2,120	1,833	[Fr]
Rwanda	10,169	6,709,000	1,820	none	31
SaoTome&Principe	386	117,000	40	none	1
Senegal	75,955	7,187,000	2,840	none	65
Seychelles	175	67,000	160	127	8
Sierra Leone	27,699	3,883,000	1,170	none	10
Somalia	246,000	6,334,000	1,560	none	89
South Africa	473,290	36,840,000	59,910	41,490	2,978
Sudan,The	966,757	26,263,000	7,290	none	144
Swaziland	6,704	716,000	470	112	8
Tanzania	364,881	23,996,000	5,370	none	193
Togo	21,925	3,486,000	780	none	20
Tunisia	59,684	7,877,000	8,340	4,402	301
Uganda	93,070	15,990,000	3,290	none	53
Western Sahara	97,344	189,000	[Morocco]	[Morocco]	[Morocco]
Zaire	905,365	32,559,000	5,070	none	81
Zambia	290,586	7,384,000	2,060	none	167
Zimbabwe	150,873	8,878,000	5,410	971	322
ASIA					
Bangladesh	55,598	107,756,000	16,070	none	253
Bhutan	18,150	1,365,000	200	none	negligible
Burma (Myanmar)	261,228	39,952,000	7,450	none	209
Kampuchea	69,898	7,876,000	600	none	68
Laos	91,400	3,850,000	765	none	55
Macau	7	466,000	1,030	none	[Portugal]
Maldives	115	202,000	60	none	negligible
Sri Lanka	25,332	16,606,000	6,460	none	167
Taiwan	13,900	19,813,000	73,270	63,364	4,740
Thailand	198,115	54,862,000	42,440	15,009	1,892
Vietnam	128,052	63,807,000	18,100	none	1,300
PACIFIC/OCEANIA					
Brunei	2,226	250,000	3,590	3,465	305
Fiji	7,056	742,000	1,280	909	16
Kiribati	328	68,000	21	none	negligible
Nauru, Tuvalu	17	17,000	165	157	negligible
Papua New Guinea	178,704	3,562,000	2,470	689	38
Philippines	115,860	58,723,000	31,820	2,459	400
Solomon Is, Tonga	11,255	396,000	220	22	[NZ]
Vanuatu	4,707	149,000	118	44	negligible
Western Somoa	1,093	162,000	110	29	[NZ]
MIDDLE EAST					
Afghanistan	251,825	14,481,000	$3,520	none	$287
Bahrain	267	421,000	3,670	$3,460	151
Iran	636,372	51,225,000	188,200	162,588	11,690
Iraq	169,235	16,630,000	34,470	26,155	15,920
Israel*	10,402	5,948,000	28,712	25,738	3,678
Jordan	34,443	2,965,000	4,220	2,738	719
Kuwait	6,880	1,958,000	24,650	23,671	1,513
Lebanon	3,950	2,828,000	5,000	3,586	429
Oman	120,000	1,372,000	6,440	5,754	2,157
Qatar	4,400	420,000	4,180	3,970	2,308
Saudi Arabia	865,000	12,972,000	83,270	76,784	22,900
Syria	71,498	11,338,000	16,980	11,311	4,512
United Arab Emir.	30,000	1,774,000	20,590	19,703	1,385
Yemen Arab Rep.	75,300	8,614,000	4,510	203	424
Yemen,Peo.Dem.Rep	130,066	2,345,000	1,030	none	193

*Includes the Gaza Strip and West Bank

Table 2. (continued)

MEASURES→ COUNTRIES	AREA [Sq Miles] 1988 Data	POPULATION [nearest1000] 1988 Data	GROSS NATIONAL PRODUCT Total 1986/85 data in millions	Discretionary	MILITARY BUDGET of $ U.S.
REMAINDER STATES minus the Middle East States					
Subtotal:	13,141,619	1,052,870,000	$654,768	$285,835	$34,299
World Percentage:	25.04%	20.65%	4.17%	2.08%	3.90%
MIDDLE EAST STATES					
Subtotal:	2,409,638	135,291,000	$429,442	$365,661	$68,266
World Percentage:	4.59%	2.65%	2.73%	2.65%	7.75%
ALL REMAINDER STATES					
Subtotal:	15,551,257	1,188,161,000	$1,084,210	$651,496	$102,565
World Percentage:	29.63%	23.31%	6.90%	4.73%	11.65%
WORLD DATA [exclusive of Antarctica]					
Total:	52,490,457	5,098,285,000	$15,710,913	$13,772,134	$880,330
World Percentage:	100.00%	100.00%	100.00%	100.00%	100.00%

RECAPITULATION ON PERCENTAGES BY SUBGROUPS

SUPERPOWERS	23.48%	10.43%	41.87%	45.84%	61.43%
MAJOR POWERS	29.93%	45.93%	25.61%	23.74%	15.12%
BUFFER STATES	16.96%	20.33%	25.62%	25.69%	11.80%
REMAINDER STATES	29.63%	23.31%	6.90%	4.73%	11.65%
WORLD	100.00%	100.00%	100.00%	100.00%	100.00%

Table 2. (continued)

because the land mass data are essentially constant and the population data nearly so in proportional terms, the effect of the chronological lags is moot.

Table 3 extends the logic of discretionary GNP to military expenditures. If it is assumed that relatively low per capita military budgets can support only local defense, then global military force would be a function of expenditure above this minimal amount. Similarly, if it assumed that low defense budgets based on both land mass and population can support only local defense, then global military power would exist only above that floor. The question is, at what point do military budgets become global in their implications? That is difficult to answer, and accordingly the table provides data for a few arbitrarily selected limits. Figure 2 extends this demonstration to a wider range of factors. As the military budget setoffs are increased, the distribution of the remaining, presumably global military power among the subgroups shifts to the point where the superpowers demonstrate an even greater dominance. The Middle East states also give some evidence of global military power, but not much in comparison with the superpowers.

MEASURES→ COUNTRIES	MILITARY BUDGET	EXCESS OVER POPULATION Factor * $100/person			EXCESS OVER LAND & POP. Factor*($5K/SqMi+$50/pers)		
		1.0	2.5	5.0	1.0	2.5	5.0
SUPERPOWERS							
United States	$265,800	$241,188	$204,271	$142,743	$235,098	$189,045	$112,291
Soviet Union	275,000	246,420	203,551	132,102	217,462	131,156	0
Subtotal	$540,800	$487,608	$407,822	$274,845	$452,860	$319,560	$112,291
Percentage	61.4%	72.9%	81.4%	88.5%	70.5%	74.0%	74.6%
MAJOR POWERS							
Australia	$5,105	$3,458	$987	$0	$0	$0	$0
Brazil	2,307	0	0	0	0	0	0
Canada	7,902	5,314	1,432	0	0	0	0
China	24,870	0	0	0	0	0	0
India	7,493	0	0	0	0	0	0
Central NATO	85,436	58,895	23,554	0	68,727	43,927	12,379
Subtotal	$133,113	$67,667	$25,973	$0	$68,727	$43,927	$12,379
Percentage	15.1%	10.1%	5.2%	.0%	10.7%	10.2%	8.2%
BUFFER STATES							
Latin America	$7,523	$78	$0	$0	$131	$22	$0
Other NATO	9,074	1,500	0	0	2,325	612	0
Warsaw Pact	47,470	36,203	19,590	3,266	39,922	28,608	12,331
Other Europe	8,949	4,038	1,415	0	3,798	1,216	188
Indonesia	2,181	0	0	0	0	0	0
Japan	13,080	818	0	0	6,219	0	0
North Korea	5,400	3,209	0	0	4,068	2,071	0
Pakistan	2,378	0	0	0	0	0	0
South Korea	4,891	631	0	0	2,569	0	0
Other Asia	2,455	931	535	0	1,062	862	529
Oceania	451	116	0	0	0	0	0
Subtotal	$103,852	$47,524	$21,540	$3,266	$60,094	$33,391	$13,048
Percentage	11.8%	7.1%	4.3%	1.1%	9.4%	7.3%	8.7%
REMAINDERS							
Latin America	$3,198	$896	$0	$0	$1,138	$0	$0
Africa&Cyprus	21,658	6,060	4,146	3,067	3,438	0	0
Asia	8,684	2,758	0	0	3,679	2,089	0
Oceania	759	280	242	180	281	245	186
Subtotal	$34,299	$9,994	$4,388	$3,247	$8,536	$2,334	$186
Percentage	3.9%	1.5%	.9%	1.1%	1.3%	.5%	.1%
MIDDLE EAST	$68,226	$56,372	$41,313	$29,324	$52,101	$31,972	$12,635
Percentage	7.7%	8.4%	8.2%	9.4%	8.1%	7.4%	8.4%
TOTAL	$880,330	$669,165	$501,036	$310,682	$642,018	$431,825	$150,539
Percentage	100.0%	100.0%	100.0%	100.0%	100.0%	100.0%	100.0%
Rel.Percentage	100.0%	76.0%	56.9%	35.2%	72.9%	49.1%	17.1%

Table 3. Pragmatic Calculations of Global Military Power. All data are in millions of dollars U.S. Source: *1989 Britannica Book of the Year, World Data Section,* pp. 860–865, for the first column of data. All other data are computed.

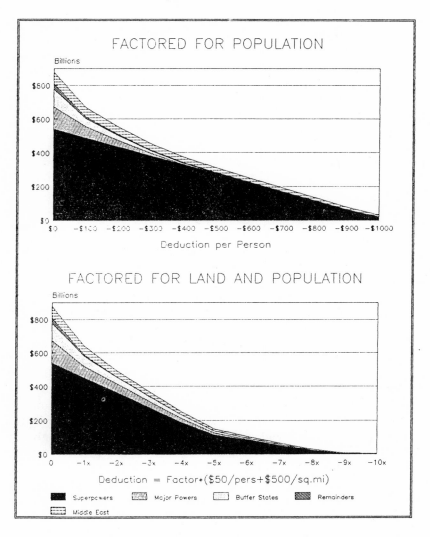

Figure 2. Gauging Global Military Power by way of Powermetrics. Source: From Table 3 on p. 18, the zero line data of which are from the *1989 Britannica Book of the Year, World Data Section,* pp. 860–865.

Chapter 3. The Elements
of National Power

Reality asserts its own logic and overrides legal arrangements.
— Hans Morgenthau

National power is a complex subject, and accordingly few writers have
tackled it. One of the few was Alfred Thayer Mahan, who identified six
elements.[1] He focused his analysis on the ability to project that power on the
high seas, but later writers were able to expand on his work with a more comprehensive perspective. Perhaps the best of them has been Frederick H. Hartmann. Hartmann expanded Mahan's six elements into seven: (1) military,
(2) infrastructure, (3) demographics, (4) geography, (5) economics, (6) scientific-technological and (7) psychological.[2]

Interestingly, Admiral Mahan had an aversion to highly technical matters.[3] He preferred the romance of sailing ships to ironclads, and his most
famous work covers the period 1660–1783, ending about 80 years before steel
ships would make their first appearance. Given the fact that Mahan commanded capital ships, Hartmann's breakdown differs from the admiral's only
by including what Mahan understood but chose to exclude. Accordingly, this
book does not veer from that breakdown, save on two points. First, the
psychological element has been renamed *ethos*. Second, military power is subdivided into conventional military power and thermonuclear power, because
the latter is not much of a viable military option anymore except in the sense
of deterrence.

Proceeding, this chapter addresses the elements of national power in two
sections. The first section briefly describes each element and how that element
is expanded upon elsewhere in the book. The second section examines some
of the relationships among these elements, both internal to a nation and with
respect to other nations, and focuses on four points: the limited opportunities
for expansion, the limits of economic and technical interdependence, the
decline in absolute dictatorships, and the resultant strengthening of subdued
nationalism. All of these points will be revisited in subsequent chapters.

The Elements in Brief

While the eight elements of national power each offer many facets, the descriptions here emphasize those aspects which contribute to an effective defense posture and deterrence against aggrandizement.

Military. This element of national power comprises: (a) forces-in-being and those readily mobilized, (b) the ability to project that power as a deterrent or maneuver it for defensive purposes, and (c) military alliances. Military power is normally a small fraction of a nation's economic power because the former does not increase net wealth, notwithstanding its contribution to the job market and technological advancement. Rather, it absorbs wealth, an investment in the preservation of national values from predators. When military power is expanded for a long period beyond the ability of a nation's economy to sustain it, the consequence may be to fatally weaken that economy.

In the nineteenth century, Helmuth von Moltke claimed that eternal peace was a bad dream and that war engendered the noble virtues of courage and dutifulness and that in the absence of war the world would sink into materialism.[4] The price of avoiding such a fate was the killing of hundreds of millions of people in the course of history, though from some perspectives it was a matter of heroic defense against invaders. It is therefore understandable that the subject fascinates historians, and perhaps it is no coincidence that the three most studied periods of American history are the Revolution, the Civil War and World War II. The four chapters of Part II concentrate on the military element of national power before any attempt is made to derive defense policy guidelines.

Thermonuclear. To the extent this element is unique, it may be best understood by reference to the organization of its potential employment. Except for the aging bomber option, the platforms are located in comfortable silos and huge submarines far from any battlefield. Only a relative handful of personnel are required to operate these systems, and the logistics are simple. And perhaps every individual who mans those platforms realizes that if the missiles are fired, what will be left topside will be grim at best. Chapter 4 examines the consequences of this element of power.

Demographic. The demographic element describes the magnitude and characteristics of population and land, and covers such items as proportionality among age groups, health, geographical distribution, and similar facets. As such, this element, like geography and economics, lends itself to quantitative analysis, which appears throughout the book. Note, however, excessive population can be a weakness as it tends to absorb the potential wealth of a nation just to survive, though by the same token such excess can discourage would-be aggressors from invasion, more so in modern times than ancient. As for population density, the results are mixed. Both Japan and Bangladesh have high population densities. The respective GNPs bear no comparison.

Geographic. The geographic element is self-explanatory, but in this case the critical aspects include land mass, access to seaports, dominant terrain and weather features, and especially the relative position of a state with respect to other states that might pose a threat to its national interests. The larger a country is, the better it can absorb aggression on a "trading space for time" basis until it is able to reorient its resources for a successful defense. The Soviet Union survived many invasions in this fashion before it rose to superpower status. Moreover, the influence of weather and climate seems to play a larger role than one might surmise. As detailed in Chapters 5, 10 and 11, most of the remainder states are located in the region bounded by 25 degrees north and south latitudes. That is, virtually all of these states exist in tropical or desert climates, and most of them are poor. The general exception are the Middle East countries, which derive wealth from a natural resource that requires little investment to make it marketable.

Economic. This element is also self-explanatory and in this application reduces to the question: "How much war can a nation afford?" This question covers both the ability of a nation to provide the necessary logistical support for armed force and the ability to sustain that force in view of the damages and other losses inevitable in war. The old adage about money being power is probably as true if not more true in international relations as it is in business. Accordingly, the gross national product of various countries, and the amount of it spent on military preparedness, is cited repeatedly in this book.

Scientific-Technological. This element tends to be an enhancer of economic and military power, though superior technology did not prove decisively beneficial to the United States in Vietnam. In the larger perspective, however, many analysts posit that the economic power of a nation is directly proportional to its technological prowess, assuming that other elements of national power are not short-changed to the point of negating the influence. Thus as a general rule the greater the technology of a nation, the greater its ability to deter or repel aggression, a point which is emphasized in Appendix A.

Ethos. This is the most elusive of all the elements. It is subject to sudden and unanticipated changes and encompasses morale, cultural bias, and emotions. It is a measure—in this instance—of the willingness of a nation's citizens, apart from governmental leadership or authority, to sustain war, and under what conditions. Most nations will defend against a direct invasion of their homeland, but support of offensive war is another issue. Hence, this element is critical when war goes beyond resisting a clear threat to national interests. Discussion of this element and that of infrastructure are woven into the book throughout, with special attention rendered in the next chapter.

Infrastructure. This element is both legal and subjective in nature. It concerns the political capability and executive machinery to invoke the use of military power and includes the ends to which that power is used. It also includes the necessary willpower of a government to use force when necessary and the recognition and acceptance of that determination by potential adversaries, and encompasses a nation's system of government with respect to the relative freedom and ingenuity its citizens exercise, which can contribute to economic power. It is the means of managing all other sources of power. Superior infrastructure gives to a nation the ability to make "the mostest out of the leastest." In combination with the national ethos, it can make for extraordinary defensive ability.

Some Key Relationships

Figure 3 illustrates the relationships among the elements of power and the four points which follow. The reader may wish to consider these four points as parameters, but the intent of the discussion here is to use them only as stepping stones, in combination with the next chapter, for the defense parameters derived in Chapter 14.

Limited Opportunities for Expansion. Though the salient powers have the power necessary to expand their territories, the opportunities for any expansion are practically nil. Virtually every square mile of land is owned and operated by a recognized national sovereignty. Antarctica is an exception only in the abstract; its utilization is governed by international treaty to which most of the salient powers are signatories. The other exception would be the handful of border disputes, most of which involve inhospitable strips of land. Thus the only means of expansion today is by outright military aggrandizement or the occasional political alignment of a remainder state with a salient power. Both options are limited. The Soviet invasion of Afghanistan may have been a prime example of such aggrandizement, but it failed, and there are few other opportunities for such aggression without either risking war with the United States or other salient power, or establishing major lines of communication and logistics that can be easily interdicted.

More significantly, if the results of the Afghanistan invasion are any indication, these expansions would drain the Soviet Union of more resources than gained—a kind of "Ransom of Red Chief" problem on a global scale. Therefore, and considering the geography, the only major conquest the Soviet Union might engineer without risking a major war with other powers would be Iran. China may have a slightly larger number of opportunities, but with the possible exception of Taiwan, it would be out of character for China to start aggrandizing neighbors beyond Tibet.[5]

The Limits of Interdependence. The magnitude of world trade has increased exponentially during the past 20 years, both in absolute terms and in percentage terms of the world collective gross national product.[6] Supposedly, this pattern serves as a damper on the potential for war, but the theory does not always square with the facts. For example, in 1974 James R. Schlesinger,

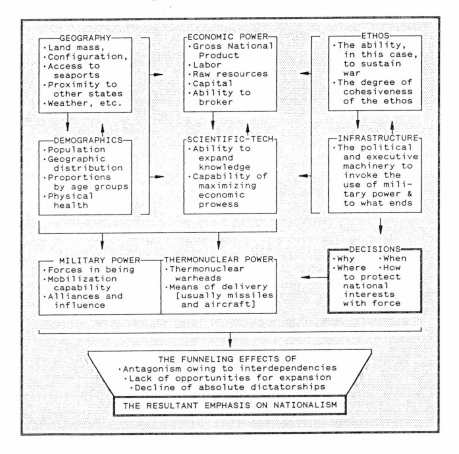

Figure 3. Relationships Among the Elements of National Power. The economic/scientific-technical pair is the main source of active military power, but the geographic/demographic pair must be extensive enough to sustain that power. The tendency of the ethos/infrastructure pair to use war to further interests, however, has been funneled inward because of geopolitical factors.

then serving as Secretary of Defense, warned OPEC nations that if the price of oil rose too high, military actions might have to be considered as an option.[7] Moreover, some countries, most notably the Soviet Union, seek maximum autarky for all essential commodities. Put another way, economic interdependence is as often considered a threat to a nation's prowess as it is a means of defusing the potential for war. And in the case of many of the remainder states, this interdependence is often perceived more as, and probably is, dependence rather than interdependence and undoubtedly generates seething discontent.

Related to economic interdependence is technical interdependence, especially communications. International television and travel have generated a greater familiarity among decision makers of the salient powers and buffer states. Also, the striking effectiveness of reconnaissance satellites makes deployment of armed forces in preparation for a major offensive difficult if not impossible to conceal, though the interpretation of such data is still subject to miscue by intransigent opinion. On the negative side, this factor can aggravate ethnocentric propensities, familiarity breeding contempt, and it can be used to enhance propaganda and disinformation tactics.

The Decline of Absolute Dictatorships. Wars of aggrandizement, with the possible exception of the British Empire, have been the products of dictators. In the main, these dictators held absolute sway over their countries at the time of the hostilities. The list is a long one and includes Alexander, Genghis Khan, Süleiman the Magnificent, Napoleon, Kaiser Wilhelm II, Adolph Hitler and Hideki Tōjō. Most of these dictators invaded countries much larger than their own, but the victims lacked the infrastructure to resist the invasion, at least initially. This situation no longer prevails.

The Soviet Union may be a totalitarian state of sorts, but it is not a dictatorship. The Soviet president is beholden to members of the Politburo for his tenure. When Khrushchev rattled the Soviet saber a little too much, he was deposed, though allowed to live on in quiet retirement. Below the Politburo exists a massive bureaucracy, arguably more resistant to change than its American counterpart. For the United States, whatever the abuses of power alleged to have been committed by various presidents over the past 40 years, the Presidency is no dictatorship. Moreover, Congress has initiated several measures—e.g., the War Powers Resolution—to control abuses which might conceivably lead to some form of dictatorial rule. As for the major powers, none evinces a government anywhere close to an absolute dictatorship, though another Mao Zedong could arise in China or another edition of military dictatorship could surface in Brazil. But neither country is noted for attempts at world aggrandizement.

That dictators, and not presiders, initiate major war arises from the prerequisite of an enormous act of unambiguous willpower and control over the elements of national power to make and enforce that decision. The larger and more powerful the country, the more absolute that dictatorship must be to do so, but the harder it is for one individual to attain such power. Bureaucracies evolve, which, combined with the difficulty of obtaining consensus among a large number of individuals, auger against any extraordinary decisiveness.

Nationalism. Given the above factors, it is no surprise that the spirit of nationalism, albeit in a subdued form, is in the ascendency. Colonialism is all but dead. The British Commonwealth has become largely one of cultural affinity. China is no longer under the sway of the Soviet Union. Whatever influence the United States formerly exercised over Latin American countries, it

STATISTICS→ COUNTRIES	Registered Communists	World %	Rank	Population	World %	% of Pop.	Indexed to USSR
SALIENT POWERS							
·China	46,012,000	(51.9%)	1	1,088,200,000	(21.3%)	4.2%	63
·Soviet Union	19,038,000	(21.5%)	2	285,796,000	(5.6%)	6.7%	100
Subtotal	65,050,000	(73.4%)	—	1,373,996,000	(26.9%)	4.7%	—
OVERT COMMUNIST STATES							
·Romania	3,640,000	(4.1%)	3	23,014,000	(0.5%)	15.8%	237
·North Korea	2,500,000	(2.8%)	4	21,903,000	(0.4%)	11.4%	171
·East Germany	2,324,000	(2.6%)	5	16,588,000	(0.3%)	14.0%	210
·Yugoslavia	2,168,000	(2.4%)	6	23,591,000	(0.5%)	9.2%	138
·Poland	2,130,000	(2.4%)	7	37,864,000	(0.7%)	5.6%	84
·Vietnam	1,900,000	(2.1%)	8	63,807,000	(1.3%)	3.0%	45
·Czechoslovakia	1,705,000	(1.9%)	9	15,604,000	(0.3%)	10.9%	164
·Bulgaria	932,000	(1.1%)	11	8,978,000	(0.2%)	10.4%	156
·Hungary	871,000*	(1.0%)	12	10,591,000	(0.2%)	8.2%	124
·Cuba	524,000	(0.6%)	14	10,421,000	(0.2%)	5.0%	76
·Albania	147,000	(0.2%)	18	3,149,000	(0.1%)	4.7%	70
·Mongolia	88,000	(0.1%)	22	2,041,000	(<.1%)	4.3%	65
Subtotal	18,929,000	(21.4%)	—	237,551,000	(4.7%)	8.0%	—
CLAIMED COMMUNIST STATES							
·Ethiopia	50,000	(0.1%)	24	47,501,000	(0.9%)	0.1%	2
·Laos	40,000	(<.1%)	26	3,850,000	(0.1%)	1.0%	16
·Afghanistan	40,000	(<.1%)	27	14,481,000	(0.3%)	0.3%	4
·Angola	35,000	(<.1%)	30	9,386,000	(0.2%)	0.4%	6
·Yemen (PDR)	31,000	(<.1%)	31	2,345,000	(<.1%)	1.3%	20
·Nicaragua	1,000	(<.1%)	73	3,622,000	(0.1%)	<.1%	0
Subtotal	197,000	(0.2%)	—	81,185,000	(1.6%)	0.2%	—
NON-COMMUNIST STATES							
·Italy	1,505,000	(1.7%)	10	57,401,000	(1.1%)	2.6%	39
·France	604,000	(0.7%)	13	55,860,000	(1.1%)	1.1%	16
·India	479,000	(0.5%)	15	801,806,000	(15.7%)	0.1%	1
·Japan	470,000	(0.5%)	16	122,620,000	(2.4%)	0.4%	6
·Portugal	200,000	(0.2%)	17	10,349,000	(0.2%)	1.9%	29
·Mozambique	130,000	(0.1%)	19	14,890,000	(0.3%)	0.9%	13
·Spain	100,000	(0.1%)	20	38,996,000	(0.8%)	0.3%	4
·Mexico	90,000	(0.1%)	21	82,659,000	(1.6%)	0.1%	2
·Argentina	80,000	(0.1%)	23	31,963,000	(0.6%)	0.3%	4
·Greece	42,000	(<.1%)	25	10,055,000	(0.3%)	0.4%	6
·West Germany	40,000	(<.1%)	28	60,782,000	(1.2%)	0.1%	1
·Finland	37,000	(<.1%)	29	4,952,000	(0.1%)	0.7%	11
·Sweden	23,000	(<.1%)	32	8,415,000	(0.2%)	0.3%	4
·Chile	20,000	(<.1%)	33	12,750,000	(0.3%)	0.2%	3
·Colombia	18,000	(<.1%)	34	30,661,000	(0.6%)	0.1%	1
·United States	18,000	(<.1%)	35	246,113,000	(4.8%)	<.1%	0
·Norway	15,000	(<.1%)	36	4,202,000	(0.1%)	0.4%	5
·Philippines	15,000	(<.1%)	37	58,723,000	(1.2%)	<.1%	4
·Brazil	15,000	(<.1%)	38	144,262,000	(2.8%)	<.1%	0
·Austria	15,000	(<.1%)	39	7,577,000	(0.1%)	0.2%	3
·Panama	13,000	(<.1%)	40	2,322,000	(<.1%)	0.6%	8
·All others	520,000	(0.6%)	—	1,598,195,000	(31.3%)	<.1%	0
Subtotal	4,449,000	(5.0%)	—	3,405,553,000	(66.8%)	0.1%	—
TOTAL	88,625,000	(100%)	—	5,098,285,000	(100%)	1.7%	—

*The Communist Party of Hungary renamed itself the Socialist Party in 1989.

Table 4. The Non-Existence of "World Communism." Source: Communist data is from the *Yearbook of International Communist Affairs 1988* (Stanford, California: Hoover Institute Press, 1988), pp. xii–xxix. Population data is from *1989 Britannica Book of the Year, World Data Section,* pp. 746–751. All data is rounded to the nearest 1,000.

is now fading rapidly. Japan may be militarily dependent on the United States, but she shows no hesitation at upstaging her benefactor economically, while one of her major industrial companies sold critical submarine technology to the Soviet Union.[8] Then, too, the OPEC nations long ago declined the "benefits" of continuing as de facto economic colonies of foreign powers. And the Soviet Union itself discovered that it will take force and embargoes to keep Lithuania and Estonia (and perhaps other states) in line.

Nor have alliances degenerated into a form of neocolonialism. NATO includes the United States as the preeminent partner, but the United States is not a member of the Common Market and has lost influence in other NATO countries on matters beyond the immediate military objectives of NATO business. And though the cultural ties between the United States and the United Kingdom undoubtedly will remain strong, there is a limit to the extent to which this abiding international friendship can be harnessed to advance incompatible interests.

Finally, the supposed threat of "world communism" has evolved from a red scare into a red herring, as shown in Table 4. The data in this table were valid *before* the iron curtain was lifted in Europe. At the time almost 95 percent of all registered Communists were concentrated in 14 countries. Another 197,000 Communists (about two-tenths of one percent of all Communists) live in five remainder states that claimed to be communist. The 5 percent balance of 4,450,000 Communists is distributed among roughly 180 other nations and weighs in at 1 percent of the combined population of those states.[9] After 73 years of "growth," that figure does not portend worldwide revolution. Moreover, with the disintegration of the Warsaw Pact and the communist parties in those countries, the strength of communism was reduced by 11,600,000 members (about 13 percent) and from 19 to 13 countries.

What has happened, of course, is that the opportunities for aggrandizement and expansion, and the means to achieve it, have shrunk. Thus the inevitable growth of the elements of national power among the salient powers and most of the buffer states has been turned inward, perhaps unintentionally, to further strengthen national postures. In the process, these nations have become increasingly resistant to aggrandizement by other national.

Chapter 4. Anvils, Swords and the Pen

If you want war, nourish a doctrine. Doctrines are the
most fearful tyrants to which men ever are subject,
because doctrines get inside of a man's own reason and
betray him against himself. Civilized men have done
their fiercest fighting for doctrines.
　　　　　　　—William Graham Sumner

　　　The anvil is a common symbol for the economic power of a nation, and
one that aptly illustrates the scriptural conflict between swords and plow-
shares. It also implies that the strength of a nation is or can be unified toward
some end, be it peaceful or otherwise. Unfortunately, two forces can work to
destroy that sense of national integrity. The first is the consequence of using
thermonuclear power and is new to this century. The second is the disruptive
power that can be exerted by ideology, a very old and established process. A
major question, then, is whether these two forces could work to negate the
effect of national power and in turn unravel the fabric of the global equilibrium.

　　　This is a question that will be addressed at various points in the third part
of the book, but for the interim it might prove helpful to examine some of
the aspects of these two forces. This examination can demonstrate why thermonuclear power is a fact of life and likely to increase rather than subside in
its potential for destruction, and why ideology no longer seems to present the
same disruptive threat it once did, at least not for most of the salient powers.
However, bear in mind that the immunization a working nationalism offers
against an ideological virus is not always effective in preventing a nation's attempt to infect others with its own ideology.

The Thermonuclear Element of National Power

　　　An increasing number of analysts hold that the destructive power of thermonuclear weapons is too great to ever justify their use under any circumstances, notwithstanding that these weapons to date have contributed to
the deterrence of global war.[1] The very existence of these weapons, however,

may or *will*— depending on the school of thought — presage their eventual use no matter how long it takes, a risk that supposedly increases or an eventuality that will occur sooner rather than later in the presence of an arms race.[2] The risk increases, so the argument goes, because the nuclear powers are opposed to a supranational authority to exercise full control over all these weapons, and the prognosis for total disarmament is unfavorable. Even if disarmament occurred, the capability to build these weapons would remain. Thus thermonuclear power keeps the peace, but it may destroy civilization some day.

In his famed *History*, Herodotus related a tale which he admitted to have no basis in fact. King Xerxes, returning to Persia after defeat in Greece, took a shortcut by sea rather than march via the Hellespont with his troops. He embarked on a Phoenician ship at Eion, so the story went, with 30 of his most trusted aides. Running into a severe storm midway, the ship "laboured heavily." Xerxes, in fear for his life, asked the captain if there was anything that could be done to lessen the danger. The captain replied that the only remedy was to lighten the load on the ship. Whereupon Xerxes turned to his aides and implored their assistance in his hour of need. All 30 jumped overboard, and upon reaching safety Xerxes summoned the captain. For the sound judgment which saved his life, he would give him his gold crown, but because the remedy cost him his most trusted aides, he would also order him beheaded.[3]

In a similar manner, thermonuclear weapons portend some good news and some bad news overshadowing the original intention. First the bad news: It is possible if not probable that the power of thermonuclear warheads might eventually be dwarfed by a new generation of weapons, propelled by missiles that could be hurled from any point on earth to any other point in ten minutes or less. Launched from a submarine within 1,000 miles of a nation's shoreline, the elapsed time would be on the order of a minute or two. At present, it takes 15 minutes or so, a critical grace period in deterrence theory, i.e., time to launch a retaliatory strike hence preserve the deterrent effect of guaranteed mutual destruction.

The potential for a new generation of weapons is the well-known $e = mc^2$ equation. Nuclear weapons operate by fission. When a fissionable atom is subdivided into two or more "lighter" atoms, a tiny fraction of its mass is converted into energy. The famed equation tells us it doesn't take much mass to produce a great deal of energy. In thermonuclear weapons, a nuclear (fission) trigger is used to activate a fusion process whereby hydrogen atoms of a heavy isotope are fused into helium. In the process a somewhat larger fraction of the mass is converted into energy, again following the same equation.

Researchers have replicated this fusion process in the laboratory, though not cheaply. Yet because commercial feasibility is not a criterion for thermonuclear weapons, it is only a matter of time before this semi-controlled fusion process is harnessed to completely annihilate a small dense mass. In this event Einstein's equation would apply to the entire mass, not just a small fraction. The explosion would likely be forceful enough to fuse considerable adjacent material until the process finally attenuated itself. Before that happened, however, the yield could prove to be on the order of 5 to 20 gigatons of TNT—enough to level the New York–to-Washington corridor in one shot.

This same semi-controlled fusion process might also be adapted as the propellant source in strategic missiles. The miniaturization of the missile body combined with the vast energy might push the missile speed from the present 18,000 miles per hour to perhaps 80,000—four or five times the current mark. True, the potential for this type of warhead and missile is only theoretical, and even if it proves feasible it might take 50 years to develop. However, 51 years have elapsed since Einstein signed the famous letter to President Roosevelt encouraging him to proceed with the research for the first atomic bomb. And in the fortunate event that this new generation of weapons never comes to pass, the present variety are lethal enough to inflict intolerable damage.

A second item of bad news is that the control over these weapons is not as secure as one might wish to believe. During the final days of Nixon's tenure in office as president, Secretary of Defense James Schlesinger issued orders to ignore any direct orders from the White House or any other source without his counter-signature.[4] By the same token, the players at shortstop might try for the pitcher's mound, i.e., in a precipitous situation, the intermediaries in the defense establishment might initiate thermonuclear war if the president waffled. Thus to the extent there is a risk it might arise not so much from a "madman at the trigger" scenario as from a "milquetoast in the armory" or waffling president syndrome.

A third item of bad news is that nuclear and thermonuclear power and technology are spreading at a fairly rapid pace, notwithstanding the Nuclear Nonproliferation Treaty. Perhaps nine nations now have or could easily obtain thermonuclear weapons, and the number will probably continue to grow.[5]

Now the good news. The most favorable aspect of the thermonuclear dilemma focuses on the misapplication of statistical probability theory to the risk of nuclear warfare. In broad brush, probability theory attempts to predict the likelihood of a specified event occurring. For example, the odds of an individual winning a jackpot in a state lottery are negligible. But if that same individual was a Methuselah and continued to buy a ticket each week ad infinitum, probability theory posits he would eventually win even if it took ten thousand years. The doomsayers believe this same logic applies to thermonuclear warheads.

Fortunately, the existence of thermonuclear weapons is not the same thing as using them. In a lottery, drawings will be held. The jackpot will eventually be claimed. This is not true with thermonuclear weapons. No inexorable crankshaft operates between the weapons and the owners. What does exist is the potential for human intervention to pull the trigger. Thus crumbles the argument that thermonuclear weapons must be abolished or otherwise safeguarded beyond access to any nation — whatever that means — in order to prevent their "certain" use. The issue joined is not how to get rid of them but how to further minimize the possibility they might be used.

A second favorable aspect addresses the waffling president syndrome. It may be true that defense officials could initiate thermonuclear warfare on their own initiative, but it would take an implausible chain of circumstances to do it. The very fact that the defense establishment puts layers of intervention between the president and the missiles also means that all of those layers must first be aligned in a conspiracy, starting with the secretary of defense — else the incumbent secretary would be able to stop the insidious game plan by alerting the president and issuing counterorders. Moreover, it is difficult to conceive of world tension so severe that a conspiracy of this magnitude could arise without the president and the secretary of defense becoming intensely involved and clamping down on any possible use of the weapons before and unless there was no other choice. It is one thing for a few misguided officers on the National Security Council to break laws to fund support of some equally misguided insurrectionist movement armed with low-grade conventional weapons, quite another to start a global war in which they realized their own families would probably be incinerated within the hour. And to reiterate, these tensions would build up over a period of time, giving everyone time to tighten controls over these weapons.

The bottom line of all this is that thermonuclear power is here to stay, and there will always be some risk, however miniscule, that it might be used. It behooves the United States, therefore, to do everything it can to further minimize that risk without unhinging the equilibrium or putting its own bonafide interests in severe jeopardy. On the other hand, the anguish of the risk has to be accepted as a fact of life. It is not a matter of playing God. Insofar as the ability to destroy civilization as we know it is concerned, mankind already has the power of God. Harry Truman understood this when he lamented, tongue in cheek, that he was unable to appoint a secretary of reaction to put the nuclear genie back in the bottle. That bottle is really the state of our knowledge and mindset. We are the genie. What we do with that knowledge and power is the issue, but the Garden of Eden option (doing away with all nuclear weapons) doesn't exist anymore and never really did. And so the abstract concept of existentialism, at least according to one dictionary, has come home to roost on the nuclear arsenal:

> . . . existence takes precedence over essence and man is totally free and responsible for his acts and that responsibility is the source of the dread and anguish that encompass him.[6]

The Influence of Ideology on Ethos and Infrastructure

Ideology has been a potent force throughout the history of civilization: the impetus of empires, of wars and revolutions, and of the rise — and fall — of numerous forms of government and religion. The books and articles written on this subject would fill a small library, and to this day many analysts essay the antagonism between the superpowers primarily in terms of democracy versus communism. That antagonism is a force with which to reckon in international affairs.

The study of ideological movements has been formalized by the field of *intellectual history,* which assesses the impact of ideas on the course of history. Perhaps the best single-volume reference on the subject is Robert B. Downs' *Books That Changed the World.*[7] Some of the ten political works he cites ignited revolutions while others lay dormant for centuries — and then ignited revolutions. It seems that most if not all these works addressed a pressing problem that was beyond the solution or capability of an existing infrastructure, that is, the ways and means of a government to deal with major problems. If the work appealed to the ethos of the people affected by the problem, it galvanized that ethos into a temporary infrastructure. But if the ethos wasn't in tune with the ideology, the message of the book remained latent until the ethos changed or the problem was resolved in the course of events, sometimes drawing on the book, sometimes not.

True, not all revolutionary movements are heralded by a specific book. A revolution may arise by virtue of a series of books or essays, or sometimes by oratory, or at other times by the issuing of a particularly odious edict. Also, the relationship of ideological movements to tyrants and dictators affords valuable insight. In most instances, the authors of these seminal works did not become the leaders of the movements, they activated, though the non-author leaders who did rise with the tides of various movements were almost always aware of the respective precursor book. Sometimes they twisted its contents to justify their own conduct, but they seldom failed to acknowledge its influence. The unusual leaders who did write books did so more to enhance their rise to power than to address a serious flaw in infrastructure. Hitler's *Mein Kampf* was the archetypical and tragic example of this.

But how does an infrastructure become immune to new ideological onslaughts? About the only way is for that infrastructure to become flexible enough to recognize and deal with major problems before the ethos of its citizens, galvanized by an insightful writer, turns against a government they consider impotent. Accordingly, the notion of further ideological upheaval in the United States, Western Europe, Canada, and Australia is implausible. It is a different story for the Soviet Union, China, Brazil, and India, but for various reasons, the event would not likely fatally weaken the global equilibrium. But first, consider the reasons for the resiliency of the

United States, which can be traced to her three major ideological movements.

The Democratic Movement. This movement is often associated with the Declaration of Independence, the draft of which was written by Thomas Jefferson in less than a week. As a state document, the Declaration formally initiated the revolutionary period, but the ethos of the American colonists was first brought to a boil by Thomas Paine's *Common Sense,* though the roots of that movement can be traced back to the writings of John Locke a century earlier, and even further back to ancient Greece and Rome. Indeed, at least one historian has suggested that the Revolutionary War was really a civil war between English conservatives on one side of the Atlantic and English liberals on the other.[8]

Sanctity of the Individual. This movement nowhere had a greater moment than in the American Civil War, resulting in the freeing of an entire race of people at the price of more than 620,000 lives. In terms of seminal works, the dominant one was Harriet Beecher Stowe's *Uncle Tom's Cabin.* It sold more than 300,000 copies in the first year of publication, a record for the time. When Mrs. Stowe visited the White House on one occasion, Abraham Lincoln greeted her as "the little lady that wrote the book that made this big war."[9] Her book galvanized the ethos of a people and in the long run solidified enough public support to sustain Lincoln through the early years of the war when the best the Union forces could do was avoid total defeat at Antietem. Interestingly, Hinton Helper's book *The Impending Crisis,* which argued that slavery was becoming economically destructive to the South, was ignored. The ethos of the Confederacy was hellbent in the opposite direction.

Civil Disobedience. Henry David Thoreau's book of that title was ignored for more than a half-century. It did not fit well with the prevailing attitude of obedience to laws. When it did spark revolution, it was in India under the leadership of the Oxford-trained lawyer Mohandas Gandhi. It would be almost 120 years before it underpinned the United States movement led by Martin Luther King, Jr. The point is, the United States absorbed the doctrine of civil disobedience without letting it destroy the fabric of government itself.

The claim was made that these movements contributed to one of the most resilient infrastructures in history. The proof resides in the Constitution and its Bill of Rights (the first ten amendments). This document has remained almost unchanged except to broaden the base of its constituency. The 16 additional amendments reduce to 14, as Article 21 repealed Article 18 (Prohibition). Article 13 outlawed slavery. Part of Article 14 extended the Bill of Rights to all citizens. Articles 15, 19, 23, 24 and 25 extended the franchise to all races, women, the District of Columbia, non-poll-tax payers, and minors over 18 years of age, respectively. Articles 11, 12, 14 (in part), 17, 20, and 25 modified election mechanics and clarified succession-of-office issues, but with the possible exception of the direct election of Senators, none of these amendments made any fundamental changes to the Constitution or the way in which the government operated.

This leaves three articles. Article 11 limited United States jurisdiction over suits of foreign origin, correcting a minor oversight. Article 16 authorized the income tax because the Constitution was not crystal clear on this point. And Article 25 limited election to the presidency for one individual to two terms, not an earthshaking change. In all, the Constitution survived the Civil War, a tenfold geographical expansion of the country, a nearly one-hundredfold increase in population, and all the technology that the American culture could produce. It works very well.

Turning the discussion to the Soviet Union, it is necessary to consider what was perhaps the most influential book in political history — Karl Marx's *Das Kapital,* as modified and interpreted by Lenin. Marx wrote his book while living in England, but apparently the plight of the lower classes was more aptly illustrated in the novels of Charles Dickens. The latter was far more in line with the English ethos, and in any event novels seem better able to convey a social truth than dry discourses. At any rate, the impact of Marx on Russian history needs no further commentary here. The masses had suffered so greatly under the tsars that Lenin had an easy time riding the tide to supreme authority.

But the potential for another revolution of equal caliber is improbable. Unlike the United States, which had pristine territory in which to expand and the insultarity to buffer against direct invasion, Russia was confronted with both existing but diversely settled territory *and* invasions. The consolidation of power into a workable infrastructure was a rough road and fell short of the resiliency developed in the United States. Yet the Soviet citizenry has become comparatively well off, and it appears that further revolution, if it must be called that, will be limited to regional conflicts.

Among the major powers, China experienced a revolution led by Mao Zedong, a prolific author of sorts though his literary contributions were more on the nature of insurrection and guerrilla tactics.[10] Another edition of this revolution might occur, but as discussed in Chapter 12, unless the Sino-Soviet pact were renewed on a global death squad basis, the equilibrium would remain intact. Australia and Canada never had revolutions, both being largely the products of British settlement, and the potential for a first time seems ludicrous.

The revolution in India, as mentioned, was by way of civil disobedience. Perhaps the intractable poverty will someday ignite another revolution, but it is difficult to see how this would undo the equilibrium. Next, Brazil avoided an outright revolution because the Portuguese government relocated to Brazil during the Napoleonic era to save itself and in the process initiated major reforms in the infrastructure. The leader, Dom Pedro, later decided to stay in Brazil rather than heed a summons to return to Portugal. This does not gainsay the potential for a future revolution, but in that event, Brazil would be too isolated to wreak havoc on global affairs. This leaves Western Europe, which is near to achieving economic if not political unity and shows no sign of any further upheavals.

Unfortunately, the tides of ideology are not so well controlled among the remainder states. Should the untold wealth in the Middle East someday contribute to development of thermonuclear power, which, impelled by the force of ideology, might then be unleashed by way of terrorism in a situation which already embroiled the superpowers, the conflict could escalate to a global war. The probability of this occurring may be low, but it is not negligible.

Chapter 5. The Powers That Be

The race is not always to the swift nor the battle to the
strong, but that's the way to bet.
— Ecclesiastes 9:11,
as revised by Murphy

Most institutions of serious intent have a few customs or traditions intended as a controlled and acceptable rebellion against authority. The Military Academy at West Point certainly has a serious intent and just as certainly provides its share of less-than-distinguished customs. One of them sets the rules how Boston cream pie would be divided among the ten cadets sitting at any of the tables in the dining hall. Knives were torqued until a winner was ascertained. He was entitled to take up to half the pie. Proceeding in a clockwise direction, each succeeding cadet could take up to half the balance, providing a tenth was left. When that point was reached, the "have nots" repeated the torquing process to determine who got the last piece.[1]

And so it is with national power, as posited repeatedly in earlier chapters. The superpowers with a tenth of the world's population possess or otherwise control about half of the world's clout. The major powers, comprising about a tenth of the world's nations, have about half of what is left. The buffer states, with two-tenths of the world population, control roughly 15 percent of the pie. The remainder states, comprising about 60 percent of all nations, divide up the tenth that is left. The statistical data presented in previous chapters attest to this distribution, but now the qualitative aspects of comparative national power need to be examined. To support this analysis, three figures have been prepared to put these considerations into perspective.

The Salient Powers

The rationale for inclusion of seven countries plus the geographical core of the NATO alliance as salient powers—two superpowers and six major powers—is outlined in Figure 4, which uses the traditional grade scale. Both superpowers rate nearly "straight A's," given the fact that with few exceptions,

36

no other nation exceeds their respective strengths in any category. The only major weakness in either power would be the economic strength of the Soviet Union, a shortcoming which has gained the attention of President Mikhail Gorbachev. The other apparent exception would be the huge populations of China and India compared to the superpowers, but in both cases these populations are as much a source of weakness by way of draining resources, as they are of indirect strength by way of disinviting aggrandizement. By contrast, none of the major powers seem to earn the same rating in *all* the elements of national power, except possibly the geographical core of NATO, which lacks political if not economic unification.

Bear in mind that the criterion for major power status elsewhere in this analysis has been the capability of deterring invasion rather than as superpower competitors. All the major powers, save India, are relatively equal in this regard, albeit this "equality" arises from different combinations of strengths among the elements of national power. Hence India is the borderline case for inclusion in this group. If it were changed to buffer state status, and some of the borderline buffer state nations were changed to remainder state status, then, as shown in Table 5, the data would change significantly in terms of population data but not much among the other measures. Moreover, the primary reason for including India among the salient powers—the mass-population-and-poverty disincentive—would not be affected.

The Buffer States

The concept of "buffer" is akin to "shock absorber." The latter softens physical blows and impacts by absorbing force rather than transmitting it elsewhere. Similarly, a geopolitical buffer absorbs the potential for war by way of posing obstacles when war may seem imminent, at the same time remaining relatively secure against direct invasion. The particular reasons for that security comprise different combinations of strengths among elements of national power among the respective buffer states.

Figure 5 depicts the reasons for inclusion of each "member" state in the buffer states subgroup. Those with the relative bulk of buffer-state power are located in South America, Europe, and east Asia. There are no buffer states in Central America, Africa, or the Middle East. The weak buffer state islands in the Caribbean and the Pacific Ocean are protectorates or dependencies of salient powers or with New Zealand. The inclusion of the two Koreas may strike some readers as odd, given the mass of troops stationed there. Yet it is precisely this military concentration that provides the stability.

The inclusion of Nepal, Pakistan, and Malaysia represents the extreme limit for buffer states, and a good case could be made for changing them to remainder state status. Malaysia could experience another foreign-supported

	Military	Infrastructure	Demographics	Geography	Economics	Scientific-Tech.	Ethos
SUPER POWERS — United States	A — The second largest military force, but with good alliances.	B- ◄ Deterrence; Defensive war. This is a matter of history.	A — High potential to sustain military force and deter invasion.	A+ — Extremely well-situated, with insularity and good neighbors.	A- — 1/4th of the world's GNP but is faced with severe budget & trade deficits.	A+ — The best in the world; the USSR cannot purloin enough of it.	C+ ◄ Deterrence; Defensive war. This parallels infrastructure.
Soviet Union	A — Largest military force in world, but with limited alliances.	A — Soviet government structure would be unsurpassed in wartime.	A- — Substantial population, though not optimally distributed.	A- — Large land mass deters invasion but global position is limiting.	C+ — Weakest point. Economy is strained; the ruble isolated.	B- — Good, but lacks national and individual initiative.	A — In wartime, but difficult to assess in peacetime.
MAJOR POWERS — China	B — Not a first-rate military power, but sheer numbers compensate.	B — Semi-dictatorial government offset by massive population.	A — Massive population serves to discourage aggrandizement.	B — Land mass equal to U.S. but borders the Soviet Union.	C- — Massive population hinders economic renaissance.	C — Not strong, but priority is given to military requirements.	A — In war, tens of millions would fight tenaciously.
Western Europe	A- — NATO is effective though its long-term future is problematic.	B- — Members will soon be joined economically, if not politically.	A — Well situated, highly skilled, large population	C — In the shadow of the U.S.S.R. and sea lanes are vulnerable.	A- — GNP is 2/3rds of the U.S. and larger than the Soviet Union's.	A- — Not far behind the United States.	B — Common dangers or needs overcome cultural differences.
Canada	B — Relatively small but proficient and allied with the U.S.	A- — Democratic government balanced with a small population.	B — Highly skilled, well distributed with respect to economic base.	A — Insular, mostly inhospitable, adjacent to the United States.	B — Strong for her population; major trading partner is U.S.	B — Good, and can rely on the United States to fill the gaps.	A- — Strikes a near perfect balance in peace and in war.
Australia	B — On a par with Canada.	B — Not far behind that of Canada.	C — Weak. The bulk of the continent is almost uninhabitable.	A — Insular and inhospitable to invasion.	B- — Adequate, and trades heavily with "free world" states.	C+ — Adequate, and can rely on British Commonwealth.	A- — Homogeneous ethnicity and culture.
Brazil	C+ — Borderline military force, but aligned with the United States	B- — Governments come and go; Brazil lacks a solid constitution.	B — Adequate enough to make Brazil a regional economic power.	A — Size inhibits local invasion and has global insularity.	C+ — Substantial, expanding rapidly, but has major debt.	C — Marginal, but can buy what she lacks.	Unknown. Little recent experience with major war.
India	C- — Sizable military force, but with few alliances.	C- — Effectiveness of India's federal structure is questionable.	A- — Massive population and poverty make for an un-inviting target.	B- — Climate and natural barriers inhibit would-be invaders.	D — India is a poor country; progress will be slow in coming.	C — Manages to invest considerable R&D in military areas.	Unknown. Difficult to assess with respect to major war.

	LAND MASS	POPULATION	GROSS NATIONAL PRODUCT		MILITARY
			Total	Discretionary	BUDGET

— AS POSITED IN TABLE 2 —

	LAND MASS	POPULATION	Total	Discretionary	MILITARY BUDGET
Superpowers	23.5%	10.4%	41.9%	45.8%	61.4%
Major Powers	29.9%	45.9%	25.6%	23.7%	15.1%
Buffer States	17.0%	20.3%	25.6%	25.7%	11.8%
Remainder States	29.6%	23.3%	6.9%	4.7%	11.7%

— SHIFTING INDIA TO BUFFER STATE STATUS —

	LAND MASS	POPULATION	Total	Discretionary	MILITARY BUDGET
Superpowers	23.5%	10.4%	41.9%	45.8%	61.4%
Major Powers	27.6% -2.3	30.2% -15.7	24.2% -1.4	23.7% none	14.3% -0.8
Buffer States	19.3% +2.3	36.0% +15.7	27.0% +1.4	25.7% none	12.6% +0.8
Remainder States	29.6%	23.3%	6.9%	4.7%	11.7%

— SHIFTING NEPAL, PAKISTAN AND MALAYSIA TO REMAINDER STATE STATUS —

	LAND MASS	POPULATION	Total	Discretionary	MILITARY BUDGET
Superpowers	23.5%	10.4%	41.9%	45.8%	61.4%
Major Powers	29.9%	45.9%	25.6%	23.7%	15.1%
Buffer States	16.0% -1.0	17.5% -2.8	25.2% -0.4	25.5% -0.2	11.4% -0.4
Remainder States	30.6% +1.0	26.1% +2.8	7.3% +0.4	4.9% +0.2	12.1% +0.4

— WITH BOTH SHIFTS —

	LAND MASS	POPULATION	Total	Discretionary	MILITARY BUDGET
Superpowers	23.5%	10.4%	41.9%	45.8%	61.4%
Major Powers	27.6% -2.3	30.2% -15.7	24.2% -1.4	23.7% none	14.3% -0.8
Buffer States	18.3% +1.3	33.2% +12.9	26.6% +1.0	25.5% -0.2	12.2% +0.4
Remainder States	30.6% +1.0	26.1% +2.8	7.3% +0.4	4.9% +0.2	12.1% +0.4

Table 5. Revised Status Statistics

insurrection. Pakistan frequently seems to be on the edge of war. And Nepal is a weak, if mountainous, country sandwiched between the two most populous countries in the world. If so, as shown in Table 5, the subgroup statistical totals would remain relatively constant—less than 1 percent in every category except population. Irrespective of the statistics, however, the main point to note is that international wars over the past 30 years involving the buffer states have been infrequent and seldom of global significance.

The Remainder States

The remainder states, which comprise a numerical majority of nations but control only a very small fraction of the world's collective national power, are described in Figure 6. They include all of Central America, the Middle East, and Africa. Elsewhere the subgroup encompasses the troubled, isolated or weak states of Asia and Oceania plus the Mediterranean island of Cyprus. Beyond the Middle East only 12 of them compile an *annual* GNP that exceeds the *daily* GNP of the United States, with none exceeding a week's worth. In the Middle East, only Saudi Arabia and Iran exceed that figure.

Opposite: **Figure 4. The Salient Powers and the Elements of National Power.**

REGION/COUNTRY   FAVORABLE ELEMENTS OF NATIONAL POWER

N A O R T H	M E R	·Mexico ·Bermuda ·St.Pierre & Miquelon	Mexico shares the continent with a super-power and a major power, while the U.S. has a substantial Hispanic population and is dependent on Mexican oil—a defacto alliance. Bermuda and the French islands are in an even more favorable position.
C A R		·Puerto Rico ·Virgin Is.[US]	The United States would not tolerate aggrandizement of its territories; the U.S.S.R. knows that.
I B B E A N		·Anguilla ·Aruba ·British Virgin Islands ·Cayman Is. ·Guadeloupe ·Martinique ·Montserrat ·Neth.Antilles	These islands are legally associated with the U.K., France, or the Netherlands, all of which are members of NATO. Any attempt at aggrandizement would likely be consid-ered a NATO concern, particularly if the the U.S.S.R. were involved. The proximity of the United States combined with the great distance to either the Soviet Union or other plausible opponents enhances the deterrence.
S O U T H	A M E R I C A	·Argentina ·Bolivia ·Chile ·Colombia ·Ecuador ·French Guiana ·Guyana ·Paraguay ·Peru ·Suriname ·Trinidad&Tobago ·Uruguay ·Venezuela	Except for civil conflict and minor con-flicts such as the recent Falkland Islands campaign, South America has seen only one war in 120 years (Chaco War, 1932-35). Spanish is the common language, except in Brazil and French Guiana, and the continent has global insularity. At times, the civil wars in some of these countries, particu-larly Columbia, and to a lesser extent in Bolivia, have been tragic. Additionally, most South American nations are saddled with considerable international debt. Yet none of these factors augers for a major war, at least not on a scale that would give U.S. defense planners any serious cause for concern.
N A T O	E U R O P E	·Greece ·Iceland ·Portugal ·Spain ·Turkey	The combined military expenditures of these five states is about 11 percent of the cen-tral NATO states, and some of these coun-tries have been demonstratively uncoopera-tive with the U.S. on basing rights. Nev-ertheless, in the event of attack, the full weight of NATO would be brought to bear.
W A R S A W	P A C T	·Bulgaria ·Czechoslovakia ·Germany[GDR] ·Hungary ·Poland ·Romania	Though the Warsaw Pact has all but disin-tegrated, the geographical position of these six countries remain in buffer status primarily favoring the West. That is, in the unlikely event the U.S.S.R. elected to attack western Europe, she would first have to reconquer these countries, and in the process give NATO all the warning needed.

Figure 5. Buffer States and Contributing Elements

E N **U E** **R U** **O T** **P R** **E A** **A L** **N S** *	·Albania ·Andorra ·Austria ·Finland .Gibraltar ·Ireland ·Liechtenstein ·Malta ·Monaco ·San Marino ·Sweden ·Switzerland ·Yugoslavia	Neutrality in Europe, given the superpower checkmate and the negligible potential for intra-European wars, is an abstract legality. Any major war in the NATO region would inevitably affect these countries and any aggrandizement of them by the U.S.S.R. would likely result in a NATO reaction. Geography also plays a major role in this defacto deterrence alliance, in that most of these neutrals are surrounded by de jure aligned powers.
D **E** **N**	·Greenland ·Faeroe Islands	These are Danish possessions. Any aggrandizement would be considered an attack on NATO, hence the deterrence is effective.
A **S** **I** **A**	·Hong Kong	Control reverts to China in 1997.
	·Indonesia ·Malaysia ·Singapore	These ASEAN treaty states are relatively isolated from the Indochina region. Indonesia, in particular, has had considerable civil war, but the passive elements of national power mean an effective deterrence.
	·Japan	The third if not the second strongest economy in the world and is an ally of the U.S., though she is highly dependent on foreign oil and is vulnerable to tariffs.
	·North Korea ·South Korea	Both are too well prepared to invite military aggression. South Korea has no intention of invading North Korea, while in the reverse case, N. Korea would face the U.S.
	·Mongolia	Politically aligned with U.S.S.R.
	·Nepal ·Pakistan	These states are the limit for buffer state status. Nepal is aligned with India, and Pakistan wields considerable regional clout. Geography favors defense.
P I **A S** **C L** **I A** **F N** **I D** **C S**	·New Zealand	Insular; latently aligned with U.S. and Australia.
	·AmerSomoa ·Guam ·Pac.Trust Terr.	The American defense umbrella obviously encompasses these islands.
	·Brit.Trust Terr ·Christmas Is. ·Cocos ·Cook Is ·Fr.Polynesia ·New Caledonia ·Niue ·NorfolkIs ·Tokelau ·Turks ·Wallis&Fortuna	These are territories or protectorates of NATO countries or New Zealand. As small islands, they may not be able to resist some forms of local aggression, but the opportunities are severely limited. The British Trust Territory, which has no permanent population, is the site of the U.S. base on the island of Diego Garcia.

*Plus the islands of Guernsey, Isle of Man, Jersey, & St. Helena.

REGION/COUNTRY	Shortcomings Contributing to the Inability to Sustain Deterrence Against Aggrandizement
ALL OF CENTRAL AMERICA ·Belize ·Costa Rica ·El Salvador ·Guatemala ·Honduras ·Nicaragua ·Panama	All of these countries have seen con-siderable war in this century, though most of it has been either civil war or intervention on the part of the United States. However, because of the proximi-ty of the U.S., the risk of a Soviet in-vasion or takeover is miniscule, notwith-standing inevitable local wars. Soviet influence in the region does exist after a fashion, but it is largely haphazard and ineffective.
REMAINING WESTERN IS. ·Antigua & Barbuda ·Bahamas ·Barbados ·Cuba .Dominica ·Dominican Republic ·Grenada ·Haiti ·Jamaica ·St.Kitts ·St.Lucia ·St.Vincent&Grenadine ·Falkland Islands	Unlike the buffer-state Caribbean islands these states are not aligned with a sal-ient power, and most of them are poor states. Their relative isolation makes them prey for proxy aggrandizement. The U.S. can easily react to a "Grenada sit-uation," but it cannot necessarily deter it from occurring. In the case of Cuba, her meddling in the affairs of other states may trigger a military reaction, even if limited to retaliatory strikes. As for the Falkland Is., Argentina still wants the U.K. to relinquish sovereignty.
EUROPE ·Cyprus	Cyprus is afflicted with a long-standing civil war, involving a number of neigh-boring countries with ethnical affinity.
AFRICA* ·Algeria ·Zaire ·Angola ·Zambia ·Cameroon ·Zimbabwe ·Egypt ·Ethiopia ·Ghana ·Ivory Coast ·Kenya ·Libya ·Morocco ·Nigeria ·South Africa ·Sudan ·Tanzania ·Tunisia	Africa is the poorest of the continents. Its collective GNP is about a tenth that of the U.S. Half of that GNP is concen-trated in just three states (Algeria, Ni-geria, South Africa), and 90 percent in 18 states listed on the left. This means the collective GNP of the poorest 37 African states is one percent of the U.S. GNP. However, with the end of colonial-ism, most of these states have become un-inviting targets for invasion, while most of the wars that do occur are either civ-il, or ethnic conflicts between adjacent states. Thus, it is a fair conclusion that while some of these states can de-fend themselves, none can *deter* war.

*The other African states: Benin, Botswana, Burkina Faso, Burundi, Cape Verde, C. African Rep., Chad, Comoros, Congo, Djibouti, Eq. Guinea, Gabon, Gambia, Guinea, Guinea-Bissau, Lesotho, Liberia, Madagascar, Malawi, Mali, Mauritania, Mauritius, Mayotte, Mozambique, Namibia, Niger, Réunion, Rwanda, São Tomé and Príncipe, Senegal, Seychelles, Sierra Leone, Somalia, Swaziland, Togo, Uganda, and Western Sahara.

Figure 6. Remainder States and Their Shortcomings

MIDDLE EAST ·Afghanistan ·Bahrain ·Iran ·Syria ·Iraq ·United Arab ·Israel Emirates ·Jordan ·Yemen Arab ·Kuwait Republic ·Lebanon ·Yemen,Peo. ·Oman Dem.Rep. ·Qatar ·Saudi Arabia	More than half of remainder-state discretionary GNP and more than two-thirds of its military expenditures are concentrated in a sixth of the remainder state land mass, most of which is uninhabitable desert. The Israel/Arab conflict, the large oil reserves, Soviet global ambitions, and religious conflicts all contribute to the history of war in this region. Israel's ability to defend herself in war is not to be denied, but to date that prowess has been insufficient to deter invasions (and terrorism).
ASIA ·Bangladesh ·Bhutan	Neither of these countries has the necessary resources to deter war, notwithstanding the mountainous terrain in Bhutan, though an invasion of either country is unlikely.
·Kampuchea ·Laos ·Vietnam	These probably are the most war-torn nations in this century. They do not have the resources to ward off invasions, especially among themselves.
·Burma(Un.of Myanmar) ·Thailand	The proximity to Indochina makes these states subject to war; Burma less so than Thailand.
·Maldives ·Sri Lanka	These island states south of India are afflicted, like Cyprus, with long-standing civil war, wars which may continue to encourage intervention by India.
·Macau ·Taiwan	China is not likely to seize Macau, but in the event, there would be no stopping it. Taking on Taiwan would be more difficult. However, if this did occur, the U.S. would not likely intervene.
PACIFIC ·Philippines	Long-standing civil war and insurrection, and a shaky political infrastructure, given major U.S. bases located there, offer some potential for war.
·Brunei ·Papua New Guinea	Invasion of these states is unlikely, but neither has the resources to deter it. Brunei, which is small, is a member of the ASEAN pact; Papua New Guinea is not.
·Fiji ·Vanuatu ·Kiribati ·Western ·Nauru Somoa ·Solomon Is ·Tonga ·Tuvalu	These are independent island nations with limited resources. They too do not have the means to defend themselves, much less the ability to deter invasion, though would-be invaders much larger than another island risk a war with the U.S.

Part II
War as an Instrument
of Geopolitical Policy

One of the surprising things in the literature of geopolitics is how few volumes really address the nature of war. Clausewitz's magnum opus *On War* stands out in part because there is little competition. Arguably, only Thucydides' *The Peloponnesian War* surpasses it in eloquence, and the latter is more history than analysis. Even more remarkable is the fact that *On War* for the most part is poorly organized. Clausewitz died before he could edit his manuscript fully; only the first 50 pages or so evince organization. This notwithstanding, his masterpiece is not likely to be supplanted any time soon.

Clausewitz's primary tenet was that wars were a continuation of policy by other means, meaning that wars were — or should be — fought for some definite political purpose and not as an exercise in lethal chivalry. But he also observed that wars are never the end of things; they only change the scenery, as it were. He then hedged his bet for a number of reasons and noted wars tend to escalate out of hand and push a country into a position from which it cannot easily extricate itself. That position causes the nation to violate the primary tenet of war: A nation should not try to reach beyond its grasp.

Abraham Lincoln, who presided over the bloodiest war in American history, understood this point well. In the early stages of the Civil War he was continuously badgered to set free the slaves in the border states. Because he realized how tenuous the loyalty of Kentucky was to the Union, he refused. His critics then weighed in with the argument that God would be on his side. The reply was to the effect that while he would like to have God on his side, he must have Kentucky.

This tale is apocryphal, albeit based on an actual incident. Yet it suffices to illustrate a point. War should be fought for a specific purpose, and then only when there is no other recourse. Moreover, no matter how worthy the cause, the leader intent on success must ensure that sufficient resources and wherewithal are available to see the war through.

This part of the book focuses first on the anatomy of war and then on what seems to be the pivotal aspect of warfare — the dynamics of what Clausewitz called the culminating point. (This term has finally gained acknowledgment in military literature.)

From this perspective, the analysis next reexamines the role of the United States in World War II. As magnificent as that period of American history was, the common interpretation of the United States role vastly overstates the facts and has generated a flawed perspective on the nature and dynamics of war and even more so on the understanding of the elements of national power. That is, war never has been all that efficient and perhaps has lost much of what efficacy it formerly offered.

That loss has given rise to terrorism, which is the subject of the final chapter in this part of the book. Terrorism, like war, is an instrument of policy, though it doesn't offer a battlefield in the normal sense of the world. On the contrary, far from being a challenge to warriors, the intent, in part, is to frustrate them. Yet because on the highest level it is a form of war, it remains a problem of defense.

Chapter 6. The Anatomy of War

Both parties deprecated war, but one of them would *make* war rather than let the nation survive; and the other would *accept* war rather than let it perish. And the war came.

— Abraham Lincoln
Second Inaugural Address

War has been described since ancient times as *ultima ratio regum* — the final argument of kings. It has also been said that truth is the first victim of war, in that most wars of aggrandizement are based on strained rationalizations. Internal criticism of a war effort is likely to be suppressed. But what of the nation that must defend itself? That form of war cannot be considered rationalization unless the process of defense exceeds its purpose and the intended victim assumes the role of the original aggressor. The point is that war is not a simple concept and cannot be analyzed using one or two watershed terms. It has its own lexicon and anatomy that beckons review to understand its relationship to national and geopolitical power.

To that end, this chapter evaluates the anatomy of war as ten aspects. The first five might be considered the qualitative aspects: (1) the military *intent* of war, (2) the *forms* of war, (3) the *levels* of war, (4) the *scope* of war, and (5) the extent of *participation*. The next three aspects are factor-oriented: (6) the *quantitative* factors, (7) the *subjective* factors, and (8) *20th century* factors, which are the inordinate factors introduced only within this century. The last two comprise the polemics of war, the degrees of (9) *definition,* and (10) *controllability.* Figure 7 provides an overview of these terms and their respective meanings.

Military Intent

The famed Clausewitz divided wars into two types pegged on intent: *absolute* wars and *limited* wars.[1] The intent of absolute war is to effectively eliminate an opponent's ability to wage war or alternatively to cause him to surrender unconditionally. A limited war is any conflict with lesser intent.

47

QUALITATIVE ASPECTS

```
MILITARY INTENT
 ·ABSOLUTE WAR - To effectively eliminate an opponent's means of war.
 ·LIMITED WAR  - A military campaign or action short of absolute war.

FORMS OF WAR
 ·DEFENSIVE - To maintain, restore, but not exceed the status quo.
 ·GRAY-AREA - Deterrence, denial and counterdenial operations.
 ·OFFENSIVE - To exceed the status quo on any scale for any reason.

LEVELS OF WAR
 ·NATIONAL    - The political context of a war and sum of operations.
 ·OPERATIONAL - A region & period of time in which battles are fought.
 ·TACTICAL    - The battlefield and its immediate environment.

SCOPE OF WAR
 ·INTERNATIONAL - War between or among sovereignties on any scale.
 ·CONSOLIDATION - War to consolidate ethnically related sovereignties.
 ·CIVIL         - War within a sovereignty, with or sans foreign aid.

EXTENT OF PARTICIPATION
 ·PRIMARY    - One sovereignty dominates the side under consideration.
 ·COALITION  - Two or more sovereignties allied on at least one side.
 ·SUPPORTIVE - Support of an ally, short of tactical engagement.
```

FACTORIAL ASPECTS

```
QUANTITATIVE FACTORS
 ·PROXIMITY      - Comparative distance to the site of hostilities.
 ·FORCE RATIO    - The net effective military strength ratio.
 ·ESCALATION RISK - The risk of more war than bargained for.

SUBJECTIVE FACTORS
 ·NATIONAL INTERESTS - The perceived aim and purpose of the war.
 ·NATIONAL RESOLVE   - Largely the ethos & infrastructure of a state.
 ·POLITICAL JUDGMENT - Perception & character of a nation's leaders.

20TH CENTURY FACTORS
 ·LOGISTICS        - Requirements increasing at an exponential rate.
 ·TECHNOLOGY       - Tends increasingly to favor defense of nations.
 ·GAS/GERM WARFARE - Essentially intolerable among developed nations.
 ·NUCLEAR WEAPONS  - Incomprehensible and intolerable damage.
```

POLEMIC ASPECTS

```
DEGREE OF DEFINITION
 ·A range from     - Defensive wars tend to have a clear definition,
  CLEAR to OBSCURE    while offensive wars tend to become obscure.

CONTROLLABILITY
 ·From CONTROLLABLE - Defensive wars tend to be highly controllable;
  to UNCONTROLLABLE    offensive wars quickly lose controllability.
```

Figure 7. A Lexicon of War

Absolute wars do not necessarily incur more casualties and damage than limited wars, and both types can evince high or low intensity warfare. The United States has fought three absolute wars: the Civil War from the Union perspective, the American Indian "wars," and World War II. The Indian wars were low intensity; the other two, high. All other American wars and conflicts have been limited, including its participation in World War I. In that war the carnage was deplorable, but in the end Germany still had the ability to wage war and did not surrender unconditionally.

The significance of the difference between absolute versus limited wars is greater than it appears. First, if the military intent is anything less than the elimination of the opponent's ability to wage war, then the opponent may not give in to the political intent of the conflict as easily as anticipated. Second, and because of the preceding item, the initial military intent of a limited war may change within the course of a war and can escalate to the absolute level without a studied decision to do so. This cannot happen in an absolute war, though additional countries can be dragged into the conflict. Third, limited wars may have a wide range of specific intent and in some cases are "fought" without actual hostilities, though the heightened potential for actual warfare is obvious in these circumstances. As such, the political and economic objectives in limited wars tend to be more pronounced than in absolute wars.

The Forms of War

Most wars are variations on a single paradigm; one side is on the offensive and the other on the defensive. This refers to the national perspective, not to offensive and defensive tactics employed in military operations. These national roles, however, are often reversed in the course of a war. When this happens the nature of the war changes for both participants. The criterion for a national defensive posture is to restore or maintain the status quo; for an offensive posture, to go beyond the status quo. In more detail:

Wars of Defense. A war of defense usually translates to the expulsion of an invader from one's own or an ally's territory or possessions but may or may not amount to the crushing of the invader's ability to wage war. However, even if the defender is waging only a limited war, the opponent may be conducting an absolute war. For example, the political goal of the Confederacy was to sever ties with the Union, which meant going beyond the status quo, notwithstanding the military goal was limited, i.e. to merely expel Union forces from the South. By contrast, the political intent of the Union was to preserve the Union—the status quo—but militarily it had to fight an absolute war to achieve that goal.

Wars of defense also include: (1) preemptive attacks aimed solely at forces poised to invade one's own or an ally's territory, (2) defense against an insurrection, and (3) rescue operations, though in each case the tactics will differ. The first variation is self-explanatory. The second hinges on the criterion of maintaining the status quo. The third—rescue operations—entails the retrieval of hostages (or conceivably, material objects of extraordinary importance) held by a foreign power or terrorists and thus also seeks only to restore the status quo. The fact that the action may occur on foreign soil or international water and that the tactics give the appearance of offensive action are immaterial provided the objective is restricted to obtaining the release of the hostages. However, any damage or casualties inflicted must be incidental to the rescue operation for the conflict to remain defensive. Retaliation would transform the conflict to offensive warfare irrespective of how justified that retaliation might be.

Wars of Offense. This form of war is any war which goes beyond maintaining the status quo but may range from naked aggrandizement of territory belonging to an established sovereignty to a half-hearted attempt to persuade another country to revise its policy. The former case, of course, tends to absolute war though the invader will usually settle for unconditional surrender. Here, attainment of the political objective in part coincides with the attainment of the military objectives. This is not true in limited wars of intervention. These wars are waged not so much against military force as against a political opponent with the objective of persuading that opponent to alter (a) his geopolitical posture, (b) his form of government, or (c) some policy.

Conflicts in the Gray Area. A few conflicts fail to fit neatly into either a defensive or an offensive national posture. The intent is to maintain the status quo, but the methods used are either offensive in nature or pose an obvious risk that they will escalate to that form. Deterrence is the most common example of this form of "conflict." If and when deterrence fails, the ensuing war will inevitably and immediately change to an offensive-defensive paradigm, but in the interim the conflict remains in the gray-area form. This is no small point. The overwhelming use of military force among the salient powers today is in the form of deterrent "warfare."

Another type of this gray-area form comprises self-standing denial or counterdenial operations. Denial operations inevitably translate into blockades or barrier plans, mixing military force with terrain features or choke points at sea. A denial operation uses firepower only when the opponent attempts to break through the barrier and then only to the extent of preventing that breakthough. The immediate military objective of a denial operation may be to contain an opponent within a specified area or to prevent him from entering a specified area. The purpose of the denial operation is usually to prevent the opponent from gaining some form of military advantage or to prevent access to a critical material or to necessary trade. A counterdenial operation would be the inverse of this—to gain a military advantage or to continue access to the material or trade, providing those objectives could be achieved by the breakthrough alone. If and when a limited war exceeds these restrictions, its form usually changes to an offensive-defensive paradigm in which a denial operation occurs.

In practice, most operations of this form occur within the context of larger wars, e.g. the blockade of the Confederacy (denial) in the Civil War, and the Battle of the Atlantic during World War II (counterdenial), and thus should not be considered as a gray-area form of war. Two genuine examples of this form were the blockade (or "quarantine") solution to the Cuban missile crisis (denial) and the Berlin Airlift (counterdenial). A third example would be the U.S. military operations in the Persian Gulf—which amount to a preemptive counterdenial operation. The first two cases simmered without boiling over, though the potential in both was obvious, and in the Cuban case, perhaps greater than surmised. In the Persian Gulf, the actual combat has been limited to isolated events, but again the risk of a far more extensive war is self-evident.

The Levels of War

The military has always relied on chains of command. War, too, has its own chain of command, in three tiers: the national, operational and tactical levels. They differ significantly from each other. Chapters 7 and 8 focus on the differences between the national and operational levels; Appendix B, the operational and tactical levels, albeit with a reprise on the national level.

The National Level. This level equates with the preservation and advancement of national aims and interests and demands a sense of justice and a refined sense of priorities. When war is fought defensively to survive as a nation, the relationship is obvious. When war is used as an instrument of imprudent policy, the relationship becomes increasingly strained. Irrespective of the situation, however, the national level regards war as a means to an end. Hence, in wartime the head of state may be the commander-in-chief.

The Operational Level. Military operations are usually conducted in a defined geographical region for a sustained period of time, under military command that must answer to political leadership and normally comprises a series or sequence of tactical engagements. For the most part, logistical considerations seem to take priority over warrior abilities. The hallmarks of a successful operational commander are preseverance and perspective.

The Tactical Level. The tactical level equates with the battlefield and is marked by intensity of combat and a premium on warrior ability. It is where the action is. In contrast to the operational commander, the hallmarks of a tactical commander are willfulness and courage. Perhaps that is the reason most military history concentrates on battles and tends to equate war with the sum of its battles. No more serious mistake has ever been made.

Scope of Wars

Most wars are either *international,* that is, between or among nations, or *civil,* between factions within a single nation. The exception is a war of *consolidation,* which usually manifests itself in an attempt to forcefully consolidate strongly ethnically related peoples currently under two or more sovereignties. Bismarck's campaign to unify the states which would make up Germany is probably the outstanding example of this exception.

In most cases of international war, identifying the attacker and the defender — at least of the moment — is fairly easy. In the case of civil war, such identification can be more difficult. But if defensive war is defined as a means of maintaining or restoring the status quo, the resolution is facilitated. The player in power, i.e., the one respecting or enforcing the sovereignty of a nation, should be presumed to be on the defensive; the insurrectionists, the offensive — even if the government in power was tyrannical and conducted offensive military operations against the insurrectionists.

However, where the latter manages to establish a bona fide sovereignty of its own, recognized by other nations, then a civil war transforms into an international conflict. Thus the American Revolutionary War became an international war when France recognized the new government. By contrast, the American Civil War remained a civil war because no other country ever recognized the Confederacy. The *Trent* affair was between Great Britain and the United States. Though the Southern emissaries on board the *Trent* were not recognized as diplomats, Great Britain did not take kindly to the forceful boarding of its ship. Had Lincoln not backed down and apologized, the incident might have resulted in British recognition of the Confederacy and perhaps changed the course of the war.

Extent of Participation

A country or insurrectionist group at war usually falls into one of three categories: (1) the *primary* defender or aggressor, with or without support by other countries; (2) a member nation in *coalition* warfare; or (3) in *support* of another nation without becoming a full-fledged participant. Analysis of wars must take into account the role of each player. This can and does lead to confusion. For example, in the Revolutionary War, Great Britain was fighting an absolute war against the United States, while the latter was content merely to expel the English from America. France aligned herself with and supported the United States though more to inflict damage on a common enemy rather than for any great love of America. Had Napoleon arisen in Germany rather than France and a little earlier than he did, the United States might not have prevailed in the Revolution or perhaps the war might not have been necessary at all. In Vietnam 200 years later, the confusion became unintangible. There is no such word, of course, but then hopefully there will never be another such war.

The Quantitative Factors of War

At least three quantitative factors affect the outcome of war: (a) the comparative *proximity* of the players to the scene of the conflict; (b) the effective *military force strength radio* that is or can be invested in the conflict, which may include deployment speed; and (c) the *risk* or probability of the conflict escalating into a wider war within the same or into a different intent, form or scope. The effects of these factors are dependent, in part, on the subjective factors discussed shortly.

Relative Proximity. As a general rule, the closer to home a war is fought, the greater the chance of success, all other things being equal. Fighting on or near home turf reduces the cost of logistical support and its vulnerability to interdiction. On the other hand, the further away from one's territory a war is fought, the less likely it would be a serious threat to national interests except when it involves a global imbalance of power or when access to a critical resource or trade has been denied with no alternative supplies.

Military Force Strength Ratio. This factor needs little explanation per se, but the ratio is modified by the facets of tactical ability, appropriateness of equipment to the environment, status of training and moral, and anything else which serves to multiply or reduce the *effective* strength. As a general rule, military strength deteriorates when committed to an operation and therefore to prevail requires either marked — very marked — superiority or the capability of continuous reinforcement and regeneration.

Risk of Escalation. Risk is inherently quantitative though seldom reduced to precise numbers. Thus to the extent a proposed use of military force wicks more war than a nation is willing to wage, so much less inclined will it be to pursue that course of action. But subjective factors can and do cloud political judgment, either by underestimating the risk of escalation or by presuming such escalation can be controlled. This is more of a problem in the poorly charted waters of limited wars than in absolute war.

The Subjective Factors

Aristotle remarked that man was a political animal. Nothing in the intervening 2,400 years suggests that his observation was in error. Politics is inherently subjective, and as politics usually governs whether war will be initiated, or defended against, and if so to what extent, it is not surprising that subjective factors exercise a dominant influence in war. These factors may be considered under three headings:

National Interests. In general, a strong correlation exists between the criticality of national interests affected by a threat and the successful prosecution of war to the end of parrying or otherwise defusing that threat. An attack on one's homeland, a threatened loss of critical supplies or trade, or a bona fide worldwide imbalance of power are all examples of unmistakable threats to critical national interests, which will be discussed in Chapter 10. But when it comes to interventions based on ideological differences or in remainder-state

civil wars, the national interests served are less clear and difficult to translate
into effective military operations.

National Resolve. National resolve is closely linked with national interests, but the two do not always operate in tandem. When threatened with
defeat, one nation may fight to the death, e.g. Israel at Masada; another may
capitulate without much of a struggle. For lesser struggles, resolve may be an
inverse function of the duration of war. In the aftermath of Vietnam, the U.S.
Army nearly added political support as a tenth principle of war.[2] It's always
been there, of course, except that it is the first, not the tenth, principle.

Political Judgment. History evinces untold carnage and destruction from
wars fought unnecessarily or pursued past the point of diminishing returns.
Even Clausewitz, who argued wars should be subordinated to political purpose, pointed out that altogether too many wars ran amuck.[3] Other analysts
suggest that bad judgment at the national level is more the rule than the exception.[4] Whatever the truth may be, the one thing certain is that imprudent political judgment is a very old problem. Consider, for example, this
harangue:

> Your country has a right to your services in sustaining the glories of her posi-
> tion. These are a common source of pride to you all, and you cannot decline
> the burdens of empire and still expect to share its honours. You should
> remember also that what you are fighting against is not merely slavery as an
> exchange for independence, but also loss of empire and danger from
> animosities incurred in its exercise. Besides, to recede is no longer possible, if
> indeed any of you in the alarm of the moment has become enamoured of the
> honesty of such an unambitious part. For what you hold is, to speak somewhat
> plainly, a tyranny; to take it perhaps was wrong, but to let it go unsafe.[5]

That speech may seem like an eloquent version of the Axis rationale during World War II, but in point of fact it was spoken by Pericles early in the
Peloponnesian war, a war which Athens—in its "golden age"—pursued for 25
years until she was thoroughly trounced by Sparta. The history of that war, including this speech, comes down to us by courtesy of an Athenian general. It
is mandatory reading in at least one senior service college.[6]

Twentieth Century Factors

Howard K. Smith is wont to relate his first encounter—as a Rhodes
Scholar—with a don at Oxford University. "I want to study modern history,"
proffered Smith, "not eighteenth century history, mind you, but modern
history." The don replied, "But my dear fellow, the eighteenth century *is*
modern history."

In the case of war, however, the eighteenth century is not really modern. Four factors have arisen in the twentieth century that radically change the conduct if not the nature of war: (1) the exponentially increasing weight of logistical support required per man per day in battle; (2) the increasing technological effectiveness of defensive weapons; (3) large-scale biological and chemical warfare; and (4) nuclear and thermonuclear weapons. The overall significance of these factors is to make war prohibitively expensive—in more than financial terms—for the potential gains sought in most cases, at least for the salient powers.

Logistical Support Requirements. As shown in Figure 8, the pounds-per-day required to sustain one man in combat is rising at an exponential rate. The significance is fairly obvious in that for every pound of military or combat support material required, the elements of national power of a nation must be taxed at a greater rate, not only in terms of production and transportation but by denial or delay of production of domestic requirements.

Technology. As discussed in Appendix A, technology increasingly favors the defensive, except in the Armageddon sense of thermonuclear warfare, in which case neither side can really claim any kind of victory. Advantages accrue to defensive technology because offensive weapons tend to evolve into behemoths and in the process are more easily defeated by lighter, more maneuverable, cheaper, defensive counterweapons, at a time when the behemoths are reaching their maximum feasible size.

Gas and Germ Warfare. This is an old form of warfare but was not widely used until World War I. Its use is now considered repugnant by most of the salient powers and buffer states. Since 1918, these countries have used it only in a few limited cases.[7] On the other hand, these weapons are sometimes considered to be "the poor nation's nuclear power." The new chemical weapons plant in Libya has focused world attention on the issue.

Various estimates conclude that at least twenty nations now produce or have chemical weapons and that ten nations have stockpiled biological agents.[8] Also it is fairly certain that both Iraq and Iran employed chemical agents during their recent long war. If the results of the Nuclear Nonproliferation Treaty are any indication, attempts to halt the proliferation of toxic agents may prove even less successful. The significance is that aggressive nations must be prepared to suffer retaliation by this form of warfare.

Nuclear and Thermonuclear Weapons. This factor, of course, overshadows all the other twentieth century factors combined. As discussed in Chapter 4, the use of these weapons makes the issue of war as an instrument of policy a moot point, except in the limited sense of deterrence. If anything, the extent of their destructive potential has been underestimated.

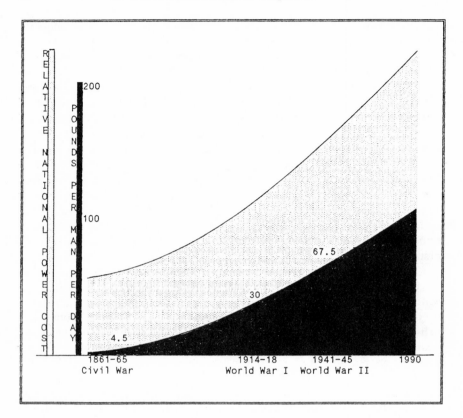

Figure 8. The Exponentially Rising Cost of War. The logistical cost of war in terms of national power is a proportional multiple of weight, due to: (1) the economic cost of producing the material, (2) the high cost of transporting and distributing the material, (3) losses from interdiction en route to the theater of operations, and (4) the increasing vulnerability of expensive implements of war—ships, aircraft, and tanks—to relatively inexpensive missiles. No singular index of national power exists and therefore it remains undimensioned, but successful prosecution of wars of aggression or intervention must scale the increasingly steep curve of national power cost. Source of the data: Eston T. White and Val E. Hendrix, *Defense Acquisition and Logistics Management* (Washington, DC: National Defense University, 1984), p. 6.

The Polemic Facets of War

The last two facets comprise two scalar dimensions that aptly describe the effects of shifting from the defensive to the offensive form of warfare, especially in limited war situations. In general, a nation on the defensive has the advantages of a war which is definable and controllable. That is, when a war shifts from the defensive to the offensive, the attributes of that war tend to shift from clearly defined objectives to ambiguity, and from controllable circumstances to uncontrollable.

Degree of Definition. A war of self-defense provides a crystal-clear paradigm of definition. In this situation an aggressor has invaded or otherwise occupied territory under the rightful sovereignty of another nation. The object of the defensive war is to expel the invader from that territory or, alternatively, to preempt him from the invasion itself. No more; no less. A rescue operation is self-defense with a change of venue. The slight loss of definition arises not so much from the military action required but from various side issues as (a) the option of paying a ransom in some cases, and (b) the possibility that the hostages have been removed from the location where originally held, or alternatively, uncertainty as to where the hostages are being held and if they are still alive.

The attribute of definition begins to cloud up in the case of gray-area conflict due to a wide range of factors, such as (a) the criteria for denial of passage, (b) the alternative approaches the opponent may use, and (c) and the occasional difficulty of defining the area. Yet the military paradigm is still reasonably clear irrespective of the probability of success for the resources invested. The same is rarely true of limited wars of intervention, where the relationship between military objectives and political or ideological purpose is more abstract than self-defense, a rescue operation, or a blockade. Absolute wars of aggression suffer from the same defect unless the aggressor has overwhelming superiority and can ensure that no other nations join in alliance against him other than those he intends to fight and against whom he can prevail. Ancient history evinces many wars in which these conditions were common; modern history does not. However, defenders have succeeded in turning back aggressive nations and then inflicting total defeat on them, most notably in World War II.

Controllability. Controllability means the extent to which a nation can keep a conflict within boundaries: geographical, funding, military forces employed, and nations involved. As such, controllability ranks high in wars of self-defense almost by definition. The territory is limited to the area invaded, and therefore as long as war is restricted to the expulsion of the aggressor, it is controllable even if the defender loses. Rescue operations are only slightly less controllable. There is always some risk the rescue attempt will be considered aggression and lead to more serious war.

Controllability is further weakened in gray-area conflicts, particularly when insufficient forces are available to cover the waterfront, as it were. More significantly, preemptive attacks against approaching units, or the pursuit of units which slip through the net, tend to escalate hostilities to a war of intervention. Offensive wars, of course, have the least controllability. The military objectives may or may not support the political objectives, and moreover, the opponent may throw more military force into the conflict than the intervening state cares to deal with. In many cases this encourages the latter to up the ante when he really cannot afford it.

The Special Case of Guerrilla Warfare

Guerrilla warfare has become a popular subject in military literature over the last 30 years. Supposedly, it is radically different from conventional forms, suggesting that attempts to combat it by conventional means are doomed to failure. Perhaps so, in the tactical sense, but war is war. To begin with, guerrilla warfare typically relies on hit-and-run tactics until a more conventional means of warfare can be applied, except when the targeted infrastructure is so weak the hit-and-run tactics suffice, for example, Cuba's revolution under Fidel Castro. As such, guerrilla warfare can be either absolute or limited, with the political purposes in both cases equal to the perspective of the revolutionary leaders.

Further, guerrilla warfare is usually but not always civil in nature, though it may require the support of sympathizers and perhaps coalition warfare. And guerrillas normally have the advantage of proximity and make up in astute tactics what they lack in strength. Their operations are often well defined and well controlled. In short, once the perspective is raised above the battlefield, guerrilla warfare isn't all that different from conventional forms. It is a serious error to consider it otherwise, as the United States did in Vietnam.[9] This point is again examined in Chapter 8.

Chapter 7. Culminating Points: When Reach Exceeds Grasp

When valor preys on reason,
It eats the sword it fights with.
                    — Shakespeare

The anatomy of war generates its own dynamics, its own physiology, as it were. But compared to physiology, the dynamics of war offer a clearer perspective. In most instances, a nation, coalition, or faction takes the initiative, while one or more opponents must defend against that onslaught. The surprising thing about most wars is that the side taking the initiative usually loses. Even when that side prevails, the advantages gained are often short-lived or prove illusory. If so, the phenomenon must have its roots and causes.

What happens is deceptively simple. The side which takes the initiative must have the power and wherewithal to prevail in what can be a protracted struggle. Because almost all of the aspects of war, as discussed in the previous chapter, tend to favor the defensive from the national if not the tactical perspective, the resources of the aggressor are drained at a greater rate than those of the defender. The reach quickly exceeds the grasp unless that aggressor possesses overwhelming resources with respect to the object of the aggression.

The reader may ask, if this process is so simple and obvious, and if it superintends the whole of war and of battle, why hasn't it been documented before? It has. Clausewitz developed the idea in his *On War,* published in 1832. More than 150 years later, it was finally recognized as a "key concept of operational design" in the current edition of Army Field Manual 100-5 *Operations.* Why it took so long is a matter of speculation, but it is not unusual for profound concepts to take a century or more to burrow their own tap roots. Clausewitz himself brought up the issue only toward the end of his book, and FM 100-5 includes it only as the last item in the next-to-last appendix. Moreover, the subject is rarely mentioned, if at all, at the senior service colleges.

The Meaning of Culminating Point

FM 100-5 starts the discussion on culminating points in clear terms which immediately convey both the meaning and the significance of the concept.

> Unless it is strategically decisive, every offensive operation will sooner or later reach a point where the strength of the attacker no longer significantly exceeds that of the defender, and beyond which continued offensive operations therefore risk overextension, counterattack, and defeat. In operational theory, this point is called the culminating point. The art of attack at all levels is to achieve decision objectives *before* the culminating point is reached. Conversely, the art of defense is to hasten the culmination of the attack, recognize its advent, and be prepared to go over to the offense when it arrives.[1]

The manual lists a number of reasons for this phenomenon followed by examples. The reasons include insufficient logistical support, increasing vulnerability of lines of communication, and losses sustained during the offensive before decisive battle begins. The discussion concludes:

> For his part, the defender must seek to bring the enemy attack to or past its culminating point before it reaches an operationally decisive objective. To do so, he must operate not only on the enemy force itself, but also on its sustainment system. The more readily the defender can trade space for time without unacceptable operational or strategic loss, the easier this will be. Once operations begin, the attacking commander must sense when he has reached or is about to reach his culminating point, whether intended or not, and revert to the defense at a time and place of his own choosing. For his part, the defender must be alert to recognize when his opponent has become overextended and be prepared to pass over to the counteroffensive before the attacker is able to recover his strength.[2]

A well-written description of this caliber needs little commentary, but three aspects beg emphasis. First, the culminating point for the defending and the attacking commanders is one and the same, though it is not a static point on the ground. The defender tries to move the point away from the attacker toward himself to wear down the latter's effective strength, whereas the attacker tries to prevent that shift, or, failing in that, should break off the attack when it is obvious he has passed the point. It is a tug of war of sorts with the knot in the rope analogous to the culminating point.

Second, FM 100-5 implies the offensive may continue after the culminating point is reached, subject to defeat. By contrast, Clausewitz implied once the culminating point is passed, the chance of victory is lost unless the enemy yields from fear. If he chooses to fight it out, he will prevail. Restated, when the attacker passes the culminating point, further progress is merely forward motion on the road to perdition. The renowned analyst wrote:

Once the mind is set on a certain course toward its goal . . . it may easily happen that the arguments which would compel one man to stop, and justify another in acting, will not easily be fully appreciated. Meanwhile the action continues, and in the sweep of motion one crosses . . . the line of culmination, without knowing it. . . . We believe that this demonstrates without inconsistency how an attacker can overshoot the point at which, if he stopped and assumed the defensive, there would still be a chance of success. . . . It is therefore important to calculate this point correctly when planning the campaign. An attacker may otherwise take on more than he can manage and, as it were, get into debt; a defender must be able to recognize this error if the enemy commits it, and exploit it to the full.[3]

In the same chapter he also said:

This culminating point of victory is bound to recur in every future war in which the destruction of the enemy cannot be the military aim, and this will presumably be true of most wars. The natural goal of all campaigns, therefore, is the turning point at which the attack becomes the defense. If one were to go beyond that point, it would not merely be a *useless* effort which could not add to success. It would in fact be a *damaging* one, which would lead to a reaction; and experience goes to show that such reactions usually have completely disproportionate effects.[4]

Third, the culminating point can be a moot consideration. When the attacker has overwhelming strength and resolve, the point occurs only as an imaginary locus far behind the opponent's main battle lines. Conversely, when the attacker is hopelessly weak, the point coincides with the line of departure. During the 1987 Wimbleton tennis matches, Pam Shriver, having been thoroughly trounced in the semi-finals, said afterward that the "turning point" — read culminating point — of the match occurred when she walked out onto the court. With these aspects in mind, the dynamics of the culminating point concept explain the outcome of the most famous battle in American history.

Gettysburg

The climactic time and place of the battle of Gettysburg occurred during the early afternoon of July 3, 1863, and is said to have been the high water mark of the Confederacy. The great cyclorama maintained near the battlefield depicts the drama on Seminary Ridge in magnificent detail, but Seminary Ridge did not mark the culminating point. That point was passed on the approach to the ridge. The ensuing battle was the foreclosure on the debt — to use Clausewitz's analogy — incurred by Lee when he ordered the attack. For as capable and distinguished a general as Lee was, he suffered a momentary lapse of judgment that day. He had ordered an attack uphill across an open field against an experienced, entrenched defender fighting on his own soil and having the advantages of interior lines, reinforcement from reserves without interdiction, and leadership in the person of Lieutenant General George G. Meade.

Longstreet had recognized the futility of the plan of attack and had tried to dissuade Lee from pursuing it.[5] Lee persisted but admitted later the same day: "All this has been my fault. It is I that have lost the fight."[6] He recognized, after the fact, that he had ordered a decisive battle beyond the culminating point, and as such the Union decided it for him.

Yet this does not imply the culminating point functions like the law of gravity. On the contrary, an astute tactic can shift the point beyond the decisive place and time. As mentioned, Longstreet had recommended some form of tactical envelopment of the Union forces on Seminary Ridge. Had Lee accepted his advice, the battle might gone to the Confederacy. But not the war. In the larger perspective of Lee's operation and indeed the entire war itself, the South arguably had passed the culminating point before Gettysburg. She was expending irreplaceable resources while the North was able to replace her losses. Worse, the Confederacy was betting on the wrong horse. Bruce Catton put the case this way:

> Lee at Gettysburg was fighting against a man who never wore a uniform or fought a battle: the eminent Illinois civilian Abraham Lincoln. The whole rationale of the Confederate offensive that summer . . . was the belief that the Northern government would crack under the strain — that it would take troops away from General Grant, lose confidence in final victory when it saw Confederate troops in the Northern heartland, find the price of war too great to pay, and so consent at last to a formal separation. None of this happened.[7]

Recall Clausewitz's prediction that the culminating point was bound to recur in any future war in which the destruction of the opponent's forces was not the objective. The South intended only a limited war with the objective of securing recognition of the Confederacy. The North, by contrast, was intent on the absolute defeat of the South's ability to wage war. Since the North had the resources to prevail, and the South had neither the intention or ability to destroy those resources, the culminating point of the Civil War was reached and passed long before Lee intruded into Pennsylvania.

El Alamein and Gallipoli

FM 100-5 provides a number of other examples of passage of the culminating point, e.g. Rommel's drive into Egypt which ended at El Alamein.[8] But paralleling the Confederate experience at Seminary Ridge, El Alamein was not the culminating point, per se. That point, from an operational perspective, occurred earlier when superiority of resources accrued to Montgomery. Either Rommel failed to recognize the culminating point or, recognizing it, passed it due to Hitler's order to fight to the last man irrespective of the futility.

Another critical demonstration of the culminating point occurred at Gallipoli during World War I. The British national objective was naive, but the operational failure did not foreshadow national or Entente failure. The national objective had been to end the war early and decisively. This objective was translated into an operational objective to put the British fleet opposite Istanbul (then Constantinople). The theory was that Turkey would crumble politically at the sight of the fleet, withdraw from the Triple Alliance, join the Entente, and thus bring Kaiser Wilhelm to his knees.[9]

The operational objective was within range of the possible even if the hoped-for national goal was ludicrous. But this objective required passage of the Dardanelles. The strait was heavily mined at its narrowest part and was protected by Turkish forts out of range of effective naval bombardment. Precipitous as the risk was, sagacious tactics might have won the day. Instead the British forces committed multiple mistakes, resulting in a protracted struggle and dismal failure.[10] In short, the passage of the tactical and operational culminating points coincided, whereas passage of the national culminating point occurred when the British forces sailed into the region.

That the failure to prevail in the operation did *not* result in national defeat is due the fact the Entente had sufficient resources and resolve to pursue the war on the main, western front. Also the distant failure gave Germany no particular advantage on that front to exploit. Yet it should be asked if the expenditure of force at Gallipoli reduced the Entente forces on the western front below the point where victory might have been attained much earlier and without U.S. intervention some years later.

Analysis

The loss of sufficient combat strength prior to decisive conflict in these examples, as elsewhere, ensues from many causes. Some were mentioned above. In more detail, unofficial doctrine holds that it takes a three-to-one strength ratio for an attacker to dislodge a defender. In some cases, determined defenders have held out against ratios ten-to-one or even higher, for example, the Pusan perimeter during the early months of the Korean conflict. Now if the attacker tends to sustain greater losses during an approach and if the uncertainties of war tend to work hardest against the side in motion, how much strength is required at the line of departure to ensure a three-to-one, or possibly much higher, force ratio at the decisive times and places of battle? Moreover, because the defender can usually "trade space for time" in order to

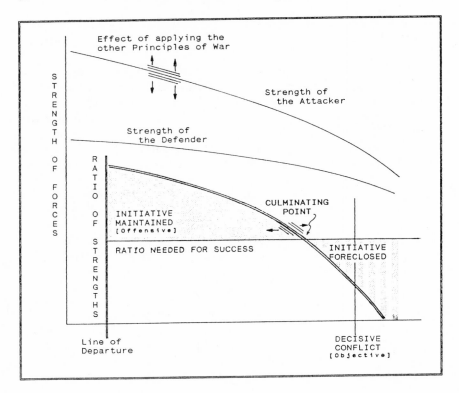

Figure 9. Dynamics of the Culminating Point. The ratio of the strengths of the attacker and defender are represented by the double-line curve in the inner graph. On this graph, the culminating point — which means insufficient mass — occurs when the ratio falls below the necessary value to inflict a decisive defeat on the opponent *before* the opportune time to do so. The ratio must be increased to prevent this from occurring. However, applying the principles of maneuver (in particular), simplicity, surprise, security, and unity of command can also push the culminating point back by virtue of increasing the effective strength ratio in favor of the attacker. Restated, if the strength ratio is insufficient before decisive conflict is engaged in, then the initiative is lost, and with it the battle, operation, or war as the case may be.

move himself to the beneficial side of the culminating point, the required initial force ratio can be much higher than estimated.

In fine, the culminating point thesis gives literal meaning to the expression *battle calculus.* Figure 9 illustrates this phenomenon in terms of the principles of war. If superior *mass* is dissipated prior to attaining the *objective,* the principle of the *offensive,* which means to retain the initiative, is foreclosed. This loss is tantamount to loss of the battle. The attacking commander has bought the farm irrespective of delays in settlement.

The position of the culminating point, however, is not fixed. When the strengths of the attacker and defender are relatively constant, the point can be shifted to the right or left respectively by brilliant or inadequate maneuver. This shifting can be further enhanced, or retarded, by a similar application or misapplication of the remaining principles of war. These enhancements have the effect of multiplying combat strength without additional cost. In a close contest, the difference between victory and defeat is often attributable to how well these supporting principles are utilized.

The analysis also applies to the operational level of warfare even though the principles of war are stated primarily in tactical terms. That is, culminating points operate at these higher levels, but the principles of war themselves take on different meanings. For example, at the operational level the principle of mass evolves into a stress on sustainability of military strength. This may require a more discrete sequence of tactical objectives in lieu of fewer, larger battles. Appendix B provides a detailed discussion on this matter, noting that while most operations can and do sustain at least a few tactical losses, usually by passing beyond local culminating points, they can ill afford to pass those points with respect to the operation as a whole.

Restated, success in war comes only when the attacker has sufficient clout to remain the superior force in spite of losses incurred before decisive engagement. This means a sufficient number of tactical engagements must succeed to guarantee the nation and the military will prevail in the theater, presuming the military objectives will yield the geopolitical goal. Warriors may elect to ignore this fine print; the calculus of battle, and of war, does not.

The Reasons Why

Even a cursory review of military history suggests that passage of the culminating point is a common occurrence, and if so, it is fair to ask why. At least four reasons exist, discussed in descending order of justification.

Operational Trade-Offs. The first reason includes acceptable losses at lower levels of command for the sake of success at higher levels, tactical bunts, as it were. Calculated risks at the tactical level will occasionally meet defeat, but collectively, these risks can increase the overall efficiency of operations. A variation on this is the sacrifice of a forward unit to enable the main but otherwise outnumbered force to inflict decisive damage. The forward element of Stonewall Jackson's forces during the Valley Campaign sustained repeated mauling, but the operation was a brilliant success.

Misperception. The second reason is the difficulty of perceiving the culminating point, particularly in pitched battles. This reason is further justified by the standard of conduct imposed on battlefield leaders. At Gettysburg, Pickett, who led the Confederate attack up Seminary Ridge, would have been branded a coward had he retreated before reaching the top, not-withstanding Longstreet had correctly foreseen the defeat. This reason, of course, is less justifiable at higher levels of command because commanders at these levels have more time and are expected to reflect on the course of the operation.

Excessive Heroism. The third reason comprises mistaken notions of heroism. Unquestionably, heroism and courage are the prime virtues of the man in uniform. It is natural to admire great courage even in futile cir-cumstances, a human attribute which raises the conduct of war to a sometimes undeserved level of merit. Lieutenant Colonel (later Supreme Court Justice) Oliver Wendell Holmes, Jr., a thrice-wounded veteran of the Civil War, reminisced there was nothing more commendable than the "faith which leads a soldier to throw away his life in obedience to a blindly accepted duty, in a cause which he little understands, in a plan of campaign of which he has no notion, under tactics of which he does not see the use."[11] But courage is not something senior commanders should attempt to organize into brigades, light or heavy.

Obsession. The fourth reason is obsession and egotism, which in some cases may be a mistaken notion of heroism carried to an extreme. As discussed in the previous chapters, the subjective factors of war often work to push a na-tion past the point of good judgment, in which case the scope of the war may erupt. Clausewitz said the reasons were "excessive emotionalism" and "greed for honor."[12] This is a shortcoming which can afflict the most prudent of soldiers. Colonel T.E. Lawrence, whose distinguished performance during World War I may be unparalleled and who was humble enough to decline the award of the *Victoria Cross,* later admitted:

> As time went by our need to fight for the ideal increased to an unquestioning possession, riding spur and rein over our doubts. . . . It became a faith. We had sold ourselves into its slavery, manacled ourselves together in its chain-gang, bowed ourselves to serve its holiness with all our good and ill content. . . . By our own act we were drained of morality, of volition, of responsibility.[13]

B.H. Liddell Hart saw the case in less philosophical terms, indicating that non-aggressive states were likely to fight to extremes compared to aggressive na-tions. The latter, he continued, viewed war more or less as business and would back off if an opponent proved too strong. By contrast, the former, motivated by ideals, tended to press a conflict "to the bitter end."[14]

Since the end of World War II, Hart's observation and the repeated and unfortunate run-ins with the culminating point seem to describe many ap-plications of military force. What has happened is that the United States has misinterpreted the unusual parameters that operated during World War II and in the process has developed a mistaken notion on the efficacy of war. Moreover, many of the twentieth century factors of war have served to make war even less efficacious. The culminating point of war is becoming harder and harder to avoid before decisive engagement.

To the end of better understanding the phenomenon of the culminating point, Figure 10 provides an overview of its operation in most of the wars and conflicts in American history, and the next chapter examines, in more detail, the process from the time of World War II forward.

	U.S. PERSPECTIVE ·Intent ·Form ·Role	SCOPE	COUNTRY, ALLIANCE or INSURRECTIONISTS initiating the war or conflict, and the occurrence of the culminating point in that offensive
Revolu- tionary War	·Limited ·Defensive ·Primary	CIVIL, then INTER- NATIONAL	GREAT BRITAIN. The U.S. was unprepared but Washington's leadership and the French alliance pushed the culminating point back over the long ocean tether.
War of 1812	·Limited ·Defensive ·Primary	INTER- NATIONAL	UNITED KINGDOM. The U.S. declared war to avenge British raids at sea. Growing resources offset the lack of alliances.
Mexican- American War	·Limited ·Offensive ·Primary	INTER- NATIONAL	UNITED STATES. Overwhelming resources surgically employed made the culminating point issue moot. In the end, Mexico agreed to sell the disputed territory.
Civil War	—UNION— ·Absolute ·Defensive ·Primary —SOUTH— ·Limited ·Offensive ·Primary	CIVIL	CONFEDERACY. The South was fighting a limited war to rid herself of the Union presence, while the Union was intent on fighting to the death to preserve the Union. The South was out-gunned, out- attritioned, and in the political if not the military sense, out-led.
Indian Wars	·Absolute ·Offensive ·Primary	INTER- NATIONAL changing gradually to CIVIL	ENGLAND/GREAT BRITAIN/SPAIN/U.S. The Indians were regarded as savages to be annihilated unless they bowed uncondi- tionally to immigrant demands. The overwhelming resources of the latter eventually pushed the culminating point to the far east.
Spanish- American War 1898	·Limited ·Offensive ·Primary	INTER- NATIONAL	UNITED STATES. Spain was too weak to protect her interests in the Caribbean and the Philippines. The U.S. had su- perior resources. No contest.
Latin American Interven- tions 1900-1922	·Limited ·Offensive ·Primary	INTER- NATIONAL	UNITED STATES. Again, the superior re- sources directed at the weak states of Latin America—compounded by weak infra- structures—made the U.S. an unwelcomed but irresistible denizen.
World War I	·Limited, nearly Absolute ·Defensive ·Coalition	INTER- NATIONAL	GERMANY/TRIPLE ALLIANCE. The resources of the Entente eventually prevailed over those of Germany and the Triple Alliance though it took four years to discover the lay of the culminating point.
World War II	·Absolute ·Defensive changing to the Offensive ·Coalition	INTER- NATIONAL	THE AXIS POWERS. The combined national resources of the allied powers, and the absorbtion of Axis military power by Russia and China eventually overwhelmed Italy, Germany and Japan. At the end, the Allies evinced enormous military strength; the Axis, very little.
Berlin Airlift 1948-1949	·Limited, ·Gray-Area ·Coalition	INTER- NATIONAL	SOVIET UNION. The Soviets were not pre- pared to fight and the blockade affected East German interests more than West.

Figure 10. Culminating Points in American Wars and Conflicts

Korean Conflict Jun 1950– Oct 1951	·Limited ·Defensive ·Coalition *nominally*	CONSOLI-DATION then INTER-NATIONAL	NORTH KOREA. A classic case of an invader who presumed his victim would be a piece of cake, only to encounter a superpower who pushed the culminating point back to the 38th parallel.
Korean Conflict Nov 1950– Jul 1953	·Limited ·Offensive ·Coalition *nominally*	INTER-NATIONAL nearly a CONSOLI-DATION	UN/UNITED STATES. The roles became reversed. The U.S. was fighting a limited war on the Asian mainland against the world's most populous state and had to threaten nuclear war to gain a draw.
Cuban Missile Crisis 1962	·Limited ·Gray-Area ·Primary	INTER-NATIONAL	SOVIET UNION. The choice was (1) thermonuclear war, (2) conventional war with the U.S., or (3) acquiescence. She had passed the culminating point and knew it
Domincan Republic 1965–1966	·Limited ·Offensive ·Support	INTER-NATIONAL interven-tion in a CIVIL war	UNITED STATES. The U.S. prevailed because she could focus on a civil war largely confined to a single city. Had that war spread to the entire country, the outcome might have been different.
Vietnam Conflict 1962–1975	·Limited ·Defensive then Offensive ·Support	CIVIL, CONSOLI-DATION & INTER-NATIONAL	NORTH VIETNAM & VIET CONG INSURGENTS. Probably the most complex war in history taxonomically, but the bottom line was inability of the U.S. to expend the enormous resources required to prevail.
Yom Kippur War 1973	·Limited ·Defensive ·Support	INTER-NATIONAL	EGYPT/SYRIA. Superior Israel fighting ability offset the numerically superior attackers. The pushing back of the culminating point was physically obvious.
Lebanon Inter-vention 1983	·Limited, ·Offensive ·Primary	INTER-NATIONAL	UNITED STATES. A lack of clear objectives coupled with inadequate forces committed to a hopeless situation put the culminating point in Washington, DC.
Grenada Raid 1985	·Limited, nearly Absolute ·Offensive ·Primary	INTER-NATIONAL interven-tion in a CIVIL war	UNITED STATES. The U.S. intervened with overwhelming resources on a par with the Washington Redskins vs. Tuckahoe Elementary School. The U.S.S.R. was too distant to risk war over an isolated proxy.
Support of Contras in Nicaragua 1981–1988	·Limited ·Offensive ·Support	INTER-NATIONAL interven-tion in a CIVIL war	UNITED STATES. The poorly organized contras waged a war against a government the U.S. formally recognized. And the Iran-contra scandal eliminated any further America support.
Support of Mujahedin 1980–1988	·Limited ·Defensive ·Support	INTER-NATIONAL	SOVIET UNION. The Stinger missile and the desolate land mass served to push the culminating point back to Kabul.
Persian Gulf In-tervention	·Limited ·Gray-Area ·Primary	INTER-NATIONAL	UNITED STATES. The point was crossed when the U.S. shot down an Iranian civilian aircraft in error. She could not function effectively after that.
Panama Interven-tion 1989	·Limited ·Defensive ·Primary	INTER-NATIONAL	PANAMA. Noreiga had an American killed, others shot at, and declared war on the U.S., which promptly obliged him. Noriega's culminating point was in his mouth.

This chart omits the *Pueblo* and *Mayaguez* incidents and the current blockade of Iraq.

Chapter 8. The Flawed Perspective of a Good War

However absorbed a commander is in the elaboration of
his own thoughts, it is sometimes necessary to take the
enemy into account.
— Sir Winston Churchill

World War II was among the more distinguished periods of American history. It was a time of global crisis and great sacrifice. Worldwide, the war inflicted death on 60,000,000 people. An equal or greater number were scarred for life, physically or psychologically. America's contribution in bringing that devastation to an end was no small matter. On the other hand, the United States has perhaps magnified her share out of proportion to the total contributions of the Allied nations and in the process developed an exaggerated opinion of her national military prowess. Arguably, this exaggerated opinion — in combination with an inadequate comprehension of national power and the dynamics of the culminating point — has contributed to subsequent military failures. As a corollary, it inflates the perception of the potential for war with the Soviet Union and the ability to prevail in conflict elsewhere.

The Contribution of the United States in World War II

In World War II, the political will of the Axis powers grasped for territory well beyond the reach of their resources to sustain it. As such, the superior resources of the Allied nations — depicted in Figure 11 — first circumscribed and then destroyed the exercise of that political will. But with the exceptions of the battles of Midway and Guadalcanal, the United States did not become decisively engaged on the battlefield until after the Axis powers reached their high water mark in the respective theater.[1] When she did engage in war, it was in theaters considered secondary fronts by the Axis powers.

At the time of the counterinvasion in North Africa (November 1942), the Soviet Union was on the verge of containing the main German advance. The Battle of Stalingrad was two weeks away. In Africa, the turning point — El

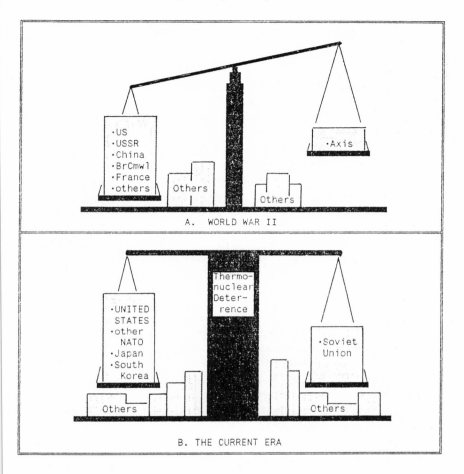

Figure 11. Changing Balance of Geopolitical Power. In World War II, the national power of the Allies vastly outweighed that of the Axis states, though the resolve and infrastructure were initially too weak to serve as a deterrent. The nations that did not participate were of little geopolitical consequence. The current era evinces a radical change. The two superpowers and their principal allies dominate geopolitics and are heavily armed to fend off aggression from each other and any upstart lesser powers. Thermonuclear power makes the minor imbalance moot. The remaining nations exercise somewhat more geopolitical influence, but many of them are unaligned, which serves as a buffer to further dampen prospects for major war between the superpowers.

Alamein—was won by British forces after 26 months of hard fighting, four days before the American landings in North Africa. And by that time, Italian forces were no longer a serious threat. The counterinvasion of Europe proper did not begin until June 1944, 18 months after the Soviet Union had gone on the offensive and reduced the *Wehrmacht* to more manageable proportions. The western European and Italian fronts accounted for less than 10 percent of the Allied forces combat man-years in Europe, and a sizable fraction of that comprised British forces.[2]

In the Pacific theater about three-fourths of the Japanese army was deployed on mainland Asia.[3] Though the Chinese did not field an effective defense, the sheer mass of their population absorbed the blows from Japan while the war in Southeast Asia was fought largely by British forces.[4] This meant the Pacific basin was a secondary front. Further, Japan placed itself at a three-fold disadvantage. First, the Japanese merchant fleet was stretched to its limit and was prey to submarine attacks.[5] Second, the geography of the Pacific basin, given the long distances between island groups, meant that Allied forces could isolate some of the Japanese strongholds without ground combat and defeat the balance piecemeal. Third, as time progressed, United States production of ships and aircraft increased while Japanese production declined, exemplified by the ratio of carriers on August 15, 1945: the United States, 100 (29 regular, 71 escort); Japan, 4 (*sans* planes, pilots or fuel).[6]

Before the Battle of Midway—June 1942—the Japanese were still the dominant force at sea, but Admiral Spruance's pilots fatally weakened the Imperial fleet by sinking four carriers. The Japanese high water mark was reached a month later with the occupation of the Solomon Islands, but this was offset by the offensive at Guadalcanal. From that time forward, the United States dominated the Pacific basin, but it must be reiterated that the bulk of the Japanese defense effort was expended on mainland Asia.

None of this gainsays the courage demonstrated by Americans during World War II. Approximately 292,000 servicemen died as a result of combat in that war. But as shown in Table 6, for every American who fell, 46 Allied servicemen also died. When civilian casualties are added—and the United States sustained few of these—the ratio increases to 1-to-99. In terms of damage to civil property, the merchant marine excepted, there is no comparison. The United States was largely untouched by the war, which enabled her to make the great logistical contribution, producing about half the armaments used by the Allies in the war effort.[7] However, this vast mobilization effort was probably an economic blessing, and in any event, it was paced to avoid harming the economy.[8]

The last observation is perforce hypothetical. The estimated casualties from the planned invasion of the Japanese mainland were widely presumed to be upward of a million, notwithstanding the Japanese air force and industrial base were in ruins. The magnitude of that prediction should evoke some empathy for the actual casualties sustained by China, the Soviet Union, and other Allies and ought to generate some understanding of just how much national power must be expended to defeat a determined country, even in *extremis*.

	Military		Civilian		Total	
British Commonwealth	373,000	2.7%	93,000	.6%	466,000	1.6%
China	1,310,000	9.5%	650,000	4.1%	1,960,000	6.6%
France	213,000	1.6%	350,000	2.2%	563,000	1.9%
Poland	123,000	.9%	5,675,000	35.7%	5,798,000	19.5%
United States	292,000	2.1%	6,000	<.1%	298,000	1.0%
U.S.S.R.	11,000,000	79.9%	7,000,000	44.0%	18,000,000	60.7%
Yugoslavia	305,000	2.2%	1,200,000	7.6%	1,505,000	5.1%
All others	151,000	1.1%	916,000	5.8%	1,067,000	3.6%
ALLIED TOTAL	13,767,000	100.0%	15,890,000	100.0%	29,657,000	100.0%
TOTAL minus U.S.	13,475,000	97.9%	15,884,000	>99.9%	29,359,000	99.0%

Table 6. Allied Fatalities in World War II. Source: "World Wars," *Encyclopaedia Britannica,* Volume 23 (Chicago: Encyclopaedia Britannica, Inc., 1973), p. 802j, except Chinese civilian casualties: Ruth Leger Sivard, *World Military and Social Expenditures 1987–1988* (Washington, D.C., World Priorities, 1987), p. 30. Data rounded to nearest 1,000.

Subsequent Conflicts

For a few years after World War II, the United States was undoubtedly the most powerful nation the world had ever seen. The subsequent stalemate in Korea and the defeat in Vietnam served to change that image. But the perceived change was inaccurate. If anything, the strength of the United States increased, though the strength of many other nations increased at a much more rapid pace. What happened was that the United States failed to recognize that her battlefield role in World War II was only a small fraction of the total Allied effort expended. When she tackled new opponents, largely on her own, and more in an offensive than defensive frame at the national level, she lost definition and controllability and in this condition crossed the culminating point almost routinely. Recall the issues discussed in Chapters 6 and 7 while considering the record of her military involvement since World War II.

Berlin Airlift. This operation airlifted 2,300,000 tons of mostly non-military supplies during a 15-month period over air routes on the order of 150–200 miles to West Berlin after the Soviet Union denied land access.[9] The drama captured world attention, but the logistics of it were minor compared to World War II and there were no overt hostilities to contend with. The Allies faced down the Soviet decision without much risk of war. The Soviet Union was still recovering from World War II, did not then possess nuclear power, and would have had a difficult time commanding the East Germans to wage war on their fellow countrymen. The policy forged a strongly negative world opinion and blocked critical trade to East Germany. In the end, the Soviet Union relented. She did not possess sufficient national clout to enforce her will, while the airlift did not overtax Allied resources.

Korea. This conflict was really two consecutive wars and should be considered in those terms. The first war lasted four months, during which the North Korean offensive was halted along the Pusan perimeter and then expelled by way of the operational envelopment at Inchon harbor. The second war was the counterinvasion of North Korea, which caused China to enter the fray and resulted in a protracted stalemate.[10] Two years later President Eisenhower threatened to use nuclear weapons to motivate the Chinese to agree only to a truce, not to quit North Korea.[11]

The success of the first war was attributable to the superior resources of the United States, as supported by several allies, against the second-rate forces of North Korea.[12] But when the conflict evolved into a larger war, this time directed at China (though the fighting was confined to Korea) she no longer had superiority of available resources. The Chinese, with the advantage of proximity, were willing to throw the full weight of their army into the war to expel the invaders from North Korea and to continue fighting to prevent their reentry irrespective of how many lives it cost. By contrast, the United States did not seem to have any specific objectives in mind, other than to avoid an all-out war with China, and obviously was not willing to expend the necessary resources to expel the Chinese from North Korea.[13]

The Cuban Missile Crisis. Here, the United States took the position that emplacement in Cuba of missiles under Soviet control capable of hurling nuclear warheads at her homeland was unacceptable. After much internal debate, President Kennedy approved the minimum action believed necessary — a blockade — to cause the missiles to be removed.[14] This gave the Soviet Union three choices: (1) to initiate thermonuclear warfare, (2) to engage in local war against U.S. forces in order to finish the missile sites, or (3) to acquiesce. The thermonuclear war option was moot. At the time the United States had superiority among such weapons and their means of delivery. The local conflict option wasn't much better. Cuba was 90 miles from the United States but more than 5,000 miles from the USSR, and that by way of sea routes straddled by American allies. This left the Soviet Union with Hobson's choice. To Kennedy's credit, he further dampened the risk of war by prudent judgment, but the long and short of it was that the rash and ambitious grasp of the Soviet Union far exceeded the reach of her national power at the time, even at full throttle.

Vietnam. The United States pursued this war doggedly for ten years, incurred more than 58,000 military fatalities (20 percent of the World War II fatalities), expended at least $300,000,000,000 and in the end neither gained nor preserved anything of note.[15] Almost every factor that contributed to the success of the Allied powers in World War II was decidedly absent in this conflict. First, Vietnam was not an imbalance-of-world-power threat on a par with the Axis aggression. Second, the United States was almost alone in its fight. Third, while she possessed far greater national power than North Vietnam, geopolitical restrictions limited how much of that power could be expended. Fourth, the war was on the Asian mainland. The casualties the Japanese sustained trying to subdue China in World War II (and the projected casualties for the planned United States invasion of Japan 1945–46) suggest what would have been required to prevail in Vietnam. Fifth, the United States did not formulate consistent political or military objectives.[16]

Dominican Republic (1965–1966). This conflict was the unilateral and un-invited intervention in a civil war in the Dominican Republic, primarily in the capital city of Santo Domingo. The object was to prevent a leftist takeover of the government. Whether or not the leftists would have succeeded without the intervention is speculation, but there is no doubt American forces quelled the fighting and enforced peace until political stability was restored and an open election held.[17] But in the longer run, the United States may have done more damage than good. The intervention abrogated the postwar policy of nonintervention in Latin America and recreated considerable mistrust. Twenty years later, she would find it had little support in Latin America for its abortive attempt to support the contras in Nicaragua.

Support of the Yom Kippur War (1973). While this was strictly a logistical endeavor, the entanglement of Soviet support and interests among Israel's attackers supposedly risked escalating hostilities into a much larger war.[18] Israel had been caught by surprise due to a failure to correctly interpret intelligence data, but with heavy U.S. support they soon proved their mettle. This meant Egypt and Syria faced defeat and perhaps occupation. That prospect was unacceptable to the Soviet Union, and the United States did not exactly look forward to it either. Kissinger's shuttle diplomacy brought the war to a halt before it reached this stage, but whether the superpowers would have come to blows had Israel proceeded to subdue Egypt is very doubtful.

Lebanon. The 1983 intervention in Lebanon cost the lives of 241 marines in a so-called terrorist strike; it was a military strike employing terrorist tactics, a subject considered in more detail in Chapter 9. In a rare exception to protocol, the Department of Defense openly criticized the White House for the intervention, and later President Reagan accepted personal responsibility for the failure.[19] This was another example of the inability of a major power to interfere militarily in the affairs of a minor state with only miniscule national resources. Lebanon posed no serious threat to national interests and accordingly the United States was not about to support a major military effort there. But Lebanon, or at least certain Lebanese factions, did not hesitate to do what was necessary to get rid of the Americans. The Israeli intervention in Lebanon the previous year, which entailed a far greater military effort, did not fare much better.

Grenada. In marked contrast to Lebanon, Grenada was an absolute success, but that is attributable to overwhelming national strength of, and the proximity of Grenada to the United States versus the great distance to, and tenuous support of, the Soviet Union. Unfortunately, this obvious outcome was so successful, the "victory" has reinforced the exaggerated notion America has of her military prowess.

Support of the Contras and the Mujahedin. The irony here is the support of the conflict 10,000 miles away in Afghanistan was effective, while the one in the United States' backyard—Nicaragua—was a washout. Four factors explain the difference.

First, the Afghan resistance fighters represented what most of the free world—especially the Congress of the United States—regarded as the legitimate government of a nation invaded by the Soviet Union without good cause. By contrast, the Sandinistas, not the contras, were the legally established government in Nicaragua, however inimical their ideology to the United States.

Second, the *mujahedin* concentrated their entire effort against Soviet military forces, did so with remarkable efficiency, and avoided committing atrocities on innocent civilians. By contrast, the contras lacked (and still do) infrastructure, firmness of purpose, and the clear objectives that might have compensated for the shortage of resources.[20]

Third, the barren reaches of Afghanistan and Stinger missiles contained the Soviet air force. The geography of the country worked against full Soviet occupation, while the missiles were effective in the destruction of the one means the Soviets had of marking their presence. In Nicaragua, geography and demographics negated the effect of contra missiles.

Fourth, the Soviet Union would have suffered major geopolitical damage had she unleashed the full weight of her national power to annihilate Afghanistan. Moreover, the gain would not have yielded any particular national advantage without a subsequent invasion of Iran in order to preside at the Strait of Hormuz and obtain warm water ports on the Indian Ocean. That option would have destroyed her influence elsewhere in the Middle East, cost a fortune in military outlays, and perhaps risked a direct confrontation with the United States. Similarly, if the United States had invaded Nicaragua, the expense would have been high and more than likely she would have lost all influence in Latin America.

Panama Intervention 1989. This one-day military intervention succeeded in protecting bona fide national interests by toppling the unpopular regime of General Manuel Noriega. Apparently, the rest of Latin America was also fed up with Noriega, because the predictable OAS criticism of "intervention" was perfunctory this time. However, the United States did err by stating outright that it was attempting a forced extradition of a head of state rather than limit the stated objective to protecting the lives of U.S. personnel stationed there. Further, the allegations persist that several hundred or more Panamanian civilians were needlessly and wantonly killed to keep U.S. casualties from potential sniper fire to a minimum.

To review the bidding, counting Korea as two conflicts, the record for the United States has been eight successes for twelve tries. But among those conflicts which thrust the United States into a combat role, the record is four for seven. Of the four successes, the first part of the Korean war ended 38 years ago and evolved into a failure in the attempted counterinvasion of North Korea. Next, the intervention in the Dominican Republic was only at the price of abrogation of agreements with Latin American states. This leaves Grenada and Panama, both of which were military pieces of cake by any standard, and in any event hardly compensate the loss of more than 88,000 American serviceman, and countless hundreds of thousands of allies, killed in the futility of pursuing the Korean conflict into North Korea and later in Vietnam and in Lebanon.[21]

All this confirms that limited wars yield limited success at best. As witnessed by World War II, it takes overwhelming power to subdue small but aggressive nations. Thus when a single major power expends limited force against all but the weakest states, it begs defeat, especially when the lesser state pulls out the stops. The only consolation is that the Soviet Union has not done too well either. Her once firm grip on the eastern European nations has evaporated, and her record elsewhere is dismal. At the present time, she can claim Cuba (for $6,000,000,000 per year), Ethiopia after a fashion, perhaps Angola, and some influence in a few other destitute locales—economic carrion in terms of national power. And even at that, the Soviets have indicated that they are getting tired of bailing out Castro.

Deterrence Vis-à-vis *the Soviet Union*

Offsetting this unfavorable record in limited wars is the undeniable success of the United States in deterring both thermonuclear war and major conventional war between the superpowers, no small accomplishment. Also, no coalition among lesser states has remotely threatened either superpower, in marked contrast to the geopolitical ambitions of the Axis powers 50 years ago. Now if it takes far more national power than presupposed to prevail in limited war, what explains this apparent contradiction? The answer begins with a review of some macro statistical data on the elements of national power.

Recalling the discussion initiated in previous chapters, and recapitulated in Table 7, the superpowers and their principal allies control 80.6 percent of the world GNP and account for 81 percent of world military expenditures. The balance of 19 percent is divided among the rest of the world's nations, about 180 in number. As shown in Figure 11 (B), this paradigm is radically different from the one existing during World War II. It is this concentrated national clout that in part accounts for the success of deterrence. Moreover, a conventional-forces war between the superpowers would almost certainly involve a NATO scenario and would instantly pit 23 countries, controlling or allied with the bulk of the world's economic and military resources, into a lethal struggle in a theater occupying no more than 3 percent of the earth's land

	Land Mass Except Antarctica [Sq. Miles]	%	Population [Thousands]	%	Gross National Product [Both in millions	%	Military Spending of dollars]	%
U.S.	3,679,192	7.0	246,113	4.8	4,221,350	26.9	265,800	30.2
Other NATO	8,125,371	15.5	421,533	8.3	3,558,110	22.7	107,517	12.2
Japan	145,875	.3	122,620	2.4	1,559,720	9.9	13,080	1.5
S.Korea	38,291	.1	42,593	.8	98,370	.6	4,891	.6
Subtotal	11,988,729	22.9	832,859	16.3	9,437,550	60.1	391,288	44.5
U.S.S.R.	8,649,500	16.5	285,796	5.6	2,356,700	15.0	275,000	31.2
Warsaw Pact	382,409	.7	112,639	2.2	871,595	5.5	47,470	5.4
Subtotal	9,031,909	17.2	398,435	7.8	3,228,295	20.5	322,470	36.6
China	3,696,100	7.0	1,088,200	21.4	314,800	2.0	24,870	2.8
All Others	27,773,719	52.9	2,778,791	54.5	2,730,068	17.4	141,702	16.1
Subtotal	31,469,819	59.9	3,866,991	75.9	3,044,868	19.4	166,572	18.9
Total	52,490,457	100.0	5,098,285	100.0	15,710,713	100.0	880,330	100.0

Table 7. World Data in Terms of the Superpowers and Their Allies. Source: Data extracted and compiled from tables in the *1989 Britannica Book of the Year, World Data Section,* pp. 746–751, 770–775, and 860–865.

surface. And equally certain is that if war occurred, the Soviet Union would initiate it. But in order to do so, she would first have to patch a number of debilitating cracks in the walls of her national power.

First, as the Soviet president is not a true dictator, he would need the consent of the Politburo, each member of which must be prepared to risk his comfortable life style in a conflict that might well eliminate it. Next the president would have to accept the price of reinvading the former Warsaw Pact nations in order to reach western Europe, during which time NATO would have all the warning it needed. Then, too, the desired Sino-Soviet rapprochement would have to be put on hold while beefing up deterrence against a potential Chinese counteroffensive.

Also, the Soviet Union would have to risk an immediate cut-off of the sea lane of communication from eastern Russia through the Strait of Malacca, the Suez Canal, and the Dardenelles, without which the industrial base in her west could not continue adequate production.[22] Finally, the Soviets must assure themselves that neither NATO, nor the French nuclear defense force, nor the United States acting independently, would resort to nuclear weapons and thereby risk escalation to thermonuclear warfare.

As such, the risk of thermonuclear war may be considered a special case of NATO deterrence. It would be absurd for the Soviet Union to directly unleash thermonuclear warfare if she were at the same time greatly concerned that a NATO scenario could escalate to that level. To be sure, Soviet doctrine runs counter to the concept of mutually assured destruction by presuming that Russia can and will prevail in a nuclear contest, but this is not the same thing as advocating that kind of war.[23] No matter how low the risk of thermonuclear war might be, the potential consequences would be intolerable.

As for a conventional war in Korea, as Paul Kennedy noted in *The Rise and Fall of the Great Powers,* probably no greater geopolitical anachronism exists today.[24] When the treaty between South Korea and the United States was implemented, the Soviet Union and China were regarded as the twin kingpins of monolithic world-aggrandizing communism. Today, China is decidedly neutral and presumably has no intention of letting the Soviet Union pass through on land to support North Korea in an invasion of South Korea. Thus for North Korea to initiate hostilities, she must (1) go it alone, (2) risk a counterinvasion by China from the north, and (3) face the full weight of South Korean forces as supported by the United States. That would be tantamount to national suicide.

In a word, as battle is a consequence of war, not its cause, so the success or failure of military force is a consequence of relative national power, not its essence. The essence of national power resides in political will and the resources available, sufficient or insufficient, which can be focused to gain new assets or to protect existing ones. War is an option to that end, but it is an option the success, cost, and mutual devastation of which demands an exponentially increasing investment and willingness to tolerate losses far beyond what we have been willing to recognize or accept.

Chapter 9. The Rise and Limits of Terrorism

Disproportion is the root of all moral mistakes....
Within most virtues there lurks, waiting to slip its leash,
a vice in the form of excess.
—George F. Will

The decline in the efficacy of war has undoubtedly contributed to the rise of terrorism. Because the salient powers and buffer states, controlling the bulk of the world's assets, are seldom threatened by military action on the part of the remainder states, terrorism has served as a compensatory means of pursuing policy goals. That is, while the salient powers have little to be concerned about in balance-of-power terms, terrorism seems here to stay as a bona fide defense concern. However it is not something that lends itself to purely military solution. It needs to be understood on its own terms.

For starters, among all forms of warfare, terrorism has inflicted the fewest casualties, caused the least damage, but evoked nearly the greatest fear. The number of casualties worldwide per year—even if all of them were fatalities—would be less than one-tenth the people killed by drunk drivers in the United States alone.[1] But because a terrorist can strike anywhere, anytime, without provocation in the eyes of the victims, the damage from a national perspective is far more psychological than physical in nature. This damage suggests reviewing the politics and jurisprudence of terrorism, the psychopathology of terrorists, the four classes of terrorism, and the limits and the implications of this paradigm. Before proceeding, however, it might prove helpful to review the comparative statistics of war versus terrorism, as depicted in Table 8. Non-nuclear terrorism does not compare with war; nuclear terrorism would.

The Politics and Jurisprudence of Terrorism

Terrorism is the extreme form of a spectrum of political initiatives associated with the doctrine of civil disobedience, as formalized by Thoreau in the nineteenth century. This doctrine holds that laws may be disobeyed to the

WAR:	U.S. Population at the time	Fatalities	Percentage of Population	Indexed to World War II
Civil War	32,000,000	620,000	1.938%	877.7
World War I	100,000,000	117,000	.117%	53.0
World War II	135,000,000	298,000	.221%	100.0
Korea	151,000,000	34,000	.023%	10.2
Vietnam	200,000,000	58,000	.029%	13.1
Terrorism [10yrs@200/yr]	250,000,000	2,000 estimated	.001%	0.4
Thermonuclear Terrorism [single strike]	250,000,000	500,000 estimated	.200%	90.6

Table 8. Terrorist Fatalities in Perspective. Source of *historical* war and population data: *Encyclopaedia Britannica* (Chicago: Encyclopaedia Britannica, Inc., 1973): Vol. 12, p. 475; Vol. 22, p. 690; and Vol. 23, pp. 759, 802j.

end of redressing a grievance beyond solution by way of ordinary political process. The spectrum has five divisions.

Self-inflicted Martyrdom. In this form a leader does himself in to focus attention on an injustice. The photograph of a Buddhist monk immolating himself in Vietnam is difficult to forget. In other cases a leader may fast to death, if necessary, to make a point. Gandhi was a particularly effective and sincere practitioner of this (and the next) approach. The point is, the violence — and self-starvation is a quiet form of violence — is directed only at the practitioner himself. At times it is the stuff of sainthood.

Direct Civil Disobedience. This form of civil disobedience is the easiest to understand. It consists of openly disobeying a law regarded as unjust and then just as openly accepting the punishment that follows from the act. If the resulting incarceration generates sufficient public pressure, the action may lead to a repeal of the noxious law. In turn, the punishments meted out to the offenders can be rescinded.

Indirect Civil Disobedience. This alternative form can be used by individuals to protest an odious law when that law does not apply to them. Laws enforcing slavery before the Civil War were an example of this with reference to the abolitionists. Also, protesters might violate both the targeted law and just laws for the purpose of intensifying the public focus. Indirect civil disobedience can be more heroic. Repeal of the targeted law would not justify the violation of the just law, meaning the practitioner cannot always hope for a pardon even if the targeted law is repealed.

Guerrilla Tactics. This form, when applied in a civil disobedience situation rather than a military campaign, means that the practitioner hopes to escape punishment. After making a strike, he fades back into the woodwork.

while punishment is avoided, the strikes normally are directed only at facilities associated with or individuals responsible for the oppressive conditions.

Terrorism. Terrorism is guerrilla warfare carried to the extreme of killing innocent bystanders or inflicting damage on property that has no relationship with an odious law or what is perceived to be an intolerable political situation, in which case the terrorists are little more than glorified psychopaths. One of the most famous terrorists in history was a U.S. citizen by the name of John Brown. Committing random murders, arson and aimless insurrection, he was finally caught, tried, and promptly hanged. Ralph Waldo Emerson, a contemporary of Thoreau, praised him, and the song about his body moldering in his grave was sung by Union soldiers going into the war which would ensue two years later. Yet the man who would preside over that war—Abraham Lincoln—roundly condemned John Brown's conduct.[2] He understood the character of the behavior and what toleration of it could lead to.

The Psychopathology of the Terrorist

The psychopathic mindset of terrorists makes a serious field of study for psychiatry, though some in this field prefer the euphemism of "anti-social behavior." But only the poets and novelists, whom psychiatry often draws upon, seem capable of expressing matters in more understandable terms. Perhaps Herman Melville came closest to describing the mental process which pushes an individual with quirks into a craven madman. A terrorist deprived of what he believes is his rightful heritage, particularly if the disenfranchisement occurred by way of force, could be compared to the mental transformation of the character of Captain Ahab in *Moby Dick:*

> It is not probable that this monomania in him took its instant rise at the precise time of his bodily dismemberment. Then, in darting at the monster, knife in hand, he had but given loose to a sudden, passionate, corporal animosity; and when he received the stroke that tore him, he probably felt the agonizing bodily laceration, but nothing more. Yet, when by this collision forced to turn towards home, and for long months of days and weeks, Ahab and anguish lay stretched together in one hammock ... then it was, that his torn body and gashed soul bled into one another; and so interfusing, made him mad.... Human madness is ... a cunning ... thing. When you think it fled, it may have but become transfigured into still subtler form. Ahab's full lunacy subsided not, but deepeningly contracted.... As in his narrow-flowing monomania, not one jot of Ahab's broad madness had been left behind; so in that broad madness, not one jot of his great natural intellect had perished.... If such a furious trope may stand, his special lunacy stormed his general sanity, and carried it, and turned all its concentrated cannon upon its own mad mark; so that far from having lost his strength, Ahab, to that one

end, did now possess a thousand-fold more potency than ever he had sanely brought to bear upon any one reasonable object.[3]

Perhaps some insight can be gained by comparing the fictional character of Ahab with the real life William Bligh. Bligh suffered the indignity of two mutinies, of which the famed *Bounty* case was the less serious, and accordingly his caustic personality is often associated with a reign of terror. The Admiralty eventually chastised him for his overzealousness but nevertheless promoted him to the rank of Vice Admiral, due in part to his ability and high courage.[4] Moreover, it was his personal leadership that meant the survival of all but one of the other 18 men set adrift by the mutineers, during one of the most harrowing open sea voyages in the annals of naval history. Lastly, the mutineers who escaped to Pitcairn Island murdered one another until only one was left.[5] They, in effect, had become terrorists. Restated, terrorism exceeds the culminating point of acceptable political behavior and deserves nothing short of condemnation, Hollywood notwithstanding.

The Classes of Terrorism

Whatever the psychology of terrorists may prove to be, the practical problem has always been dealing with them. To this end, it could prove helpful to recognize that terrorism has four classes, each of which seems to require a different approach.

Class A. This class of terrorism is the most well known. It is practiced by or on behalf of a revolutionary group or sect not aligned with any sovereign power and is intent on gaining international recognition of its cause, or obtaining funds to support that cause, or both. The tactics include assassination, kidnapping, hijacking and sabotage. Irrespective of the tactic used, the common denominator is that its practitioners seem to believe their conduct is the only means of advancing their cause. They may or may not have the sympathies of one or more governments, but it would be incorrect to say they are acting under the direction of a head of state or a government agency.

Class B. This class is outwardly similar to class A, but these terrorists are controlled and usually funded by a sovereign power and act under its direction or at least are permitted to so act without fear of prosecution. The aims of the government supporting them and of the terrorists themselves may or may not coincide, but that subtle point is secondary to the fact they are acting as a military arm of a government in power. Thus their actions constitute an undeclared act of war on the part of the sponsor.

Class C. This class of terrorism is confined to a single country, normally in support of a civil war. If committed by government forces, it would resemble class B; if by rebel force, class A. In the latter instance, such terrorism can be thought of as guerrilla warfare and may or may not be a prelude to more conventional tactics, a point commented on at length by Mao Zedong.[6] Variations on class C terrorism might have the rebel terrorists encamped in a neighboring country, but their actions remain confined to a civil war within one country or possibly two or more countries if the civil war is an attempt to unify ethnically related sovereignties into a single power.

The significance of class C terrorism, in contrast to classes A and B, is that the terrorism itself (though not necessarily the encompassing war) seldom has a major impact on the national interests of other nations, notwithstanding the abhorrence of the tactics employed. An exception on the lack-of-impact thesis would be the recent "drug wars" in Columbia. These drug wars are in fact civil war, albeit not for the usual reasons, and the combatants, i.e., the drug dealers, have chosen to use terrorist tactics to intimidate the government to stop prosecuting them.

Class D. This class is not really terrorism but the use of terrorist tactics in open warfare. The most notable example in recent times was the so-called terrorist bombing of the Marine barracks in Lebanon in 1983. The United States had intervened in a conflict where it was not wanted, where it was not willing to sustain its presence, and where it singularly failed to formulate precise objectives to warrant its intervention in the first place. The so-called terrorist act thus served the military purpose of dislodging the American contingent from the region.

The distinction may be of small comfort to the next of kin, but it is critical from a geopolitical perspective. Specifically, what is the difference between driving a truck laden with explosives into a military facility and flying a *kamikaze* plane similarly laden into a ship? The point is, if a nation chooses or is forced into war with one or more opponents who have few compunctions about using these tactics, then that nation must be willing to combat them as best it sees fit. It may choose not to retaliate in kind, but it must be able to bear with the psychological aspects of such tactics and persevere in bringing them, as well as the war itself, to an end.

The Limits of Terrorism

If there is any fortunate aspect to terrorism in general, it is that most forms of it tend to be self-limiting, and where they are not, the means of reducing, if not eliminating it, are feasible. The dominant reason for this situation is that an excessive amount of terrorism deprecates the international recognition sought. In a distressing sort of way, people grow used to it, paralleling the way in which the general population of almost every country has grown used to and even accepted the carnage from automobile accidents. Thus class A terrorism has its own built-in limits, a fact observable in that it ebbs and flows. Class B terrorism also has this limitation, but more importantly, any access is eventually identified by counterterrorism intelligence, opening the way for retaliation. The 1986 raid on Libya fits this description and apparently did serve to reduce Libyan-sponsored acts of terrorism for a few years.

As for class C—civil war based—terrorism, there is admittedly less international incentive to control it, and accordingly it can persist for decades or longer, for example in the Philippines. On the other hand this class of terrorism is usually confined to a single country. As mentioned, the outcome of civil war among the remainder states will seldom if ever threaten the equilibrium; its continuation is normally confined to a small region without global ramifications. Moreover, civil wars are both inevitable and bloody. The United States has participated in two of them. The process of self-determination is not always a matter of holding a Constitutional convention. Thus excessive concern over other countries' civil wars, and the terrorism that may occur in them, is usually a *prima facie* case of inadequate national perspective.

This does not condone civil war terrorism but simply recognizes the inability of external powers to do much about it. If there is justification for external intervention in a civil war, it should be irrespective of the tactics employed. It makes little difference if government forces and insurrectionists shoot at each other or install bombs in each other's cars. Human rights activists may be appalled at terrorist acts committed in civil wars and may exert political pressure to reduce them, but such noble motivations will seldom justify outright military intervention. Moreover, that intervention could serve to add to the killing of innocents.

As for class D terrorism, if a nation is willing to persevere in open war that includes the use of such tactics, then it should have the means of bringing those tactics to an end. The long, successful war of Great Britain against the Malaysian insurgents in the 1950s was a first-rate example of this situation.[7]

Implications

Given the four classes of terrorism and the self-limiting aspects of most of them, or alternatively the uncertain means of limiting them, the central issue is, can there be a worldwide, consistent policy against terrorism or even a consistent policy advocated by the United States? The answer for the short run seems to be no. The difficulty arises from the psychological cacophony associated with terrorism and the attendant inability to orchestrate an effective defense against so wily an opponent. One nation may choose to appease terrorists, another to sacrifice hostages if necessary to demonstrate its resolve, still another to claim it is opposed to terrorism and then sell arms to those same terrorists to fund other covert activities.

Within a given country, the antiterrorist posture can change radically from year to year and even from incident to incident. A hijacked plane loaded with refugees from some obscure African country might not generate much public concern in the United States, but that attitude would change quickly if the daughter of a high cabinet official were on board. The Entebbe rescue mission conducted by Israel was hailed worldwide as a brilliant stroke; the 1980 proposed rescue of United States hostages then being held in Iran led Secretary of State Cyrus Vance to resign his office.[8]

In short, as the problem is international in scope, it may take an international approach to throttle it, one that would not overlook the necessity for occasional use of military force but also one that would come to grips with the jurisprudence, psychopathology, classes, and limits of terrorism.

Part III
Equilibrium and Excalibur

Legend has it that the sword known as Excalibur could be withdrawn from its stone scabbard only by the rightful king of England, which turned out to be Arthur. However, in Malory's *Morte d'Arthur,* the sword was a gift from "The Lady of the Lake," which Arthur, mortally wounded, commands to be returned to her domicile. The analogous question for the current era is whether the equilibrium only means that global war awaits a strong enough antagonist or whether the force of circumstances has caused global war to go out of style. Though this book argues that the equilibrium greatly reduces the risk of war, it would be naive to claim that risk has been eliminated. However, a better understanding of what makes it work can lead to better defense preparedness. The latter is inevitably based on risk assessment. Thus to the extent the risk of the equilibrium failing exists, defense policy cannot rely on the equilibrium, and vice-versa.

Accordingly, this part of the book attempts to assess that risk, primarily by way of evaluating the underlying causes. Superintending that answer is the concept of *homeostasis.* Ever since Walter B. Cannon advanced that idea in physiology, it has been applied analogously to geopolitics, usually in the sense of balance of power. Yet it is important to distinguish between balance of power and homeostasis. The former has been in use for more than three centuries and aims at political alignment of nations to prevent a potential opponent from gaining too much power. These alignments have witnessed continuous realignment. In the twentieth century the superpowers have been aligned and unaligned twice. Unfortunately, many balance-of-power machinations have failed, leading to war.

However, as mentioned, balance-of-power politics may have become passé. Alliances exist, but only three have worked the international scene of late, and their tenure is shaky. The Warsaw Pact was largely a euphemism to cover Soviet military occupation of her eastern European satellites, though in practice it served the purpose of an alliance. NATO, which has prevailed for 40 years, is a truer case, but the pending reunification of Germany may sound its death knell. The third is the ASEAN pact in southeast Asia, which to date has been more of a cultural than a miliary alliance. What does seem to dominate the international agenda is the fact that the salient powers are more-or-less firmly entrenched in their interrelationships or neutrality as the case may be, except for the move toward independence for some of the eastern European countries.

The underlying reasons for this state of affairs and for the equilibrium are discussed first, the most significant of which is the extension of the culminating point doctrine in military operations to the national level—what is called the *culminating reach of national influence*. The following chapter evaluates the contenders for superpower status. Only two, possibly three, give any evidence of having the wherewithal, and none would likely upset the equilibrium. The next chapter evaluates ten contingencies which might upset the equilibrium, of which only four appear sufficiently plausible to warrant serious consideration in developing an adequate defense posture. One of them would be a fatal act of bad judgment on the part of the United States itself. The roots of that problem provide the basis for the last chapter in this part, which considers the malaise versus the maladministration in the defense infrastructure.

Chapter 10. Whys and Wherefores

I intend to leave after my death a large fund for the
promotion of the peace idea, but I am skeptical as to its
results. The savants will write excellent volumes. There
will be laureates. But wars will continue just the same
until the force of circumstances renders them impossible.
— Alfred Bernhard Nobel

This analysis so far has tacitly assumed that global equilibrium results
from a disproportionate share of the world's resources being concentrated in
a few nations, combined with the deterrence afforded by mutual destruction.
Actually, that situation is the manifestation of at least six fundamental reasons
that account for the homeostatic restraint now practiced by the powers that be.

The first two reasons are the receding culminating reach of national
influence — to trade on Clausewitz's concept of the culminating point — and
the consequential increase in risk of failure for military operations that might
have succeeded in times past. The second two reasons comprise the inertial
resistance posed by the major powers and buffer states, coupled with the
physical dispersion and disparity among the already weak remainder states.
The third set of reasons would be the ascendency of complementary interests
among nations at the expense of conflicting interests, paired with a decline in
the severity or criticality of most threats to various salient power national
interests.

The Receding Culminating Reach of National Influence

Chapter 7 dwelled on the operation of the culminating point in war,
where the strength of the aggressor ebbed at a faster rate than the defender's.
When this ebbing results in excessive loss of strength before decisive battle, the
usual outcome is military defeat. Similarly, the distance between a nation and
its international objectives may be considered as the *national culminating
reach*. That reach is receding, meaning that national power, even when concentrated in the hands of a few nations, has lost international influence.

This national culminating reach, like its military counterpart, is based on

89

comparative strengths between nation and object. Perhaps the individual who best understood this point was Abraham Lincoln. The Civil War, over which he presided as victor, was no easy task. The North had the superior resources, but the South had the better generals and needed only to chase the Union army out, not defeat it, to prevail. Nevertheless, the Union, except for General Winfield Scott, believed it could put the Confederacy in its place with a few decisive battles. Scott, the aging Army commander, realized the South would fight nearly to the death to preserve its way of life, and that to subdue it, the Union would have to establish a massive blockade and either siege the Confederacy into submission or wage a long and arduous war.[1] This viewpoint was initially met with derision and nicknamed "the Anaconda Plan."[2]

At the end of the first year of fighting, the Union had yet to win a significant battle. About the only thing the North had been able to do was to establish sufficient military infrastructure in the border states to prevent their slipping back into the secessionist grip of their southern neighbors. Because of this, many Unionists, including the famed newspaper editor Horace Greeley, clamored for Lincoln to free the slaves in these states. But Lincoln correctly understood the tenuous loyalty of these states, namely that while they seemed to prefer the Union to the Confederacy, they were not sure the Union would prevail in the war and in the event certainly had few compunctions about slavery. Lincoln would write to Senator Orville H. Browning of Ohio:

> I think to lose Kentucky is nearly the same as to lose the whole game. Kentucky gone, we can not hold Missouri, nor, I think, Maryland. These against us, and the job on our hands is too large for us. We would as well consent to separation at once, including the surrender of this capitol.[3]

Eleven months later, he would respond to Greeley:

> My paramount object in this struggle *is* to save the Union, and it is *not* either to save or destroy slavery. If I could save the Union without freeing *any* slave I would do it, and if I could save it by freeing *all* the slaves I would do it; and if I could save it by freeing some and leaving others alone I would also do that. What I do about slavery . . . I do because it helps to save the Union; and what I forbear, I forbear because I do *not* believe it would help save the Union.[4]

A month later, Lincoln did issue his preliminary *Emancipation Proclamation,* but that document applied only to slaves held in states then in rebellion, not the border states.[5] As such, no slaves were freed at the time. It would take the Thirteenth Amendment to the Constitution to free those in the border states, an amendment passed only after the Union had reestablished its preeminent position and therefore no longer had to ensure the loyalty of those states. And what is especially noteworthy about Lincoln's statesmanship was that his real passion remained that of freeing the slaves, not saving the Union.[6]

The latter he regarded only as a means to an end. However, once the war began, it was the means that took first priority and moreover one that could be gained only by ensuring the North did not prematurely expend the elements of its national power—its culminating reach.

A more comprehensive account of the culminating reach of nations can be found in Robert Asprey's *War in the Shadows.*[7] The ostensible intent of this book was to bring history to bear on the failure in Vietnam, stressing, as the title suggests, the record on guerrilla warfare. In the process, however, Asprey wrote a succinct history of war from the national perspective, noting wars seldom attained the political goals sought with any degree of permanence.

The Higher Risk of Military Failure

It follows that if the culminating reach of nations is receding, the risk of failure of military operations has increased. To the end of understanding the phenomenon better, this form of risk can be considered a spectrum with five segments. These segments of risk range from *negligible,* to *moderate,* to *calculated,* to *precipitous,* and finally to *insurmountable.* As the culminating reach of national influence recedes, the risk increases.

Negligible Risk. Negligible risk occurs when a nation exerts its influence well within the boundaries of its influence, for example the United States' reinforced raid on Grenada in 1983. For obvious reasons, the risk was also negligible in the case of the American Indian wars, notwithstanding the superior tactical ability of the Indians. Thus in a manner of speaking, objectives entailing negligible risk lie within a nation's de facto "territorial waters."

Moderate Risk. Moderate risk occurs when the attempt at influencing international affairs begins to approach the culminating reach, somewhat analogous to kicking a field goal from 25 to 30 yards out. At worse, the risk of failure faced by the Allies in World War II was moderate, given the vast resources and collective resolve of those nations.

Calculated Risk. This level of risk occurs when the stretch of policy seems to coincide with a nation's culminating reach—the objectives are within reach but just barely. An unfortunate turn of events could spell failure, but if the probability of such misfortune is less than half, the overall risk is calculated—calculated to give a better chance of success than not. An example would be the Union's position in the Civil War. The North had the necessary superiority of resources, but lacked, at least initially, military leadership and political resolve.

Precipitous Risk. When an operation stretches beyond the culminating reach the risk of failure becomes precipitous, meaning that there is more chance of failure than success. However, astute leadership and maneuvering of resources can turn the tables. Israel, in particular, has demonstrated the capacity to do this in all of her wars, except the incursion into Lebanon. The risk taken by the United States in Vietnam was also precipitous, at best. In the absence of extraordinary leadership and political judgment, it failed miserably.

Insurmountable Risk. Insurmountable risk means that no amount of leadership or ingenuity can prevent failure. The Japanese attack on Pearl Harbor and the French and later the German invasions of Russia were classic cases in point, as was the attempt of the United States to subdue Chinese forces in the second part of the Korean conflict, short of thermonuclear annihilation.

The significance to these didactics—to expand on the conclusions developed in Chapter 8—is that the United States needs to assess more carefully the risk of failure of any proposed military operation in light of the receding culminating reach of her national influence. Perhaps the record of failure since the end of World War II will hasten the day when these risks are no longer underestimated. By the same token, the idea of any other nation trying to take on the United States, or the Soviet Union, is absurd.

The Inertial Resistance of the Buffer States

The statistical presentations thus far have emphasized the cumulative strength of the salient powers and the buffer states, noting that the small balance is distributed over the numerous remainder states. Here, however, our focus shifts to the clout controlled by the major powers and buffer states in order to grasp the significance of that strength when juxtaposed between the salient powers and remainder states, as shown in Table 9.

Land. The major powers and buffer states control nearly half of the world land mass (excluding Antarctica). The superpowers control slightly under half of the balance; the remainder states, somewhat more than half. In short, half of the world serves as a geographic buffer between the other two quarters.

Population. The buffer effect for population is even more dramatic than for land mass. Two-thirds of the world's population belongs to the major powers and buffer states. True, the remaining third is not evenly divided between the superpowers and remainder states, but the disparity in favor of the latter is more a detriment than an asset, except, as mentioned, in the indirect sense of deterring invasion by way of massive poverty.

Gross National Product. In this case, the buffer controls just over half the world GNP, with the balance skewed six-to-one in favor of the superpowers—higher on a per capita basis. The buffer for the discretionary GNP data is nearly as large, and the disparity is even greater, yet the superpower share is less than the buffer intruding between them and the remainder states.

Military Expenditures. Here the buffer states control a much smaller percentage of the world total than in other categories, slightly over a quarter.

	LAND MASS [sq miles]	POPULATION [thousands]	GROSS NATIONAL PRODUCT Total Discretionary [in millions of dollars U.S.]		MILITARY BUDGET
Superpowers	12,328,592 23.5%	531,909 10.4%	$6,578,450 41.9%	$6,312,496 45.8%	$540,800 61.4%
Major Powers & Buffer States	24,610,508 46.9%	3,378,215 66.3%	$8,048,253 51.2%	$6,808,142 49.4%	$236,965 27.0%
Remainder States	15,551,257 29.6%	1,188,161 23.3%	$1,084,210 6.9%	$651,496 4.7%	$102,565 11.6%
Total	52,490,457	5,098,285	$15,710,913	$13,722,134	$880,330

Table 9. Geopolitical Buffer Statistics

For the balance, the superpowers outspend the remainder states nearly five to one, lending some credence to the observation that the superpowers have earned their exclusive sobriquets primarily from the scope of their respective military expenditures. Perhaps so, but if it takes a three-to-one ratio of military strength on the part of the aggrandizer to prevail in overt conflict, the buffer prevents that ratio from being achieved.

The Dispersion and Isolation of the Remainder States

The collective statistical shortcomings among the remainder states have been perhaps overemphasized in previous chapters. What may be more significant is the geographical dispersion of these nations with respect to the salient powers, combined with numerous other differences and the difficulty of communications among states that are located in juxtaposition.

Latin America. The Central American states occupy a long isthmus between two continents, most of which is jungle. The Caribbean islands are dispersed and interspersed with buffer-state islands. Spanish may be the common language, but it does not seem able to overcome other differences. Moreover, these states are at least 3,000 miles from remainder states elsewhere.

Africa. The African continent, occupying about a fourth of the world's land mass, gives the appearance of a unifying factor among the 55 nations ensconced on it, but the very vastness combined with the geographical barriers of major deserts and dense jungles makes intracommunications among these states difficult at best, not to mention the wide range of ethnic and cultural differences. The Mediterranean littoral is essentially Islamic; in the jungle regions, ethnicity is nonexistent except in the sense of "black heritage"; and at the southern end, a largely European culture is dedicated to permanent separation of races. These factors do not auger for unification, however worthy the goal may be.

Southeast Asia. This part of the world suffers from the same lack of intracommunication capability as does Africa, albeit on a smaller scale. The recent withdrawal of Vietnamese forces from Kampuchea suggests that Vietnam has now experienced *its* Vietnam. Moreover, while westerners tend to group various oriental populations into a common mold, sometimes under pejorative terms, the truth of the matter is that they do not share a common ethos.

The Middle East. This appears to be the one subgroup among the remainder states where intracommunications are more feasible. True, most of the region is pure desert, but the common ethnic background, notwithstanding the differences among various Islamic sects, and the enormous wealth of these states, could work to overcome the physical barriers. No other Islamic nation criticized (or endorsed) Iran's recent flagrant violation of international law in publicly ordering the execution of a British citizen, Salman Rushdie, author of *The Satanic Verses* (and strongly implying that "retaliation" would also be visited upon the publisher and on bookstores). Further, unlike other regions, the salient powers have major interests here. Finally, while European nations recalled their diplomatic representatives, no country cited Iran for what was obviously a de facto declaration of limited war. Oil is thicker than justice.

The Ascendency of Complementary Interests

One of the distressingly ironic aspects of geopolitics and international relations is that a simple formula seems to govern the propensity for war. This formula appears in a number of textbooks and may be too old to determine who originated it:

$$\text{Propensity for War} = \frac{\text{Conflicting Interests}}{\text{Complementary Interests} + \text{Conflicting Interests}}$$

The dynamic is equally simple. The extent to which two nations increase their complementary interests is the extent to which they crowd out—in relative terms—their conflicting interests and hence lower the propensity for war between themselves. In terms of the superpower rivalry, avoidance of mutual destruction is a complementary interest, however negative it may seem to be on the surface. Increases in complementary interests are not always accompanied by decreases in conflicting interests; nevertheless, if the formula is correct such changes still lower the propensity for war.

The Decline in the Severity of Threats

In 1905, Kaiser Wilhelm is reputed to have remarked that "some fool thing down in the Balkans" would usher in a world war. Later, beginning in

	DEFENSE OF HOMELAND	BALANCE OF POWER	ECONOMIC WELL-BEING	IDEOLOGICAL TENETS
S U R V I V A L	American Revolutionary War —————— Thermonuclear missile attack	None, except if the United States had further delayed her entry into World War II	None, as yet	Attempt of the Confederacy to secede from the Union
C R I T I C A L	Nuclear terrorism in the United States —————— Attempt by the U.S.S.R. to place missiles in Cuba, 1962	Axis powers during World War II —————— The Sino-Soviet alliance, had it become permanent	The Great Depression 1929-1941	Inadequacy of the Articles of Confederation 1776-1789
M A J O R	War of 1812 —————— Systemic state sponsored acts of non-nuclear terrorism	Triple Alliance in World War I: Austria, Germany & Turkey —————— Sino-Soviet alliance 1949-1971	OPEC oil prices before international market forces reacted sufficiently —————— Sustained trade deficit	Abuses of the McCarthy anti-communism era
P E R I P H E R A L	Isolated non-nuclear terrorist incidents —————— Mexican-American War 1845	Soviet invasion of Afghanistan —————— Continued suppression of Tibet by China	Closing of the Suez Canal —————— Short-term consequences of of the October 1987 stock market "crash"*	Most Soviet disinformation campaigns and also most "communist" revolutions in various Third World nations

*The long-term consequences, in light of the federal deficit increasing at a rate of at least one-half billion dollars per day, could range from the major to the survival level depending on other contributing factors.

Figure 12. Nuechterlein's Matrix of Threats and Intensities

the 1920s, defense analysts in the United States clearly envisioned a war with either Japan or Germany or both. The same is not true today. If anything, most contemporary analysts hold that the probability of war between the superpowers, or any global war for that matter, is low. Part of this is due the propensity-for-war formula just discussed, and part is due the intrinsic nature of threats. Drawing on Donald Nuechterlein's matrix of threat types and intensities, most if not all defense concerns can be reduced to four categories.[8]

This matrix is illustrated in Figure 12, with case examples. Obviously, thermonuclear attack is a survival-level defense of homeland threat, and considerable funds have been invested to develop and maintain an adequate deterrent posture to minimize this threat. Elsewhere, however, the threats have lessened in intensity over the last 40 years.

Defense of Homeland. Aside from the nuclear threat—no small matter—an invasion of the United States by the Soviet Union or any other power, as mentioned, is absurd. Attacks on overseas bases and troops are another issue, but outside of NATO, Japan, and Korea, the opportunities are limited and some of those arise from inappropriate U.S. intervention, e.g. Lebanon and the Persian Gulf (at least prior to Iraq's invasion of Kuwait). In other words, this threat plausibly exists only on the fringes of American interests.

Balance of Power. The evolving equilibrium has made this level of threat essentially moot in complete contrast to the ambience of power that permeated international relations before the two world wars. Hence, the emphasis in the defense posture should be on maintaining this situation, a point given priority in Chapter 14.

Economic Well-Being. As the two superpowers and their respective allies control the bulk of the world's economic clout, this type of threat has also become moot. The exceptions are a handful of what might be called economic "choke points," e.g. critical resources. However, as discussed in Chapter 3 and again addressed in Chapter 17, only the oil resource seems to pose a serious problem, and the global impact of that problem is limited.

Ideological Tenets. This leaves the ideological concerns of the superpowers, with the United States perhaps being more susceptible than the Soviet Union to participating in international war as a means of maintaining purity of political mindsets. Yet if the influence of ideology on the salient powers is waning, as discussed in Chapter 4, this too is no longer much of a threat.

Chapter 11. Expanding National Power on a Fixed Globe

At the present time the world evinces two great nations, starting from different points but tending towards the same end. I refer to the Russians and the Americans. Both have evolved unnoticed. While the attention of mankind was focused elsewhere, they have suddenly placed themselves in the front rank among the nations.
— Alexis de Tocqueville, 1835

An age-old question asks what happens when the irresistible force meets the immovable object. The modern version of that question might ask what happens when a handful of nations develop irresistible power on a globe that refuses to expand and accommodate that power. Do other nations gain strength at the expense of existing powers and supplant them? The potential for that process to occur is always present, but certain factors now augur against the tradition. This lends permanence to the pattern of global equilibrium that has evolved since World War II.

The equilibrium argument implies that no nation is capable of supplanting either superpower, notwithstanding, for example, that Japan's gross national product may now rank second in the world, exceeding even that of the Soviet Union.[1] The argument arises from the fact that few other nations possess both the immense, balanced array of national resources and the necessary infrastructure to bring the potential power of those resources to fruition. At best, and providing the superpowers refrain from destroying themselves by some form of geopolitical suicide, one or possibly two nations might also evolve into additional superpowers, and elsewhere a few others might become even stronger regional powers.

However, it is important to distinguish between a world superpower and a dominant regional power. Regional power is always relative to the surrounding states. For example, Algeria, Egypt, Nigeria, and South Africa are prime candidates for dominant regional power status in Africa. Yet the combined GNP of all four of these African nations is less than 6 percent of the GNP of the United States.[2] By contrast, the influence of a superpower is global, perhaps not dominantly so but strong enough to call more shots than are called against it. And thermonuclear power, which is spreading among many states, is not an equalizer except if and when it is used. That is, this form of purely defensive power may enhance deterrence against military aggrandizement, but it will not buy international clout.

The Contenders

The route to superpower status would normally be by way of extraordinary growth and development in a nation with significant resources on a par with the existing superpowers. Clearly, the superpowers dominate the world scene yet occupy only a fourth of the world's land mass and have only about a tenth of the world population. Who then are the logical contenders? One way to address this question would be to drop down the list just short of the point of absurdity, that is, where the lack of sufficient resources is patently obvious. As a minimum the list should encompass all the major powers, including the European core of NATO. To this should be added the strongest of the buffer states. Without question this would include Japan. Beyond Japan, however, no single nation seems to offer serious competition, though a few may exhibit a particular strength in one or two elements of national power. For example, Indonesia has a massive population, and Saudi Arabia has accumulated enormous wealth from its oil reserves. Yet neither nation remotely evinces the wherewithal to compete with the salient powers in the superpower sense.

To continue, Table 10 extracts data from Table 2 for the salient powers plus Japan. In this case, however, the percentages are relative to the United States, not world totals. Collectively, these nations command a definitive majority of the world's land area and population and 80 percent of the GNP. Some but not all of these statistics are subject to change. Land mass and its distribution are fixed for all practical purposes, though new resources may yet be discovered in some countries and commercially feasible means found of exploiting known but latent resources. Relative populations are nearly as fixed at least for the foreseeable future. That is, the massive populations of China and India are not likely to be reduced significantly in the next hundred years, nor those of Canada and Australia significantly increased. The GNP is far more subject to change, provided the resources, population, ethos, and infrastructure are in place to increase it. And rising above a null discretionary GNP in China and India, for example, would be a difficult task. This leaves military expenditure, but given the global equilibrium, there isn't much that can be done with it except to improve one's own deterrent posture.

On the other hand, statistical data alone cannot make the case for the more-or-less permanent status of the superpowers. A more qualitative perspective is appropriate, comparing the contenders with the elements of national

MEASURE→ ↓COUNTRY	AREA [sq miles] 1988 Data	POPULATION [nearest 1000] 1988 Data	GNP [millions] ——— 1986	GNP MINUS $500/PERSON Data ———	MIL BUDGET [millions] 1985 Data
UNITED STATES	3,679,192 100.0%	246,113,000 100.0%	$4,221,750 100.0%	$4,098,694 100.0%	$265,800 100.0%
SOVIET UNION	8,649,500 235.1%*	285,796,000 116.1%	$2,356,700 55.8%	$2,213,802 54.0%	$275,000 103.5%
CHINA	3,696,100 100.6%	1,088,200,000 442.2%	$314,800 7.5%	none 0.0%	$24,870 9.4%
WESTERN EUROPE	687,230 18.7%	265,359,000 107.8%	$2,697,940 63.9%	$2,565,262 62.6%	$85,436 32.1%
JAPAN	145,875 4.0%	122,620,000 49.8%	$1,559,720 36.9%	$1,498,410 36.6%	$13,080 4.9%
CANADA	3,849,675 104.6%	25,880,000 10.5%	$361,720 8.6%	$348,780 8.5%	$7,902 3.0%
AUSTRALIA	2,966,200 80.6%	16,470,000 6.7%	$190,420 4.5%	$182,235 4.4%	$5,105 1.9%
BRAZIL	3,286,488 89.3%	144,262,000 58.6%	$245,520 5.8%	$173,389 4.2%	$2,307 0.9%
INDIA	1,222,559 33.2%	801,806,000 325.8%	$213,440 5.1%	none 0.0%	$7,493 2.8%

*All percentages are relative to U.S. data

Table 10. Statistical Data on the Salient Powers and Japan. Source: *1989 Britannica Book of the Year, World Data Section,* **pp. 746–751, 770–775, 860–866.**

power. Figure 13 (p. 100) lists the contenders roughly in order of the apparent ability to compete. The figure omits thermonuclear power, because (as cited in Chapter 4) virtually all of the contenders either possess it or could readily obtain it.

Granted that any evaluation of this nature is inherently subjective, and unforeseen events may occur which could negate the conclusions. Yet if there is any truth to the argument that a nation's long-term standing is a function of how much of a decisive share of the elements of national power she has, then the degree of subjectively may be less than presumed.

China. Across the board, China seems to have the most balanced potential for a slow but steady rise to superpower status. The obvious drawback is the massive population. In the course of a century, however, the current policies aimed at zero-population growth and eventual reduction may work concurrently with a gradual but massive build-up of economic clout. After all, it took both the United States and the Soviet Union more than a century to rise to superpower status from the time that de Tocqueville first recognized the potential. In the interim, China's vast size, huge population and anti-hegemonic geopolitical posture served as an effective deterrent against aggrandizement.

As a last observation here, while the excesses of Mao Zedong were deplorable, he did not inflict on his country the millions of casualties that Stalin did

	MILITARY	INFRASTRUCTURE	DEMOGRAPHICS	GEOGRAPHY	ECONOMICS	SCIENTIFIC-TECH.	ETHOS
CHINA	China has the manpower and the potential resources to field the largest military force in the world.	Whether or not the present government can tolerate the give-and-take of radical growth remains to be seen.	The huge population is a major obstacle to superpower status. It will absorb much of what should be invested.	Roughly equal to the U.S. in size, but must support 4 times the population. Borders the Soviet Union.	Still a very poor economy, and so far has the distant potential is there, perhaps a century away.	Slow in coming, and so far has been invested to military ends, but the potential is considerable.	China has an undeniably strong national ethos, which can be aroused sometimes too easily.
JAPAN	Japan's Constitution proscribes a major military force, but even one percent of her GNP is considerable.	Superb. Japan manages her resources perhaps better than any other nation and can leverage world trade very well.	High density in a small country is at best a problem and may prove counter-productive in the quest for power.	An uncorrectable major weakness. Not much land, few natural resources, and in the shadow of China and USSR.	Awesome and unbeatable for her size; it may be the second largest GNP in the world.	Second only to the United States and seems to be closing the gap.	The Japanese national ethos may be stronger than Israel's, and it is based on a large population.
WESTERN EUROPE	The combined forces are strong but not in the superpower class. Defense budget is a third that of the U.S.	Exists only in the form of the NATO alliance structure, the Common Market and a few other joint functions.	Population is on a par with the superpowers and may be the healthiest in the world. Evenly distributed.	Relatively small land mass is a weakness, and it has an unfortunate proximity to the Soviet Union.	Would be second only to the U.S., clearly surpassing both Japan and the Soviet Union.	Collectively, it might exceed that of Japan and perhaps someday even that of the U.S.	The obvious weakness. There is no superintending ethos that could effectively bind these states.
CANADA	Canada evinces a fine military presence, allied with the U.S., but it was never intended to be dominant.	Already first-rate and one that could accommodate major growth, though there is little potential for it.	The population is remarkably balanced and healthy, but at 25,000,000, it is not a superpower contender.	Second in size only to U.S.S.R., has major resources but limited access to much of it.	Per capita GNP is high, but exponential growth in population would be required for superpower status.	Adequate and has the potential for major growth, but Canada will tend to be overshadowed by the U.S.	Canada is homogeneous, notwithstanding the French culture in Quebec. It is an admirable ethos.
AUSTRALIA	Australia follows in Canada's footsteps for the military element, but has even fewer resources.	Adequate, but would probably require major reworking for superpower status, toward which there is little motivation.	Almost as balanced and healthy as Canada's but with only 16,000,000, Australia is even less of a contender	Roughly equal to the U.S., but mostly desert with relatively few natural resources.	Less than half of Canada's, with little potential for exponential growth.	Not strong. Australia is still somewhat of a "frontier" country; tends to import technology.	Once again, Australia tends to parallel Canada; even more homogeneous but also more spread out.
BRAZIL	Has the potential to field a substantial military force but South American states seldom think in those terms.	This is improving and will probably continue to do so as her economic prowess grows.	Much of Brazil is jungle and sparsely inhabited. Yet she makes the most of the more inhabitable areas.	A country roughly equal in size to the U.S. with many untapped resources plus insularity.	A regional economic power, small by superpower standards, but it has the potential for much growth.	Brazil is not a leader in technology. The potential for major change and growth is problematic.	The potential to regear infrastructure toward massive growth is too difficult to assess.
INDIA	India's potential military power is hard to assess; the lack of infrastructure and poverty intervene.	Perhaps India's weakest point. She has not been able to deal effectively with major internal problems.	Three times the U.S. population on one-third of the land. Disease is prevalent.	Not favorable. Natural resources are nearly depleted. Proximity to even more poverty makes things worse.	Unfavorable. Most of the nation operates at a bare subsistence level with real growth many decades away.	India may have some potential here, but more pressing problems take priority for resources.	The country is largely Hindu, but nationalism is not a dominant trait.

on Russia, estimated at 18,000,000, not counting the second 18,000,000 or so that resulted from military unpreparedness in World War II. If anything, Mao set the stage for a national infrastructure to evolve without a second revolution (notwithstanding the recent student revolt) and wisely chose Zhou En-lai to preside over the actual administration of his country.[3]

Western Europe. The central European core members of NATO— Belgium, Denmark, France, the Federal Republic of Germany, Italy, Luxembourg, the Netherlands, Norway, and the United Kingdom—offer an admirable combination of population, economic capability, and favorable geographic position, at least for trade purposes. The combined land mass, which is less than one-fifth that of the United States, is at least all highly developed. The obvious weakness—the lack of a common ethos on which to form a common nation—is the one that augurs heavily against the potential. Moreover, British Prime Minister Margaret Thatcher seems as intent on further defusing the potential as Chancellor Bismarck was on unifying the states that would make up Germany. The compromise will likely remain what is already a certainty—an economic union.

Japan. Japan's economic prowess is awesome, but as a nation she suffers from a fatal defect; her geopolitically miniscule land mass and lack of natural resources force her into a power-broker role rather than what might be called an intrinsic power. This imposes on Japan a vulnerability that cannot be covered by compensating factors as long as she seeks superpower economic status, a lesson Great Britain learned with respect to her Empire.

There are three ways of accumulating wealth: (1) building on natural resources, (2) brokering and improving on the resources of others, and (3) stealing it. Japan tried the last option starting in 1931, under the euphemism of the Greater East Asia Co-Prosperity Sphere, and in the process inflicted death on at least 8,000,000 people. In the end, she suffered abject defeat. As the first option was beyond reach, this left brokering.

The vulnerability of brokering on a geopolitical scale, however, is demonstrated by the fact that Japan's impressive economy could be shut down overnight either by a cutoff of oil or by two or three countries throwing up prohibitive tariffs. The same does not apply to any of the salient powers. Additionally, competing Asian nations, particularly South Korea, Taiwan, and Thailand, have succeeded in imitating the Japanese economic model.

Canada. Among the salient powers, Canada could be considered a geopolitical garden of Eden. The blend of her elements of national power is admirable. The obvious weaknesses are a small population and the equivalent of Siberia for most of her land mass. These weaknesses could be overcome by a concerted effort to increase her population massively by immigration, and to

Opposite: **Figure 13. Potential contenders for superpower status.**

tame the northern wilderness, yet there are no signs of the population increasing, in the absence of which there is little need to settle the wilderness. In all probability, Canada will remain in the shadow of the United States, if for no other reason than the GNP ratio, but the relationship is about as even-keeled as possible between two economically disparate states.

Australia. The 8,000-mile distance from the United States may eliminate the in-the-shadow problem for Australia, but the prospect of its reaching superpower status is even less than for Canada. The population and per capita GNP are smaller. About the only thing that could turn the tables would be a massive emigration to Australia from overcrowded Asia followed by 50 years of economic development. Paralleling Canada, the Australian government does not seem disposed in that direction, though some of the social problems in southeast Asia may exert pressures that will be difficult to resist.

Brazil. There is no question that Brazil is the dominant economic power in South America, but its GNP is less than 6 percent that of the United States, and at least a third of it must be directed at bare subsistence. To reach superpower status would require an eightfold or higher increase in GNP with roughly the same population, not an easy task. However, the long-term potential for growth to even greater regional power status exists, and moreover, there is no need to reduce a massive population to achieve it.

India. Among the contenders, India seems to face the steepest climb between present and superpower status. The sheer mass of obstacles blocks the route at every step, and even if each one could be overcome, undoubtedly China would get there first, leaving India a distant fourth in the down-the-road geopolitical pecking order at best. Additionally, the various traditions, such as the de facto caste system, that permeate the ethos of this nation may work against the development of the potential that does exist.

In review, it would appear that only China, Western Europe, Australia, Canada, and India have the *theoretical* potential to attain superpower status within the twenty-first century. Of these, Australia and Canada can be ruled out on the practical grounds of either a reluctance or an inability to vastly expand their populations to manifest the potential. The concept of a politically unified western Europe is nearly as implausible, though the process of integrating economic exchange mechanics may create a de facto superpower.

India might make the grade some day in the distant future, but the prognosis is not favorable. This leaves China, which may in the course of a century rise to superpower status. Japan might have different ideas, but in global leverage as elsewhere, there is a major difference between a sprint or relay and a marathon. The latter mandates endurance, which requires intrinsic resources. With these, China is richly endowed. Japan is not.

The significance, of course, is that the superpower standoff between the United States and the Soviet Union is likely to remain a permanent fact of geopolitical life. China's predictable rise to competing superpower status will probably serve to increase the anti-hegemonic posture she set out to engender, while the rise of a western European economic superpower, if it comes pass, can only serve to enhance the geopolitical buffer.

Chapter 12. Potential Sources of Disequilibrium

"Universal history?" the captain inquired.
"Yes, universal history! It's the study of the successive follies of mankind and nothing more."
—Fyodor Dostoevsky, *The Brothers Karamazov*

Every newspaper has its front page, its editorial page, its pundits, analysts, and other writers. In the absence of genuine threats to national interests, the pages of one paper are sometimes filled with speculation of threats such as the "potential" for the whole of Africa becoming a Soviet camp. Another paper may speculate on the opposite polemic—that world peace is just around the corner and that the American military machine should be dismantled or at least severely reduced to hasten the process. Perhaps an international edition of Murphy's Law would suggest otherwise—that the equilibrium is bound to fail sooner or later—but if so, some prepossessing event would be required. For in practice, few contingencies seem plausible enough to upset the balance. This chapter reviews ten of these potential events, some of which were identified in previous chapters. Of the ten, four seem to have sufficient gravity to induce a global tilt.

The "Madman at the Nuclear Trigger" Scenario

The first contingency is the "madman at the nuclear trigger" scenario, where a head of state or other high official of either superpower, or any nuclear power for that matter, momentarily goes berserk, conceivably over some provocation best left to diplomatic solution, and in the process unleashes thermonuclear war. This has been a recurring theme in films and books and was discussed in Chapter 4. The potential for this event occurring is remote, but if it did occur the consequences would be disastrous and might very well trigger a complete unleashing of everything in the nuclear arsenal. In short, this threat may be no more than a mere toenail in the doorway, but that toenail belongs to a military giant.

Fortunately, the remedy may exist in the Strategic Defense Initiative. This system might not prove effective against thousands of incoming missiles, at least not for its initial employment, but it would undoubtedly offer that capability against a small number of missiles launched by error or by an act of bad judgment. This is an expensive solution yet a bargain when compared to the costs of the damage ensuing from even a "minor" thermonuclear strike. Moreover, while the U.S. populace seems pleased with the thaw in Soviet-American relations, there is no guarantee that Mikhail Gorbachev's policies will remain in effect forever.

Nuclear Terrorism

The second contingency—the potential for nuclear terrorism—is more plausible than the "madman at the nuclear trigger" scenario. An attack of this kind might be suicidal, but many terrorists are suicidal by nature. Moreover, the Strategic Defense Initiative would not be useful in countering such a threat. The "warhead" probably would be smuggled to its target in pieces and assembled on or near the site.[1] The resulting casualties and damage would be tragic, but the potential for disrupting the global equilibrium—that is, the perpetrator successfully mimicking one of the superpowers and generating a mutual exchange of thermonuclear weapons—is more appropriate for James Bond novels than critical defense policy analysis.

Major Civil War in Either the Soviet Union or China

The third contingency is the potential of a major civil war in either the Soviet Union or in China. In the former case, the ostensible cause would be a conflict between the so-called "white" Russians and the various Russian ethnic sects, which in their mass comprise a majority of Soviet citizens. The recent civil discontent in Azerbaidzhan (over a territorial dispute with the Armenians), Lithuania, Estonia, the Ukraine, and Soviet Georgia is thought by some writers to herald a much larger civil war.[2] The theory continues that the Soviet Union might initiate hostilities as a diversion to offset such an uprising. However, the last serious uprising in the Soviet Union was in 1917, at a time when poverty racked most Russians and the Tsar was indifferent.[3]

Moreover, the effectiveness of the Soviet internal intelligence network is not to be underestimated—a network whose task, in this regard, is lessened by the relative economic well-being of most Soviet citizens. This well-being may not be on a par with Western standards, but it serves to prevent the massive civil discontent that preceded the 1917 revolution. Moreover, the various ethnic populations in Russia reside, for the most part, in separate geographical regions, and to some extent allowances are made for ethnic differences in enforcing central policy. In fine, this contingency, in terms of its potential for igniting global war, seems grossly inflated.

A major civil war within China is somewhat more plausible, but there is little chance of it regenerating an unshakeable alliance with the Soviet Union or inviting, as a matter of opportunity, a Soviet invasion of China. Further, a civil war in China, even if it did occur, would not likely erupt overnight. The delay would provide time for affected nations to prepare for the eventuality.

A Worldwide Resurgence of the Muslim Religion or Other Third World Coalition

The fourth contingency comprises the supposed possibility of a resurgence of the Muslim religion as an ideological force to spawn a world revolution inimical to salient-power interests. This is far-fetched. For starters, the Muslim nations (1) lack ideological consistency, (2) seldom offer ideological appeal to non–Muslim countries, and (3) in any event lack the global horsepower to threaten the salient powers even if they could enlist the whole-hearted support of every remainder state on earth.

Other forms of coalition might arise from perceived economic disparities between the "have" and the "have not" nations, disregarding the fact that a few of the remainder states possess considerable wealth, e.g., most of the Middle East nations and a few African nations. But if all of the nations in the remainder state subgroup except for the Middle East coalesced into a world power and tried to blackmail the salient powers and buffer states to meet their demands, they would have to do it with few resources and virtually no global military power. We cannot deny the extreme poverty in these nations, nor is their lack of power an excuse for ignoring their plight, but this is not a realistic contingency with respect to upsetting the equilibrium.

Economic Cartels

The fifth contingency would be an insidious economic cartel and seems more plausible than the previous scenario, as it would likely endanger the economic interests of one or more salient powers without the necessity to form an alliance among a wide range of nations. To date, however, only OPEC has shown any evidence of being able to materialize this threat, and that threat has been ameliorated by a number of measures: (1) non–OPEC producers increasing their oil production, (2) strategic petroleum reserves, and (3) the need of OPEC nations for incomes as much as her customers need oil. In short, this once plausible contingency seems to have lost most of its steam.

A Catastrophic Chain of Events

The sixth contingency would be an application of catastrophe theory, where a chain reaction of unfortunate circumstances and antagonisms escalates into global war, e.g. the events that triggered World War I. This scenario was reflected in General Sir John Hackett's book *The Third World War,* albeit that fictional war did not escalate to the use of thermonuclear weapons. The plausibility of Hackett's thesis arises from the Middle East environment — the Balkans of the late twentieth century. The brew here could draw on (1) Iran's recent bid to the Soviet Union to form closer ties and her public encouragement of terrorist acts committed against the United States; (2) the headstrong Soviet approach to international relations; (3) the almost certain possession of thermonuclear weapons by Israel; (4) terrorism in general; (5) oil; and (6) the predictable continued bad judgment on the part of the United States.

German Reunification Followed by Soviet Hegemony

The seventh contingency is paradoxically the most feasible and the most far-fetched. In mid–1989, the concept of German reunification was an idea that did not seem possible until well into the next century. By mid–1990, it was a certainty within six months. One concern is that this will lead to the disbandment of NATO. Thus, harkening back to Halford J. MacKinder's 1904 paper "The Geographic Pivot of History," the Soviet Union would finally gain Eurasian hegemony, at least over the "high rent district" in the west. From this position, without firing a shot, she could permanently unbalance world power.

The far-fetchedness of this scenario is that the combined economic clout of the western European nations far outweighs their giant neighbor. Yet this may not always be the case. The Soviet Union is cutting its losses. By abandoning her former satellites in eastern Europe, she has in effect passed the debt to the West. In this way, the Soviet GNP could increase at the expense of the western powers. In addition, the residual fears in France, the Benelux countries, and the United Kingdom of a resurgence of German nationalism might further subdue international cooperation in Europe.

In the interim, the current euphoria could lead the present NATO members to discount the importance of retaining a military deterrent posture. For that reason, Chapter 16 outlines a different approach to the NATO defense, one that would more easily make the transition into a reunified Germany, quell the unnecessary fears of her neighbors, still remain effective with the potential absence of NATO forces in Germany, and not antagonize the Soviets.

But because military thinking does not always run along those lines, Germany may eventually demand that NATO be disbanded, which would then put the United States into a semi-isolated world position, and which would then give the Soviets more leeway elsewhere on the globe. It was said long ago that "good fences make good neighbors." That advice still applies.

Economic Collapse Within the United States

The mounting federal and trade deficits in the United States have spawned a number of doomsayer books prophesying another depression just around the corner. Many of the interviews conducted by Bill Moyers in his *World of Ideas* television series (later published in book form) seem to support the thesis. Some of the notables interviewed believed that it would take a major crisis for the country to deal with these issues. Thus this eighth potential continency could be fueled by the demands of a growing elderly population coupled with a smaller percentage of the population taxed to fund the demands; by a decaying physical infrastructure; by widespread functional illiteracy; and by many other factors. The legacy of politics is intractable debt.

Unfortunately, there is no way of evaluating this prognosis other than to surmise it is a possibility. But the issue is, could another major depression fatally weaken the equilibrium, and if so under what conditions? Any analysis along these lines would be highly speculative, but even if the United States did experience another major depression, the strategic defense missiles would still be in place as would all of the natural resources of the country. In the face of imminent danger affecting the survival of the nation, martial law could be declared and the necessary infrastructure imposed over the discordant conditions generated by the supposed depression to react to the threat. In short, an economic collapse of the United States would be more than unfortunate, but it would not likely weaken the elements of national power sufficiently to upset the world balance of power, or if it did, it would only be in conjunction with the previous contingency involving western Europe.

Worldwide Malthusian Catastrophe

This ninth contingency is also speculative and might arise if the accelerating world growth of population reached beyond the point where the earth, as presently managed, could sustain the population. It would be a case of nature reaching her own culminating limit. Disease and starvation could become epidemic on an astronomical scale. Yet the resources of the salient powers would undoubtedly be applied to attentuate their own losses far more effectively than would occur within the remainder states. Therefore, it is difficult to imagine how so unfortunate a chain of events could serve to rend the fabric of the equilibrium, even if it triggered an unprecedented number of terrorist acts. This is not to say the roots of this potential catastrophe should be ignored, but only that it is as much if not more of a political and economic problem than a challenge to defense policy.

Fatally Erroneous Geopolitical Judgment

This brings the review to the last contingency, which is not so much a different one as it is the compounding of previously discussed contingencies with bad judgment. This is no small problem, though two factors would act to reduce the severity of the consequences. First, the United States evinces an enormous resiliency arising from its vast resources, its ethos and infrastructure, and its insularity. Second, other nations are prone to the same error. In fine, providing bad judgment does not push the United States past a geopolitical culminating point, the equilibrium should be maintained by default if nothing else. Nevertheless, such an error could be fatal, and therefore the sources of this problem are considered in further detail in the next chapter.

In sum, the four contingencies short of a direct thermonuclear holocaust that appear to have the potential for destabilizing the global equilibrium are: (1) a "minor" thermonuclear strike launched by error or bad judgment; (2) a catastrophic sequence of events, ostensibly arising in the Middle East; (3) disbandment of NATO following the reunification of Germany, followed by increased global isolation for the United States and Eurasian hegemony for the Soviet Union; and (4) an unprecedented and fatal act of bad geopolitical judgment on the part of the United States, probably in the Middle East.

The thermonuclear contingency can be addressed by SDI. The Middle East scene unfortunately does not lend itself to a simple solution and is probably the one area where the United States needs to be the most concerned. The NATO disbandment scenario can be addressed by rethinking current defense methodology, at least sufficiently to defuse the potential of the Soviet Union becoming too powerful. This leaves the bad-judgment contingency, which in some ways can be considered only in tandem with other contingencies, but the sources of the problem must be addressed internally.

Chapter 13. Malaise Versus Maladministration in the Defense Infrastructure

A nation never falls but by suicide.
> —Ralph Waldo Emerson

The previous chapter posited that bad judgment was perhaps a more serious destabilizer than global contingencies. If so, the sources of bad judgment need to be identified in order to buffer the development and maintenance of an adequate defense policy against their influence. Few of these sources will come as any surprise to readers familiar with the defense establishment. On the contrary, most of them are discussed at length in the defense literature, especially at the senior service college level. More often than not the authors are well-known critics, but the services are willing to publish or republish the criticisms.[1] However, the source that could prove fatal—malaise—and the source common to virtually all organizations and institutions—maladministration—should be carefully distinguished from one another.

Lack of Stated, Consistent National Aims and Purposes

The Constitution nowhere requires the president to formulate the aims and purposes of the United States, save what may be inferred from the proviso to report on the State of the Union periodically. Accordingly, few presidents have elected to do so, relying instead on the pragmatism essential to election and achievement in the method of government established by the Constitution. Moreover, even if presidents did formulate such programs, they would probably change from administration to administration if not from year to year. Some of these changes would be occasioned by changing circumstances, but it's a safe bet others could be traced to political whims and preferences. This absence of consistent aims and purposes makes the formulation of a consistent defense policy difficult at best.

110

As mentioned previously, defense of homeland against foreign aggrandizement is an universally accepted national interest, but the last time the non-territorial United States was invaded by a foreign power was 1812–1815 and that was by courtesy of the mother country after the United States declared war on her. The attack on Pearl Harbor was an attack, not an invasion, against military targets, located in a then territory, with the cumulative time of the bombing and torpedo runs amounting to less than an hour. Nevertheless, this attack led immediately to a declaration of war against Japan. Only one dissenting vote in Congress was cast, and that individual wisely did not stand for reelection in 1942.[2] The subsequent declarations of war against Germany and Italy three days later followed only upon those countries first declaring war against the United States. But the consensus for war in 1941 has not been repeated since that time. Congress did not declare war in the case of Korea or Vietnam and has opposed some military actions initiated by executive authority.

As many presidents prefer to act in spite of Congressional restrictions, it is not likely the country can expect definitive statements on national aims and purposes emanating from the White House. Fortunately, the Nuechterlein matrix of threat types and intensities described in Chapter 10, in combination with the superpower status and defensive posture of the United States, permits the development of sound policy without these statements. Whether or not this will be done is another issue, but at least the supposed lack of foundation is no obstacle.

Conflicts Between the Legislative and Executive Branches of Government

The War Powers Resolution of 1973 and the Congressional report on the Iran-Contra hearings may be examples of the conflict between the two "operative" branches of government, but that conflict is not new. The *Federalist Papers* foresaw the conflict and praised it as a necessary check and balance against an usurpation of the strong authority deemed essential for the chief executive. It was not long before the checks and balances were implemented. Congress refused to confirm George Washington's first replacement for a Supreme Court justice, notwithstanding the nominee had previously served on the Supreme Court and had participated in the Constitutional Convention.[3]

The dominant complaint seems to be that the restriction resulting from conflict has stymied the Chief Executive in carrying out his responsibilities in the defense and international arena. Yet it is evident this conflict has flared over abuse of authority, and then only when that abuse has failed to yield any sterling accomplishments. In fine, these supposed restrictions do not impose on or restrict Presidential decision-making. If anything, Congress seems willing to give the President the benefit of the doubt in borderline cases and has permitted him to act in emergencies without consulting the legislature beforehand. About the only way Congress has routinely interfered in defense matters has been in the area of contracts.[4] This interference in part stems from the desire to direct as much defense work as possible to their constituents, some wags labeling the process as the "pork gunbarrel." At the extreme, by way of example, this results in shipping coal to coal-rich Germany, at high cost, to heat the barracks of American servicemen stationed there.[5]

Dual Military Chains of Command and Service Parochialism

The military operational chain of command runs from the president, to the secretary of defense, to the chairman of the Joint Chiefs of Staff, to commanders of unified and unspecified commands, to (or alternatively to) joint task force commanders, to the commanders of units assigned to those commands. However, control of personnel and administration remains with the separate services, and in practice most unified commands have army, navy, and air force component commanders. The direction of logistical support is subdivided down both sides of this dual chain of command. Most wholesale logistical support is now directed by defense-wide commands, such as the Defense Logistics Agency, but a considerable amount remains in the hands of separate services and for some items, a single service has defense-wide responsibility for support.

Obviously, this organizational maze violates one of the cardinal principles of war: unity of command. On the other hand, this situation should be recognized as a long-term transition from the acceptable separation of the army and navy in times past to the imperative for joint service operations today. As discussed in the first chapter, Congress has imposed joint responsibility on the separate services, starting in 1947 with the creation of a unified Department of Defense. It was a ragged tent erected over a three-ring circus, but it was a start.

Many iterations later, a major Congressional initiative, inspired in part by occasional outspoken military support, increased the command clout of the Joint Chiefs of Staff and their subordinate commands at the expense of service prerogatives.[6] Finally, the service comptroller functions were transferred to the respective service secretariats, where presumably they will be more amenable to Department of Defense perspectives.[7] The long-term result of these changes, whether intended or not, will be to transform the separate services into "wholesalers" of military force, responsible for training and administration of such force but with budgetary and operational control consolidated in the Defense/OJCS arena. The only battles the separate services are destined to fight are the rearguard actions to retard the inevitable transformation.

This form of "battle" often goes by the name *service parochialism* and results in the separate services advocating and obtaining competing and overlapping weapon systems to the detriment of an efficient defense posture. The problem is more than understandable. Each officer is reared in the lore of his own service and moreover experiences intense rivalry among the branches or their equivalent within his own service, e.g. artillery versus armor, submarines versus naval aviation, and tactical versus strategic air. Undoubtedly, much of this competition is healthy and inspires better performance. To the extent it is detrimental, the process of consolidating authority at the DOD/OJCS level should eventually serve as the remedy.

The Sheer Mass of the Defense Establishment

The mass of the defense bureaucracy fuels excessive compromise among senior officials, a problem exacerbated by service parochialism. The number of defense staffers in the Washington, D.C., area, exclusive of clerical and contract personnel, exceeds 60,000. That is a lot of management, and it makes the statistics associated with Parkinson's Law pale by comparison.[8] The offsets are a constant turnover and rotation of military personnel between the Pentagon and field assignments, and frequent reorganizations. Moreover, to borrow from naval terminology, most senior officers accept that the Pentagon is inundated with three-foot-deep institutional bilgewater. They do what must be done to negotiate this minimum bilgewater level (MBL). It is remarkable how much is accomplished by a substantial number of dedicated personnel. Unfortunately, the MBL seems to rise each year, and this can degrade the ability of the defense posture to react decisively when the circumstances warrant it.

The Annual Defense Budget Process

The short-sighted one-year budget cycle is a product of the Constitution and the way Congress does business. Authorizations may extend for many years, but appropriations are annual. No other salient power is faced with the same restriction.[9] The consequence is incrementalism. This means new systems are hard to introduce and antiquated systems are equally hard to get rid of.

This is not all bad. Major weapon systems take many years to bring to fruition. They are not something that can or should be turned off and on annually. Moreover, the majority of the defense budget covers active and retired pay of personnel and "housekeeping" functions, the bulk of which does not change much from year to year. Finally, a number of measures have been instituted to bypass some of the worst difficulties of the one-year budget cycle with the blessings of Congress. Most notable is the five-year defense contract, which if cancelled in the interim requires a penalty payment to the contractor up to $100,000,000 but not to exceed 50 percent of the remaining value.[10] To the end of further abating the deficiencies of the annual budget cycle, a modest proposal to use computer-based expert system technology has been included in Appendix D.

The Fixation on Technology

A common maxim in the defense establishment is that advanced technology will compensate in quality what the United States and her allies may lack in quantity *vis-à-vis* the armament of the USSR (which has 40,000 tanks).[11] This is debatable, especially when (1) the equipment becomes too complex for troops to operate effectively; (2) it breaks down too often under field operating conditions; (3) it becomes too expensive to buy in sufficient quantities; or (4) it causes, by way of budget trade-offs, shortages to occur in repair, parts and operating expenses, strategic lift, and other less glamorous budget items. This conflict reaches beyond the immediate concerns of the Pentagon; witness the continual haggling between the Air Force and NASA over space technology.[12] Another side effect of the technological fixation is the disdain it generates for the human element in war and deterrence.

On the other hand, technology has served to make offensive warfare increasingly expensive and therefore a politically unacceptable means of furthering national policy, a point addressed in Appendix A. This applies to both nuclear and conventional warfare and extends to the near-instant public perception of changes in international relations via satellite television. In fine, the technological sword has probably cut more in favor of improving the defense posture than against it, though this does not justify the excesses.

Fraud and Abuse of Power

The allegations of fraud throughout the defense establishment are too pervasive to be ignored. All doubt was removed by the current investigation into the systematic selling of sealed bid information to competitors by high officials within the service secretariats. The problem runs deep enough for Defense Inspector General June Gibbs Brown to state that the 1,000 inspectors hired to track down defense contractor fraud were insufficient; at least 450 more were needed.[13] On the other hand, this situation is not much different from that in earlier times or in other large organizations. Abraham Lincoln had to dismiss his first Secretary of War, Simon Cameron, for defrauding the War Department.[14] Worse, an investigation of New York state officials revealed that of 106 individuals offered bribes, 105 accepted and the other balked because the money was insufficient.[15] This potential fraud is compounded by the legal but questionable "revolving door" practice—the frequent rotation of key personnel between Defense, Congressional staffs, and private industry. Fortunately, criminal fraud and abuse will seldom denigrate sound national policy though they can weaken warfighting capabilities.

Repackaging the Apple

Ever since Adam and Eve tasted an apple's worth of the knowledge of good and evil, their offspring in all successive generations have been trying to stuff it back in, particularly the bad news. The Department of Defense is no exception. Like most organizations, it experiences difficulty owning up to serious errors and rarely tolerates whistle blowers. At times, this trait can reach ludicrous dimensions, as when test officials evaluating the Army's Division Air Defense gun (the "Sergeant York") used radio activated detonators in the target drones to conceal the inadequacies of the gun itself.[16]

A far more serious incident involved the killing of four students at Kent State University, who were protesting involvement in the Vietnam conflict but who hardly posed a threat to the interests of the United States. To this day, not a single Defense official, at least not while in office, has ever admitted to the overwhelmingly bad judgment exercised during that era, while others remain convinced that it was the media that "lost the war." For example, General William Westmoreland attempted to sue a reporter for libel over allegations he had suppressed negative intelligence in Vietnam. In mid-trial, Westmoreland agreed to drop the suit in return for a statement by the defendant that the latter did not intend to reflect unfavorably on Westmoreland's sense of duty. It was a sad encore for a dedicated soldier.

The "Military Mind"

The expression "military mind" has never been accurately defined, but most descriptions dwell on an overdue emphasis on military solutions to problems requiring a wider perspective. In a 1957 film, an Army major is portrayed as having been assigned as advisor to a junior ROTC detachment at a parochial school. Upon his arrival, the Mother Superior gives him the grand tour of the facilities, stopping before a large oil painting. "This was Father So-and-So," she says, following with a brief account of Father So-and-So's many accomplishments, concluding with: "He was canonized in the year 18 such-and-such." Replies the major: "Oh, I'm sorry to hear that."[17]

It is easy to be critical of the military mind, but this mindset is often the product of distinguished battlefield leaders, men who were more than willing to lay down their lives without hestitation for a higher purpose. Some of the arguments they have advanced must at times be countered or even ignored, but the respect due them for their conduct on the battlefield cannot be denied. While there are many situations where a military solution is imprudent at the national level or even the operational level of conflict, to the individual at the tactical level, this imprudence is hard to recognize. He is called upon to be a warrier, not a statesman, regardless of the larger perspective. This having been said, the problem should be confronted.

Unfortunately, the military mind is difficult to recognize within the profession of arms itself. General Omar Bradley claimed that he had never met a soldier with a "military mind" in the whole of his career.[18] Yet when General Mac Arthur, the most decorated soldier in United States history and the only individual to serve as a general officer in three major wars, wanted to pursue the Korean conflict to a point where it might involve an all-out war with China, Bradley, then serving as chairman of the Joint Chiefs of Staff, stated to Congress: "[It] would [be] the wrong war at the wrong place at the wrong time, with the wrong enemy."[19] Much later, Colonel David Hackworth (U.S. Army, retired), the most decorated soldier in the Vietnam conflict, would write an outspoken article for the *Washington Post*.[20] In it he lambasted the inadequate performance of the United States since World War II, advocating a return to the General Patton style of warfare. He has a point, but the truth of the matter, as discussed in Chapter 8, is that most of those post–World War II conflicts should either have been avoided or have been far more limited in their military objectives.

The State-Defense-Intelligence Triad

This final item is probably more of a strength than a weakness in the defense infrastructure, notwithstanding ample criticism to the contrary, because the three perspectives serve as a defense checks-and-balance system. Briefly, the overall defense perspective is not the sole prerogative of the Department of Defense. DOD shares that perspective with the State Department. International relations affecting defense requirements are influenced by Foggy Bottom as much as, if not more than, the Pentagon.

To this is added the Central Intelligence Agency, which conducts a number of covert operations and the director of which is designated as the coordinator of all United States intelligence efforts. Many of the efforts are imbedded in the State and Defense departments. Responsibility for overall direction resides in the National Security Council, though in practice it falls on the president's national security advisor, as often as not an active-duty or retired military officer. It is true too much power can momentarily be concentrated in this position, but when that happens the bureaucracies lose their patience and pull the incumbent's plug one way or the other, usually by way of leaking fatally damning evidence.

In review, many of these shortcomings are common to all organizations. In the case of Defense, however, Congressional initiatives, the rapid turnover of personnel, and a willingness to admit to the problems — in the literature, if not directly to the public — reduce the severity of some of the consequences. Other shortcomings persist, but few seem inimical to the equilibrium. The exceptions are: (1) the tendency of many defense officials to seek or at least advocate military solutions to problems that are best left to diplomatic and political initiatives, particularly in the absence of a clear statement of national aims and purposes; and (2) the somnambulistic decision-making inherent in the massive bureaucracy, the dual chains of commands, and the political aspects of the annual defense budget process, all of which retard effective decision-making in times of crisis. A good defense policy should take these two problems into account. However, because they are subjective and apply to almost all tiers of defense concerns, they are addressed in Part V, perspectives, rather than Part IV, which concentrates on specific implications.

Part IV
Implications for Defense

Some books of this genre concentrate on the theoretical aspects of defense policy but seem to avoid applying the points advocated to specific defense problems. Perhaps the authors believe it is beneath the dignity of scholarly writing to be practical or perhaps they fear that the resulting manuscript will give the appearance of being a geopolitical cook book. Risking that fault, the arguments thus far advanced in this book will now be restated as seven defense parameters from which four suggested policy guidelines are derived and compared with various levels of concern relevant to an adequate defense posture.

The subdivision of defense into the five areas—(1) nuclear defense, (2) Western Europe, Korea and Japan, (3) the Middle East flash points, (4) contingencies among the remainder states, and (5) defense against terrorism—is arbitrary, but it was based on a number of considerations. First, nuclear defense is very nearly a unique division of the armed forces, comprising the navy's strategic nuclear submarine element and the air force's Strategic Air Command. The latter has additional missions, e.g. conventional bombing, but the nuclear defense mission dominates. Moreover, the logicstical requirements are relatively small, few supporting forces are required, and the United States is fully prepared to act unilaterally, that is, there is no prerequisite for coalition warfare. By contrast, American commitments in Europe, Korea, and Japan could be said to present logistical nightmares and involve millions of personnel who could not be effective without coalition warfare.

The third area—the Middle East—presents some serious concerns for the United States, the severest of which is the potential of a local war escalating to global proportions. Next, the fourth area addresses Central America, Africa, and many of the Asian states beyond China, Japan, and Korea. For the most part, the United States has avoided any overt military commitments in Africa, and in the aftermath of Vietnam, is properly gun-shy about becoming involved in Asia beyond Japan and Korea. But she still practices intervention in Central America. With very little success.

The last area is terrorism, which is not restricted to any region in the world. It is not a problem fully amenable to ordinary military solution, and will likely take the concerted efforts of many nations, over many generations, to throttle. In the interim, defense against terrorism must address some difficult issues in international law.

These five areas of defense concerns can be thought of as analogous to baseball. Nuclear defense obviously represents homeplate, while Western Europe, Korea and Japan would be the infield. The Middle East contingencies could be considered as shortstop, on the grounds that it would be in the best interests of the United States to stop short any potential for global war that might arise from that region. The remainder states beyond the Middle East, of course, would be the outfield, and terrorism, given its inability to inflict much actual damage — nuclear terrorism excepted — would occupy the bleachers.

As for the report of the Pentagon's Commission on Integrated Long-Term Strategy ("Discriminate Deterrence"), which was not seen until after this book was largely complete, the thrust of the recommendations was to change the defense focus from an increasingly improbable nuclear or conventional war in Western Europe to lesser conflicts elsewhere. Perhaps so, but it seems imperative that deterrence against the larger potential conflicts be maintained for the sake of the equilibrium while at the same time recognizing that success with military initiatives elsewhere seems increasingly difficult to achieve.

Chapter 14. Parameters and Policy

My experience teaches me that men and nations behave
wisely, once they have exhausted all other alternatives.
                                        — Abba Eban

The factors which contribute to the global equilibrium and to slimmer
pickings for U.S. military force, considering some of the shortcomings in the
defense policy infrastructure and with a few additional observations, can be
restated as seven defense parameters. These parameters in turn suggest four
policy guidelines. These guidelines then serve as the basis for an appropriate
defense posture against various levels of threats and contingencies.

The reader may be puzzled at first why the equilibrium is not one of the
defense parameters. The reason is that it is more of a long-term effect than a
cause, a situation analogous to the practice of medicine. In theory, the principal object in medical practice is to assist the body's homeostatic mechanisms
to defeat or contain a dysfunction that might otherwise do that body in. Yet
the actual practice concentrates on less abstract concepts, ranging among
various chemical balances, cell counts, surgical removal or repair of tissue
beyond the body's ability to cope, and so forth.

And so it seems to be with defense policy. The equilibrium is something
to harness, but the route to understanding and making use of the process arises
from less abstract parameters. That is, the equilibrium is something to bear in
mind but should only peak as a statement in the highest order of policy
guidelines, followed by a quick descent into the specific aspects of defense
policy. It should be the focal point, rather than the focus per se, of policy.

The Permanence of Thermonuclear Power

As intolerable if not unthinkable as a thermonuclear war would be, the
potential for it will likely continue to rest in the hands of the salient powers
for the foreseeable future. Moreover, thermonuclear technology continues to
spread among other nations, a technology which may open the door to even
greater destructive power by way of harnessing the fusion process to transform

a small unit of mass entirely to energy. Lastly, crude but devastating thermonuclear technology will in all probability some day fall into the hands of
one or more terrorist groups. How long it takes is immaterial.

Attempts to suppress this trend — most notably the Nuclear Nonproliferation Treaty — have met with little success beyond a few delays and in some cases
have worked strongly against the grain of U.S. interests. For example, Pakistan
threatened to cut off transshipment of American military aid to the Afghan
resistance fighters if the United States persisted in trying to stop Pakistan's
development of nuclear material, ostensibly weapons grade. Also, the nonproliferation treaty was not signed by France, which is responsible for roughly
26 percent of the world arms sales beyond those of the superpowers.[1]

Nationalism as the Dominant Force in International Relations

Nationalism is the dominant force in international relations. Nothing appears on the political horizon to supplant it. Five factors in particular support
this assertion.

Weakening of Political Ideology. Neither communism nor democracy nor
any other political dogma seems to be a primary force in world affairs. Political
dogma may appear as a dominant force in some situations, but nationalism
and the centers of power attendant thereto are the final arbiters in conflicts and
disputes. Democracy may prevail in the United States, in Western Europe, in
Canada and Australia, in Japan, and after a fashion in a number of other countries, but the majority of nations live either under some form of totalitarian
regime or within a somewhat less imposing regime with a modicum of personal
liberties tolerated (though this situation is improving).[2] On the other hand,
communism has singularly failed to spawn a world revolution. The domino
theory works only in reverse, as recent events in eastern Europe, or for that matter within the Soviet Union itself, have indicated.

Lack of Any Supranational Authority. The likelihood of any sustainable
supranational power or institution for the enforcement of international law or
prevention of armed conflicts appears nil for the foreseeable future. The
United Nations offers only limited effectiveness. Far and away, the most effective means of enforcement seems to be the threat of retaliation from one or
more nations affected by an offending state. This does not overlook the influence and moral authority of international law, but that influence is usually
insufficient by itself to prevent major war.

Aging Limited Alliances. The past 40 years have demonstrated a reduction in the number of alliances offset by an increase in their stability. And the
few that do exist seem headed for the archives. The reason seems to be the
decrease in the number of major threats, leaving primarily the view the superpowers and their respective allies have of each other. But alliances rarely serve

to advance the interests of one member if those interests are perceived as inimical to the interests of the others. For example, NATO members seldom support United States policy in the Middle East, particularly with reference to Israel. Moreover, alliances tend to disintegrate whenever the members are expected to share too much of the common burden or perceive adherence to alliance conditions as more onerous than the mutually perceived threat itself. Thus New Zealand backed out of the ANZUS pact when she felt permitting ships laden with nuclear warheads into her harbors was more disruptive to her ethos than the threat of an invasion by the Soviet Union or possibly China.

Lack of Opportunities for Expansion. Opportunities for the salient powers to expand their real estate holdings have become virtually nonexistent, save by means of outright aggrandizement. Even that method has proven largely futile in the last 10 to 15 years. The remainder states may continue to engage in various wars, but even here the territorial gains are small. Iraq restored the bits and pieces she wrested from Iran after eight years of fighting, while her invasion of Kuwait may prove ephemeral.

The Limited Effectiveness of Interdependence. Economic and technological interdependence may have served to defuse the potential for war, but the sense of dependency created by this phenomenon seems to have heightened rather than ameliorated awareness of national aims and interests. For example, the arguments heard in this country in favor of tariffs and import quotas, seem to be stronger than they have been in many decades.

The United States and the USSR as Permanent Antagonists

The United States and the Soviet Union are likely to remain antagonists for the foreseeable future, notwithstanding—in fact, probably reinforced by—the difficulty of resolving conflicts by mutual war and the limited opportunities for exploiting the remainder states. Moreover, the Soviet Union sustained the highest losses during World War II and had been invaded several times before then. Further, the recent loss of the Warsaw Pact buffer states has made the USSR more fearful—witness the digging in of heels when it came to the issue of letting Estonia and Lithuania go. And the fact the western nations hold to a different perspective on this matter fuels the animosity.

Even more important is the fact that all seven of the other salient powers are either aligned against the Soviet Union or at best are neutral, while a majority of the buffer states also tend to be aligned with the United States or at least are more inclined to be associated with "western" policy than Soviet ambitions. This, too, serves to keep relationships cool between the superpowers. And as at least one writer has pointed out, the international behavior of the Soviet Union today would be no different if communism had never been invented.[3]

Other sources of antagonism include the Soviet Union's being a superpower primarily due to her military strength, substantial population, and massive land area, though she is trying to upgrade her economic clout. With two-and-one-half times the land mass and a somewhat larger population, her GNP is only 56 percent that of the United States. Moreover, and as discussed in Chapter 8, the sea lane of communication by way of the Indian Ocean and through at least three major choke points is another sore point. The trans–Siberian railway, and a subsidiary track to the south of it, are incapable of carrying the raw materials and resources so plentiful in eastern Russia to the industrial sectors of her west, hence the extreme reliance on this sea route. As there is no practical alternative to this route and no end in sight to the volatility of the Middle East, this vulnerability is apt to grow more serious.

Still other sources of antagonism have been the Soviet Union's recently ended slaughter of Afghans for eight years, her persistent disinformation campaigns, and her long record of deception in international relations. One such campaign spread the rumor in Africa that the Acquired Immune Deficiency Syndrome (AIDS) was the result of medical experiments in the United States, though the United States has in the past exacerbated this antagonism by her moral pronouncements on the state of the Soviet Union, most notably Ronald Reagan's "evil empire" allegations. Next, spying on each other has reached a new high.[4] Finally, the two superpowers remain engaged in a proxy war in Afghanistan. Whether the Soviet Union still intends to become the dominant world power is speculation, but it seems imperative that she not be given the opportunity to rise to this position by default on the part of the United States.

The Global Scope and Unaffordability of a Superpower Conflict

Because the superpowers control or are formally aligned with the overwhelming bulk of the world's economic strength, military power, and thermonuclear weapons, the concept of some form of minor or limited war between them is either naive or runs a severe risk of escalating to global proportions almost immediately. Both countries span the respective continental masses on which they are situated. Moreover, as demonstrated in Chapter 2, the preponderance of their military prowess is even more significant in global terms, perhaps comprising between 90 and 95 percent of the real international military clout. Indeed, the superpowers are the only nations left which have the wherewithal to invest in truly global navies.

As for the unaffordability aspect, consider that any global war would likely be prolonged. The resulting devastation would virtually eliminate the industrial base and inflict tens of millions of casualties, the survivors of which would take priority for all remaining resources. If the war centered in NATO, the counterinvasion would entail an operation against the entire weight of the

Soviet Union. That would be a far cry from the situation during World War II, in which the Soviet Union and the United States, and many others, fought on the same side to crush a comparatively small upstart opponent with less than one-tenth the actual and potential resources.

Moreover, in that war, the United States was still reeling from a major depression and had no significant national debt. Economically speaking, World War II was a blessing. Today the national debt is astronomical and the unemployment rate in the 5 to 6 percent range. The price of modern weapons systems is nearly prohibitive, and replacing them at the rate they would likely be destroyed in heavy fighting is arguably beyond the capabilities of the entire industrial base. Lastly, the exponentially increasing logistical requirements of war, cited in Chapter 6, would bankrupt the United States in a major war that dragged on for years. One only need consider the extremely high cost of the 1973 Middle East war between Israel and her opponents Syria and Egypt. That short, local war burned up more (and more expensive) tanks in a few weeks than were destroyed in the most intense, extended campaign in World War II.[5]

The Middle East as the Region of Volatile Flash Points

An ancient tale has it that a scorpion hailed a passing crocodile along the Tigres river to ask for a ride across. The crocodile at first demurred on the grounds that he would get fatally stung. The scorpion reasoned that this fear had no basis. If he stung him, they would both go under. So the crocodile relented and bade his new friend come on board. Half way across, the scorpion inflicted the sting, whereupon his victim asked why. "Who knows?" replied his rider. "This is the Middle East."

It comes as no surprise that most if not all the world's more volatile flash points are located in the Middle East. First among the reasons is that many nations continue to depend on the Middle East oil producers, though U.S. dependency has shrunk to less than 10 percent of requirements. Second, the United States continued support Israel notwithstanding the deep-seated enmity between Israel and the balance of the Levant, is exacerbated by Israel's possession of nuclear weapons. Third, most of the world's terrorist groups emanate from this region. Fourth, Iran in particular demonstrates a violent, disregard for international law. Fifth, the Soviet's critical sea lane of communication runs through this region. Sixth, Iraq's Saddam Hussein seems intent on following in Hitler's footsteps.

To all of this must be added the fact the United States is 10,000 miles from the region, while the Soviet Union borders directly on Iran. Further, the United States has very few bases in the area and is not exactly welcomed by the Arab states, given American support of Israel. True, the Arab states will on occasion police themselves. A few years ago, during the Iran-Iraq war, Saudi

Arabia felt impelled to warn Iran that if the latter's international behavior grew any worse, she might have to intervene.[6] But that tendency is not one to count on, hence this region will likely remain the source of the flash points. In 1976, an instructor at the U.S. Army Command & General Staff College summarized the situation by noting it was the juncture of three continents and that there was a lot of oil there.[7] That is an oversimplification, of course, but not bad as an aphorism.

The Weakness of the Remainder States

With the exception of the Middle East region, the global horsepower of the remainder states, individually or collectively, bears no comparison with the clout exercised by the salient powers. This point, plus the growing effectiveness of easily afforded defensive weapons, has been dwelled on so extensively throughout the analysis that it may insult the reader's intelligence to bring the matter up again. Yet so much defense planning seems to focus on various so-called Third World contingencies that the lack of any real threat emanating from them bears repeating. The problems in these regions are largely those of state, not defense.

The possible exception would be a cutoff of a particularly critical material, either without alternate suppliers or with the alternative being the Soviet Union. Only a few of these situations exist, and they are somewhat offset by Congressionally mandated strategic reserves.[8] Moreover, it would seem far less expensive to increase these reserve stockpiles than to prepare for war in the event of a cutoff.

A Nation As Its Own Worse Enemy

One of the more memorable utterances of the cartoon character *Pogo* was his observation to the effect that "we have met the enemy and *they* is *us!*" As outlined in Chapter 8, the United States demonstrated bad judgment in most of its significant attempts to use military force since the end of World War II, including Korea (after South Korea was resecured), Vietnam and Lebanon. Bad judgment was also in evidence in the U.S. presence in the Persian Gulf, and according to at least one analyst was responsible for incorrectly sizing up the situation in that region prior to the overthrow of the Shah of Iran.[9] And it did not deter Iraq's invasion of Kuwait.

That the United States escaped the devastating consequences of bad judgment in the past was due, arguably, to the fact that her political resiliency and vast economic potential absorbed the consequences without falling apart at the seams, though the bitter aftertaste of the Vietnam era lingers. Whether or not future contingencies will continue to draw down on resources at the subcritical level is problematic, but imprudent military involvement, particularly in the Middle East, might escalate to a level that begs untoward global consequences.

To look at matters another way, while continued bad judgment in international relations might not severely jeopardize the defense interests of the United States, that margin of safety is no justification for continuing it. On the other hand, the nearly insatiable appetite to manipulate world balance of power, ostensibly to thwart the mythical power of "world communism," seems too deeply embedded in the American ethos to be ignored. It is a political reality to be addressed without denigrating a consistent defense policy. But one thing seems certain: If it comes to another major war, there will be no new edition of *Victory at Sea* and no Bill Mauldin will arise to interject a little humor into an otherwise tragic situation. The mutual devastation will have been too great to celebrate the outcome.[10]

Significance

The principal significance of these defense parameters is that the resultant global equilibrium should be the essence of defense policy. Insofar as controlling international factors that may work to distend that equilibrium, deterrence and not war would be the method of choice. The reasons comprise a restatement and resequencing of the defense parameters:

• War, at least if it involved the salient powers, would be too destructive even if it could be financed. This applies whether or not nuclear and thermonuclear weapons were used.

• Thermonuclear power is here to stay and will probably proliferate among nations and become even more destructive.

• Notwithstanding the potential devastation of major war, the two superpowers are apt to remain antagonists for the foreseeable future, hence continued deterrence is virtually mandatory.

• The remainder states, beyond the Middle East, pose few serious threats to the superpowers, while the growing superiority of inexpensive defensive weapons makes military intervention in those states a questionable proposition. The Middle East, unfortunately, does pose serious threats, but because of the global consequences, the ideal defense posture would be damage limitation to the extent deterrence may fail.

• The United States can thus well afford to let other nations pursue their own goals, irrespective of differences in political ideology. Moreover, any posture to the contrary will likely be thwarted by the forces of nationalism. If anything, she could strength her influence by helping the poorest of these nations to overcome weaknesses in their infrastructure which prevent them from becoming more self-sufficient.

POLICY GUIDELINES

PARAMETERS	RECOGNIZING THE PERMANENCE OF NUCLEAR POWER	MAINTAINING THE GLOBAL EQUILIBRIUM	EMPHASIZING DETERRENCE & DAMAGE LIMITATION	EMPHASIZING NATIONAL SELF-DETERMINATION
PERMANENT EXISTENCE OF THERMONUCLEAR POWER	Inevitable, though recognition of the inevitable can be difficult.	The existence of this form of power is a major cause of the equilibrium, but its potential devastation mandates an absolute emphasis on deterrence.		The spread of thermonuclear power clearly supports this policy.
THE DOMINANT FORCE OF NATIONALISM	This contributes to the inexorable spread of this form of power.	The force of nationalism, to the extent it motivates other states to strengthen their respective infrastructures, contributes to the equilibrium.		There are few, if any, practical alternatives.
LASTING ANTAGONISM BETWEEN THE SUPER-POWERS	The possession of thermonuclear weapons adds to the antagonism.	Similar to the reasoning for the continued existence of thermonuclear power, the long-standing antagonism between the superpowers is a major cause of the equilibrium while the consequences of war involving nuclear power mandate its prevention.		A genuine mutual recognition of the sovereignty of the superpowers can lower the threshold of global war.
GLOBAL SCOPE AND HIGH COST OF SUPER-POWER WAR	The costs of waging thermonuclear war are incalculable.			
VOLATILITY OF MIDDLE EAST FLASHPOINTS	As this region is the one plausible source of contingencies which might trigger a chain reaction of events that could lead to global confrontations, the salient powers need to keep the threshold below "critical mass."			Because nationalism is inevitable, a different course of action can only serve to exacerbate the threats that do exist.
FEW THREATS FROM REMAINDER STATES	Because there are so few threats emanating from these states, this parameter supports primarily the fourth policy guideline, almost to the exclusion of the first three.			
A NATION AS ITS OWN WORSE EMENY	Bad judgment can lead to international initiatives on the part of the United States, which might under some contingencies exacerbate the risk of global war arising from volatile conditions among remainder states, especially in the Middle East, or which might NATO to weaken NATO before its usefulness ends.			

Figure 14. Comparison of Defense Parameters and Guidelines

The relationships of the defense parameters to the suggested defense policy guidelines which follow shortly are further illustrated in Figure 14. Before stating those guidelines, however, it might prove useful to examine the concept of deterrence itself. Deterrence is an instrument of war in its own right—a psychological weapon aimed at the mindset of a potential aggrandizing opponent. To be effective, that mindset must: (1) be convinced that retaliatory damage will prove intolerable in comparison to the gain sought; (2) be assured that the retaliating state has the means and the willpower to make good on its "promise"; (3) be convinced that it is essentially impossible to disable the retaliatory means by a preemptive first strike or by other preconflict means; and (4) be persuaded—which presumes sufficient rationality—to react prudently to the above perceptions. But if the potential opponent believes that lesser means can be employed or indirect objectives selected which are below the threshold value that will trigger retaliation, he is likely to try them. Hence, the Soviet Union would think twice before it invaded NATO, but obviously it did not worry about potential retaliation on the part of the United States to its invasion of Afghanistan.

There are limits, then, to deterrence. For example, is largely ineffective against terrorism, except in the sense of keeping it from becoming too extensive or too openly supported by a legitimate government in power. Therefore, the need is to determine the options when deterrence fails or is inapplicable. The alternative to deterrence at the thermonuclear level, or in potential conflicts which offer a substantial risk of escalation to that level, is more or less unthinkable; the resulting damage would be too extensive. Thus defense policy should hone that level of deterrence to perfection. In lesser circumstances, the obvious alternative is to control damage and prevent escalation of hostilities to any level that might unhinge the equilibrium.

Suggested Defense Policy Guidelines

The four policy guidelines suggested by the defense parameters are as follows:

First, the existence of the thermonuclear form of power should be recognized as a permanent fact of international relations, concentrating policy on reducing the risk of its use in war, in lieu of trying to eliminate the source.

Second, the defense posture of the United States should rely primarily on the global equilibrium among the salient powers and buffer states, endeavoring to maintain if not enhance that equilibrium, and thus should avoid any actions which could serve to weaken it.

Third, and as support for the first two guidelines, maximum reliance should be placed on deterrence, honing that posture to near perfection, but where deterrence is inadequate and force must be used as a last resort, the emphasis should be on damage limitation and prevention of escalation of hostilities to higher levels.

Fourth, except when another state seriously threatens the equilibrium, a policy of self-determination toward all states should be inviolate, irrespective of political dogma, with a further emphasis on elementary infrastructure building for the poorest of the remainder states.

The application of these guidelines to defense against terrorism works in the abstract but not as well in practical terms. Obviously, the salient powers would not want terrorism to upset the balance of things, and they would prefer to deter rather than combat it. But only a small fraction of the defense dollar is invested in reacting to the terrorist threat, and arguably most of that small amount is spent on the intelligence process and guarding critical facilities. Accordingly, the application of the guidelines to this problem goes beyond the norm of the other chapters and incorporates eventual reliance on potential advancements in international law doctrine.

Chapter 15. Nuclear Defense

More than any other time in history, mankind faces a
crossroads. One leads to despair and utter hopelessness,
the other to total extinction. Let us pray we have the
wisdom to choose correctly.
                    — Attributed to Woody Allen

The implications of the policy guidelines with reference to nuclear
defense involve the fewest changes from existing policy. That policy is already
deterrent in nature. The few occasions when the United States threatened or
otherwise hinted at the use of nuclear weapons to resolve an impasse have not
been repeated in recent times. Further, the implications accept the inevitability
of thermonuclear power for the foreseeable future. Finally, and in a negative
way, the policy of self-determination is upheld in that none of the implications
strives to stop other nations from developing the same type of weapons.

At the same time, a growing vocal minority has been advocating massive
arms reduction and eventual disarmament at all costs even if it puts the United
States at a disadvantage with respect to the Soviet Union.[1] In August 1989, a
Media-General Associated Press poll found that half of all Americans expect
World War III to occur someday and most of them anticipate nuclear devastation. Also, the policy concerning first-use or no-first-use of nuclear weapons remains fuzzy, perhaps intentionally so. Then there are subordinate issues
centering on the adequacy of command and communications abilities as well
as on the Strategic Defense Initiative (SDI). The latter has spawned an ongoing
debate. Some critics contend this system would serve to destabilize the deterrent posture afforded by nuclear weapons. Others assume SDI cannot work
because of technical limitations no matter how much money and time is invested in it. Comparing these criticisms, then, with the proposed guidelines,
the implications for nuclear defenses would be as follows:

Mutually Assured Destruction

The reliance on the mutually assured destruction (MAD) of land-based
ballistic missiles, submarine launched missiles and manned bombers should be

continued, but phasing out the use of the manned bomber leg of the triad for this purpose. The rationale is that while the Soviet Union may proclaim it will prevail in a nuclear war, it does not advocate such warfare. The Soviet reasoning presumes they would be struck first or would be forced to resort to nuclear weapons to defend against an invasion. Nowhere in the current Soviet literature is there a policy of world aggrandizement and very little about exploiting civil wars for the sake of communism, though much was written in the past. If anything, Soviet military policy is changing to one of national defense.[2] Hence the mutually assured destruction (MAD) concept is still valid and still works.

But to maintain this resilient deterrent posture, the opponent must be convinced a surprise move on his part will not disable the ability to retaliate. The triad serves this purpose because it reduces the potential damage that can be attained with a first strike on the part of the opponent. However, and as discussed in Appendix A, the manned bomber leg of the triad is nearly an anachronism, and the ponderous stealth bomber replacement even more so.

Arms Control Agreements

Arms control agreements with the Soviet Union—beyond the Intermediate-Range Nuclear Forces (INF) treaty—and with China should be continued, but primarily for the purpose of reducing political tensions rather than elimination of the nuclear threat. The reduction of political tensions that accrues as a side effect of arms reduction talks supplements the deterrent posture in that it can further reduce the risk of war, but such talks cannot eliminate the threat or risk. A very small number of warheads can inflict intolerable damage, while it is difficult to perceive how the reduced number of weapons per se can have much effect on the risk. If anything, deterrence is favored by a maximum number of weapons. And in light of the proliferation of nuclear power worldwide, it is not likely either superpower will forego its own nuclear weapons.

As for including China in the talks, the reason is simply that she possesses thermonuclear warheads and the ballistic missiles to deliver them, albeit not in the quantity and quality of the superpowers. In time, however, that nuclear arsenal could reach parity with the United States and the Soviet Union.

Technological Improvements

Within the scope of any arms control agreements, or in their absence within the scope of any reasonable limit on warheads, investment in technological improvements related to nuclear weapons should concentrate on command and control mechanisms. The United States has more than enough warheads on hand to effectively destroy the physical infrastructure of the Soviet Union, if not the world, several times over. Hence the emphasis in technological improvements should be in command and control. This would serve to further reduce the risk of accidental firing or an overreaction to a terrorist nuclear attack.

In September 1987, the United States and the Soviet Union signed an agreement on just that contingency, but several critics have pointed out how existing command and control systems may prove inadequate in a crunch.[3] It should also be noted the Department of Defense is spending a sizable amount of money to improve these communications, but the scope of that upgrade may or may not fully address the valid points raised by critics.

The Nuclear Nonproliferation Treaty

The goals of the Nuclear Nonproliferation Treaty should be discounted irrespective of any commitment to support that treaty and any persistence on the part of the United States to abide by its provisions. This would only be a matter of facing up to reality. Even if she refuses to contribute to the proliferation, it will continue. Instead, the emphasis should be on attempting to stretch arms limitation agreements and negotiations to a wider sphere of states to reduce political tensions. The roots of war, and its avoidance, are more subjective than objective.

Strategic Defense Initiative

The pursuit of the Strategic Defense Initiative should be continued, encouraging the Soviet Union to follow suit—as if she were not already doing so—but without sharing critical technical information. Additionally, the specific SDI methodology chosen should offer maximum invulnerability to future counter–SDI systems, even if the scope of such a system requires a greater investment.

Several reasons support this approach.[4] First, it would enhance deterrence in that each superpower would be more invulnerable to attack, or at least it would further reduce the effect of a first strike. Second, it could serve to all but eliminate damage from an accidental firing or a partial firing under the "madman at the nuclear trigger" scenario. Third, the supposed risk that the pursuit of SDI might destabilize MAD is based on subjective reasoning and presumes the Soviet Union is not pursuing the same line of development.[5] As such, this "risk" does not bear much weight compared to the more plausible risk of an accidental firing or other incident against which the United States now has very little defense. Fourth, as discussed in Chapter 4, if fusion-powered missiles with even more destructive warheads are developed, then the necessity for SDI against accidental strikes becomes all the more imperative. Fortunately, the same technology could be used to strengthen SDI itself.

As for advocating that the Soviet Union do likewise, the same justification applies. Not sharing critical technical information, however, improves the deterrent value. And as for the theory the Soviet Union cannot afford SDI, she already spends at least 13 percent of her gross national product on defense, more defense than she will ever need. That is, she can well afford SDI merely by reducing excess deployments in her satellite countries.

As for the emphasis on maximum invulnerability to SDI itself, the reader is referred to Appendix A. Every weapons systems eventually meets its nemesis. The Strategic Defense Initiative is expensive, but it would be a waste to build a less expensive but more vulnerable model and then find it prey to counter-measures.

No-First-Use Policy

A policy of no-first-use of strategic nuclear weapons against any country is warranted, with the proviso that the unmistakable detection of the firing of such missiles against the United States, to include possessions, territories, or troops stationed or deployed overseas, constitutes first-use of nuclear weapons. This would not mandate immediate retaliation but only the recognition that the no-first-use policy had been abrogated by the opponent initiatives.

The proviso is based on the observation that damage from even a single thermonuclear warhead, particularly if it is directed at a populated area, is politically unacceptable under any circumstances. Military analysts are wont to calculate all sorts of survival indices and to stress military targets (counterforce) over civilian targets (countervalue), but whatever influence the United States exercises in the world today would be totally destroyed by the act of initiating warfare at this level of devastation.

Also, the no-first-use proviso does not weaken second-strike (retaliatory) capability. The proviso would stand only until the firing of an opponent's missiles is detected. Hence, it would be impossible for the Soviet Union to destroy all or most United States missiles simultaneously, even if she could locate all deployed strategic submarines. It is a matter of mathematics. If the USSR fired all missiles simultaneously, the time-spread between the first and last impacts would be close to 20 minutes. If she timed the launches so that the impacts would occur simultaneously, then the earliest launches would be detected long before the balance were fired.

Policy Statement

A concisely written, comprehensive statement regarding nuclear defense policy, devoid of any rationalization or other specious reasoning, should be prepared and disseminated. The need for this statement should be obvious. Much of the public has an inordinate fear of nuclear weapons and tends to support the growing movement to reduce warheads and even disarm. Thus it is likely Congressional pressures will eventually mount to force the issue. Yet while the Soviet Union might very well prefer to avoid nuclear war, if one superpower is perceived worldwide as being the preeminent power, then the equilibrium would be weakened if not negated. To prevent this situation, a clear policy statement would be indispensable.

A higher perspective also applies here. One of the mainstays of the defense posture of the United States is to protect the American way of life. That way of life includes the right of free speech. The right of free speech extends to critics of the Defense Department. To regard such critics with disdain goes against the grain of this right if not human nature. That is, while the defense posture of the United States cannot be the handmaiden of the day-to-day predilections of public opinion, mounting negative public opinion should be addressed in straightforward terms.

Nuclear Terrorism

Briefly, while nuclear terrorism seems to be more probable than "conventional" nuclear attack, virtually none of the defensive measures against the latter would have any effect at reducing the former. First, a terrorist who tried to use a nuclear weapon probably would do so by emplacement rather than missile delivery. Second, the mindset of a terrorist is seldom swayed by the rationality inherent in conventional deterrence.

On the second point, it is difficult for the Western mind to comprehend the motivations of terrorists, particularly those who operate out of the Middle East. Iran sacrificed hundreds of thousands of her countrymen, including young children, in a senseless war against Iraq. Thus it would not be out of character for, say, an Iranian terrorist group to someday attempt to inflict nuclear damage on a superpower which it deemed to be "evil"—*the great Satan* is Iran's favorite sobriquet for the United States—sensing that the superpower probably would not retaliate in kind against their entire country. Chapter 19 addresses this issue, but it will take an entirely different approach than deterrence between superpowers.

Chapter 16. Western Europe, Korea and Japan

Austin White—Chicago, Illinois—1918
Austin White—Chicago, Illinois—1945
This is the last time I want to write my name here.
—Inscription of an American soldier found
on a wall of the fortress at Verdun

Western Europe, Korea and Japan should be addressed apart from other defense matters because of the long-standing presence of U.S. military forces in these regions. In the case of Europe, the long-term future of the NATO alliance is problematic. A number of defense analysts, among them retired General Andrew Goodpaster and Leonard Sullivan, Jr., are advocating cutting the United States contingent of 356,000 troops in half within five years. More significantly, as discussed in Chapter 12, the pending reunification of Germany may force NATO out of business altogether. This would mean that in order to continue the proven effectiveness of NATO with much smaller forces, a revised way of developing an effective defense posture is essential. And it would have to be low cost.

Korea presents a different picture. While the defense of Western Europe is complex and any war there probably would escalate to global proportions involving most of the salient powers, the defense of South Korea is relatively simple. A war there probably would be confined to the Korean peninsula and not necessarily pit the superpowers in direct conflict. That is, a NATO war would entail global damages and casualties and run the risk of escalation to nuclear warfare, whereas a Korean war could well be limited to conventional weapons and remain local.

As for Japan, her enormous wealth combined with her constitutional proscription against comparable military forces pose unique issues for the United States. The odds of a major war involving Japan are minimal, but her reliance on the United States for global if not local defense, while investing the "savings" for further economic development inimical to American interests, is one of the thorniest problems in geopolitics today.

Implications for Western Europe and NATO

The suggested policy guidelines yield seven implications for Western Europe and NATO. These measures would take cognizance of the policy guideline to maintain the global equilibrium, in that war in Europe will remain unlikely even if NATO is disbanded, provided the deterrent posture remains plausible. Preventing escalation of hostilities to global proportions, however, would be moot in this instance. Because such escalation would be probable in a European war, the deterrence must be adequate to prevent *any* war. The policy of self-determination toward all states would be honored by way of emphasizing the negative consequences to the former Warsaw Pact countries. Their future depends on keeping the Soviets out. And by strengthening the deterrent posture, the risk of the use of thermonuclear weapons would be further reduced. In more specific terms:

Political Enhancement of the Deterrent Posture. The efficacy of the deterrent posture should be enhanced by emphasizing the extreme devastation that would be inflicted on the eastern European nations in the event of hostilities, devastation that would probably exceed that borne by the Soviet Union. When the former Warsaw Pact nations were freed from Soviet control, they became part of the NATO defense by virtue of geography. In the history of Europe, this is yet another version of an old story. Still, it is valid, and by stressing the unfortunate geographical position, they would become a de facto part of the deterrent posture.

Mobilization Preparedness. The mobilization posture of the United States should be improved by making the mobilization process itself an instrument of deterrence, with especial emphasis on the legal and management infrastructure to manifest and project military power overseas. The more ready the United States appears to be in terms of the ability to mobilize its resources, and to do so quickly, the more deterrence in NATO is enhanced. As discussed in Appendix C, this would not entail increased resources for defense but a streamlining of the mechanics of mobilization—the legal and managerial infrastructure essential to facilitate mobilization. Then, too, if NATO is disbanded, the ability of the United States to mobilize with greater efficiency will improve the deterrent bearing of the remaining forces.

Nonintegration of Nuclear Forces. No attempt to integrate control of the independent French nuclear force with the nuclear elements of NATO should be made. Moreover, the issue of employment of tactical nuclear weapons (for those weapons not excluded by the Intermediate-Range Nuclear Forces treaty) in the defense of NATO should be left an open issue, aside from no-first-use of any form of strategic nuclear missiles against the Soviet Union itself. Separation of control over nuclear forces would sow further doubt in the opponent's mindset. It is one thing to estimate the probability of employment of nuclear forces by a single power, quite another to predict the actions of two independent entities. Hence, France's preference to go her own way better serves the interests of NATO than would any integrated control.

No Counterinvasion of the Soviet Union. If there are any war plans for a counterinvasion of the Soviet Union, in the event of a Soviet attack, they should be eliminated and that elimination publicized. It would be difficult to imagine a more insane war plan. It is one thing to deter the potential for an invasion, or that failing to repel it; quite another to take on the Soviet Union itself. Napoleon and Hitler both learned that lesson the hard way, and the USSR would be infinitely better prepared this time. Moreover, the emphasis must be on deterrence. When the Soviet Union recognizes that the West seeks only to protect its own interests, it may junk her once-justified paranoia from the harsh experience of World War II.

De facto Defense Utilization of the former Warsaw Pact States. The former Warsaw Pact states should be considered as a passive asset for the defense of Western Europe. Having just shed their Soviet yoke, it is perfectly understandable if some of them might choose to remain independent, but the accidents of geography suggest otherwise. They would unavoidably become a buffer zone for Western Europe, and suffer the brunt of the effects of any Soviet invasion.

Downplaying the "Forward Defense" Plan. The concept of the NATO defense should be shifted from an emphasis on the current "forward defense" plan to a mobile defense in depth, to include a so-called "killing zone" for a specified but variable width west and east of the border.

The "forward defense" concept in NATO is fatally flawed. It may sound good politically, but the primary mode of Soviet operations depends on sharp, massive penetrations. Reliance on forward defense denies NATO the best opportunity to inflict maximum casualties on invading forces while choosing the time and place of decisive combat on its own terms.[1] Also, forward defense can be further weakened by the use of Soviet airborne divisions and other means of "vertical envelopment." The name of the game is deterrence, the alternative being essentially intolerable. The extent to which the Soviets realize they cannot possibly succeed militarily is the extent to which deterrence works. This is one of those rare instances where military logic is justified in rapping political knuckles.

As for the concept of a "killing zone," this is not much different from the frequently proposed weapons-free zone straddling borders." The difference would be only in tactics in the event of hostilities, and that primarily to ensure maximum attrition of Soviet armored forces before decisive engagement. Hence the emphasis in the killing zone would be on well-dispersed anti-air and infantry-borne anti-armor missiles. Anything moving in the air or on the ground much bigger than a small truck would be presumed to belong to the invading force. Additionally, this method would bypass the extreme difficulty of attempting to coordinate a main defense or attack in an intense war zone.

All this is nothing more than a variation of trading space for time and is meant to enhance deterrence. The Soviets must be convinced that if the USSR elected to invade Western Europe, her forces would be decimated before they could engage in decisive combat. The idea of deterrence is to prevent war, not to utter a hopeful plea to avoid it.

Emphasis on Anti-Armor and Anti-Air Technology. The development and production of state-of-the-art anti-armor and anti-air weapons should be emphasized at the expense of standardization of weapons systems within NATO and if necessary at the expense of armor technology development.

The need for state-of-the-art anti-armor and anti-aircraft weapons is pressing, more so the former than the latter. The Soviet Union is heavy in armor, far outweighing NATO's collective tanks, though it normally takes marked superiority in numbers and mass to dislodge a determined defender. Anti-armor weapons are much cheaper than tanks, and the deterrence posture should convince the opponent that his supposed advantages will be negated before he can engage in decisive operations. Moreover, in the absence of intermediate-range nuclear missiles, these anti-armor weapons would prove all the more important in the deterrent posture mix. Appendix A provides more detail on this matter.

As for the weapons standardization program, it has proven more costly and time-consuming than anticipated.[2] Moreover, it forces the United States to compromise on some of its weapons designs when those compromises could prove inimical to the defense of United States interests elsewhere, "elsewhere" tending to favor lighter, more easily transported weapons. That is, the standardization is an expensive method to gain a minor degree of military efficiency, whereas the funds so expended could be better spent to develop state-of-the-art anti-armor weapons.

Geopolitical Limitations for the NATO Treaty. The NATO allies should not be depended upon to support U.S. policy, or the ways and means of that policy, for any U.S. interest outside commonly perceived NATO interests. Dependence on NATO allies for support of policies beyond the sphere of mutually perceived NATO interests is a misuse of the treaty and goes against the grain of nationalism and self-determination. It is understandable why the United States, contributing 60 percent to the NATO tab, sometimes expects such support, but the magnanimity of her contributions is her choice. Moreover, these expectations could hasten the eventual demise of the NATO treaty. Restated, treaties are not geopolitical rubber bands.

Korea

As mentioned, the situation in Korea differs considerably from NATO. A war involving the two Koreas could easily be confined to that peninsula.

Moreover, North Korea does not have the normal three-to-one ratio of conventional forces on hand to dislodge the South Korean defenders, who are both well prepared and well entrenched. Then, too, while it is probable that North Korea has tactical nuclear weapons, they would be no match for what the United States could throw into the mêlée. Finally, only a few potential invasion routes into South Korea exist, and the combined South Korean–U.S. forces have been training for decades to repel every conceivable invasion that might occur on those routes.

The potential of China joining forces with North Korea to initiate an attack against South Korea (hence the United States) is not likely, while for the Soviet Union to do so would require easily interdicted lines of communication and support, presuming that China would let the Soviet Union forces pass through her homeland.[3] That, too, is unlikely. Overall then, Korea is probably the garden spot of military preparedness, and as such the U.S. presence there could be safely reduced. In August 1989, the United States commander in Korea (General Louis C. Menetrey) went so far as to indicate that all U.S. forces could, under current trends, be removed by the mid–1990s.

But this discounts the Asian mind, which puts as much stock in appearances as in factual reality. The steady presence of U.S. forces in Asia (even if reduced) gives America a substantial advantage in the politics of international relations without much risk of war. It also provides some of the best field training in the world, something to be considered if NATO is disbanded. Finally, South Korea could serve as an alternative for U.S. bases if for any reason the bases in Japan must be abandoned.

Japan

Japan's constitution limits defense spending to about 1 percent of the national budget, but because that budget is so large, this defense spending exceeded $13,000,000,000 in 1985 and is growing. In the same year, only the two superpowers, China, France, West Germany, the United Kingdom, Saudi Arabia, Poland, and Iraq exceeded that figure, and the last two only by a negligible amount. More significantly, even just 1 percent of an explosive GNP growth will eventually push Japan's military spending to third or fourth in the world, behind the Soviet Union, the United States, and possibly China. Even so, at least one analyst contends that Japan has not the slightest intention of increasing her defense budget, a fact of geopolitical life that needs to be recognized.[4]

What the United States must really learn to accept is that nations prefer to make their own choices—wise or unwise—including alliances and defense spending. On the other hand, she is under no obligation to provide any set dollar amount of global defense on behalf of Japan. Thus the rationale for extending the umbrella of U.S. support over Japan should be based on her own interests. The possibility of a reduction of the U.S. defense commitment toward Japan, without a commensurate increase in defense spending by Japan, should take into account that: (a) a direct Soviet attack on Japan has little more probability than a Soviet attack on America; and (b) Japan is becoming a regional military power simply by virtue of her rising GNP.

Further, the economic rivalry between the United States and Japan might erupt into a debilitating economic trade-sanction war, given the "contribution" of Japan toward the U.S. trade deficit and the differences in outlook between the two countries on free trade issues and the proper relationship of government and business. Estimating the probability of this event would be pure speculation, and in any event it would not likely upset the equilibrium. Nevertheless, it is a contingency that would have an impact on the defense posture of the United States.

Chapter 17. Middle East Flash Points

In individuals, insanity is rare, but in groups, parties,
nations, and epochs, it is the rule.
— Frederick Nietzsche

Because the Middle East is the location of the world's more volatile flash points, the overriding defense interest should be damage limitation. The prevention of war in this region is problematic at best, but for reasons outlined elsewhere, it would be far more important to the interests of the United States — if not the world — to prevent these wars from escalating beyond local proportions than to attempt to prevent the wars per se.

That is, the United States is not a world policeman and need not be to protect bona fide interests. Only four plausible contingencies should generate cause for concern, one of which would be her own doing. And none of them risks global war if properly adjudicated. These contingencies are: (a) a cutoff of Middle East oil, either by military action or by blackmail pricing; (b) a major war involving Israel; (c) further Soviet aggression in the region or, alternatively, political intervention which might exacerbate the potential for a pivotal war in Israel; and (d) unnecessary preemptive intervention on the part of the United States in the region.

The Oil Cutoff Contingency

The seriousness of the first contingency — a cutoff of oil — depends on the duration of the cutoff. It could range from a temporary blockade of the Strait of Hormuz to a sustained war, military or economic. The United States would not be the primary victim, however, due to the low dependence on Middle East oil and the strategic petroleum reserves plus alternative suppliers, although this favorable situation may deteriorate if the suggested "super–OPEC" is established. Hence any military options or economic counterinitiatives taken by the United States should be in concert with those countries more seriously affected by the cutoff.

This suggests an alliance, formal or informal, to deal with this contingency in a constructive manner. This alliance would not likely give the appearance of threatening OPEC except in the case where OPEC itself was the originator of the cutoff, either physically or by imposing prohibitive prices. The emphasis in this alliance should be on joint alternative-source and conservation programs, using the military option only as a last resort and then only to the point where the oil supply again rises above critical shortage levels.

Additional reasons supporting an alliance include the observation that the reaction to any oil shortage must consider the alternative sources available at the time, the relationships with OPEC countries, and the price of oil that was still available. The alliance should also encourage oil importers to develop their own strategic reserves. Finally, it would support a doctrine of maximum self-determination among all states, insofar as this is possible in the face of a mutually perceived contingency threat in lieu of the United States attempting to act as a world policeman. Granted, most of the nations heavily dependent on Middle East oil do not share the American proclivity toward Israel and are much less inclined to offend Arab sensitivities. But on the other hand, it would be a mistake for the America to become their international den mother.

The Israel Contingency

The second contingency — the potential for a war involving Israel with the United States in direct support — is a more complex situation. The United States would have few allies in this instance. The contingency is further compounded by the potential for a concerted attack on Israel being launched on Christmas eve when U.S. military readiness is at its lowest, with the invading forces threatening to "cut" Israel physically in half at her narrowest point. In this case Israel could request full United States support, in the absence of which she might state it would be necessary to use nuclear and possibly thermonuclear weapons notwithstanding the risk of retaliation by the attacking states. Presume also that Israel has not changed her policies on the Palestinian homeland and West Bank/Gaza Strip issues.

The options here are: (a) to provide only logistical support as in the 1973 Yom Kippur war; (b) to provide air and possibly naval fire support; or (c) to engage in coalition warfare. The choice would be further complicated by the predictable USSR warning to stay out of the war because that participation might escalate hostilities and endanger passage on her vital sea lane of communication past the Suez canal, or might obligate the Soviets to support one or more of the attacking countries. As early as 1976, a variation of this scenario was part of the standard curriculum at the U.S. Army Command and General Staff College, substituting fictitious names for the countries involved but using "lessons learned" material from the Yom Kippur war.[1]

Of these three options, the one to provide air and naval fire support offers the most advantages with the least risk of undue consequences. At a minimum, a major outbreak of nuclear warfare in the Middle East would generate negative consequences for the salient powers for years to come and therefore must be prevented. This eliminates the logistical-support-only option. Of the remaining two options, the coalition war option is questionable. It takes considerable time to project major ground forces into a foreign country, particularly in relation to the presumed crisis on the battlefield. Then, too, commitment of ground forces would make the United States a full-fledged participant in the war, whereas air and naval fire support can be construed as just that—support of an ally in time of extreme emergency. Finally, given the lethality that can be unleashed from U.S. air support, it is doubtful if U.S. ground forces would be needed to support the already first-rate Israeli army.

Some readers will strongly disagree with this analysis, perhaps forgetting that military actions should always be subordinated to political purpose and the full perspective of national interests. War is not something intended primarily for the exercise of warrior skills; boxing and riding the New York City subways are the proper outlets for that need. It would not be in the national interests of the United States to become overly embroiled in regional conflicts when such conflicts threaten the far greater interests of global equilibrium. It would be in the national interest to support Israel and prevent her demise if it came to that.

This situation can better be understood by reference to the bombing of North Vietnam during the Vietnam conflict. Had the United States attempted a full-scale invasion of North Vietnam, the negative consequences would have been far greater than those she did suffer. In that instance, China might have intervened, repeating the intervention in the Korean conflict in late 1950, the United States not having recognized China until 1973. In the Middle East case, full-scale U.S. participation might cause Saudi Arabia and other nations to throw the full weight of their considerable military forces into the fray (after the current Iraqi crisis has passed). Irrespective of the final outcome, the damage sustained by Israel would be devastating.

The Soviet Military Intervention Contingency

Turning now to the third unlikely but plausible contingency—a Soviet invasion of Iran on the pretext of defending her new ally—the apparent options are to: (a) do nothing directly beyond supplying the resistance fighters; (b) attempt to secure the littoral on the Gulf of Oman, particularly at the Strait of Hormuz, before the Soviet Union could get there; (c) engage in direct conflict with the Soviet Union short of employing U.S. ground forces; and (d) engage in full-scale war with the Soviet Union.

The last option is probably the worse. It would be a serious mistake to become involved in a direct war with the Soviet Union over a country as desolate and ill-behaved as Iran. Moreover, the United States would have few allies, and the 10,000-mile line of communication to the region would make it almost impossible to provide sufficient force to dislodge Soviet forces short of global war. Finally, the prevalence of diseases, to which non–Iranians are particularly susceptible, would incur untold casualties in a land war that the American people would not likely support wholeheartedly.[2]

Put another way, if the deterrent posture in Korea and NATO is excellent, it is wholly inadequate in Iran. Every nation should ask itself if it is willing to engage in a war or conflict it seems incapable of deterring in the first place, and if so, then perhaps it should concentrate on developing the deterrence. On the other hand, neither of the first two options is especially inviting. Doing nothing might strike many international observers as demonstrating a fatal weakness on the part of the United States, while attempting to secure the littoral before the Soviet Union did is problematic and means accepting at least the third option by default. That is, it is fairly certain that if the Soviet Union elected to invade Iran, she would simultaneously move swiftly, by vertical envelopment, to secure the littoral at the Strait of Hormuz. As such, any attempt by the United States to secure it first would almost certainly lead to a direct conflict with the Soviet Union, at least in terms of air and sea power.

The remaining option — use of air and naval fire against the USSR — is still tantamount to full-scale war; if it were not, it would not be particularly effective in repelling the supposed Soviet invasion. In short, Iran presents one of those rare situations where an indirect policy might fill the bill. That would be to indicate in advance that the United States would have no interest in defending Iran against any foreign invasion. However, because of world dependence on Persian Gulf oil (though not necessarily on the relatively small amount now produced by Iran), in the event of war the littoral in the Gulf of Oman region would be declared an international zone and the combined forces from the alliance suggested earlier in this chapter would occupy the area immediately. The purpose would be to enforce the policy of international access, not to combat the invader. The Soviet Union, were she the invader, would be welcome to traverse and use the littoral for seaport purposes.

The policy would offer a number of advantages. First, it would prevent direct conflict between the superpowers. Second, it might encourage the Persian Gulf states to become more serious about their own defense instead of relying on the United States to do it for them. Third, it eliminates any provocation of the Soviet Union *vis-à-vis* her sea lane of communication in the region except if she attempted to override the international zone, in which instance the lane could be cut immediately and decisively. Fourth, any war between the Soviet Union and Iran would severely tax the resources of the former — if the experience in Afghanistan has been any indicator — and weaken if not destroy her political influence elsewhere in the world. Fifth, as Iran is the extreme limit of potential Soviet aggrandizement without obvious risk of global war, the invasion would not presage an eventual upsetting of the equilibrium. Sixth, the precedent would be the Neutrality Treaty for Panama, which in effect declares a major choke point to be an international zone in wartime.

This would not be a rewrite of the "peace in our times" statement made by Prime Minister Neville Chamberlain as a justification for abandoning Czechoslovakia prior to World War II. On the contrary, the policy is insidious, intended to place the Soviet Union into an untenable position should she elect to repeat her aggression in the region, all at very little cost to the United States. In this way, the policy is deterrent in nature. Finally, it would serve to put Iran in her place. Though Iran has a tendency to bad-mouth America, she detests the Soviet Union even more, notwithstanding her recent ploy seeking better relations with her great neighbor to the north. Thus the implied threat that Iran could be "fed to the Cossacks" might have some influence on her behavior. To make matters worse, from the Iranian perspective, the United States could not be blamed for interfering.

Preemptive Initiatives

As discussed at some length in Chapter 6, wars or conflicts of intervention tend to grow out of hand while gray-area operations have a tendency to explode into outright wars unless hostilities can be avoided altogether. In this vein the naval operation in the Persian Gulf was a good example how to risk a major war without any substantive protection of major U.S. interests. Many analysts have asked just what these interests are.[3] As pointed out by other analysts, it was Iraq more than Iran that posed a threat to Persian Gulf oil shipping; moreover, until late in the game, the U.S. protection extended only to a tiny fraction of the tankers in the Gulf.[4]

Henry Kissinger, who stated he initially had grave reservations on the Persian Gulf commitment, later said that the United States had achieved its objectives and ought to negotiate its differences with Iran.[5] Chief among those supposed objectives were: (a) that the very presence of U.S. forces made Iran fear a United States invasion and thus caused her to tone down her international behavior, and (b) that at minimum the U.S. presence kept the Soviet Union out of the area. The first claim is speculation, and in any event it did little to stop the Iran-Iraqi war before it had run its course, or the Iraqi takeover of Kuwait. The second claim is specious. As the Persian Gulf is international water, the Soviet Union was and is free to sail into it any time she pleases. All things considered, the best the United States could expect was to break even. When an Iranian civil passenger aircraft was shot down in a state of nerves, the world reaction gave America the benefit of the doubt. A replay of that incident, however, would severely harm U.S. influence, and it is possible that the bombing of Pan American flight 103 over Scotland in mid–December 1988 was in retaliation for that incident.

However, all of this has been overshadowed by the current Iraqi crisis. The nearly unilateral U.S. intervention may have been justified as a stop-gap measure to deter further Iraqi aggrandizement, but the continued build-up of American forces in that area, and the attempted blockade of Iraq, leave more questions than answers. There are three separate issues here: (1) the continued deterrence on behalf of Saudi Arabia, (2) the status of Kuwait, and (3) preventing the crisis from expanding beyond the immediate area.

The deterrence issue is the most well-defined, but it should be primarily a Pan-Arab effort, supported by a wide-range of foreign military force and that only until the affected Arab nations become strong enough to protect their own interests, and at their expense from their obscene oil pricing (which is already driving many remainder states, and their U.S. bankers, to ruin).

As for Kuwait, any attempt to dislodge the Iraqis by force would involve a major war against 200,000 to 300,000 troops entrenched there, backed up by another 700,000 and supported by 80,000 troops from Jordan. It would take overwhelming force to do it, and almost certainly would result in the slaughter of more than 15,000 American, British and other foreign hostages. The embargo alternative would prove equally futile, and the hostages would probably be starved to death.

And as for the damage limitation issue, the worst-case scenario would have Saddam Hussein use poison gas both against U.S. forces and against Israel, the latter of which might retaliate with nuclear and possibly thermonuclear weapons. Then when the intense radioactive fallout began to drift northward, the Soviet Union could up the ante to global warfare. Worse, at least from a long-term prospective, it is only a matter of time before Iraq develops a nuclear capability of its own.

The only permanent solution is the most long-range and difficult one, and that is for the salient powers to become as free of dependence of Mid-East oil as possible, and in the interim for the United States to make it clear to her supposed allies, including Germany and Japan, that unless they pick up their fair share of the deterrence tab—in cash and in military forces—she will withdraw from the region and let them fend for themselves. As Warren Harding put it: "I can take care of my enemies; it is my *[expletive deleted]* friends that keep me awake at night." The alternatives, barring an assassination of Hussein, are: (a) to add to the astronomical (and already accelerating) national debt, and slowly write the hostages off, or (b) to engage in a major war, and quickly write the hostages off. And Saudi Arabia has recently barred the United States from conducting offensive operations from its territory.

Chapter 18. *In the Crescents of Discontent*

Against stupidity the gods themselves fight in vain.
—J.C.F. Schiller

The remainder states, for the most part, are concentrated in two crescents. The larger of these crescents extends from Africa through the Middle East, and into parts of Asia, breaking only for India, which is the poorest of the salient powers and which herself suffers considerable internal discontent. The second crescent is much smaller and comprises only Central America and some of the Caribbean islands, though some readers might suggest it also extends into a few of the South American nations along that continent's northern littoral. It is in these crescents that war continues to rage: civil, international, and in a few cases, consolidation. But what need is there for the United States to become involved in military terms?

An aging maxim in defense is "never get involved in a ground war on the mainland of Asia." The American experience in Korea and Vietnam tends to confirm the wisdom of that maxim, while during World War II the United States confined most of her fighting in the Pacific theater to naval battles and island campaigns. The explanation arises from the fact that the United States doesn't have the resources to persevere in wars of this caliber. The corresponding outlook for Latin America — isolated small island states excepted — isn't much better, notwithstanding the proximity. On the other hand, if the salient powers and buffer states are imbedded in military equilibrium, then the United States has little to be concerned about from eastern hemispheric remainder states and arguably even less from the supposed threats emanating from her own hemisphere. This situation suggests five implementing policies.

General Policy of Noninterference. Interference in the internal affairs of all remainder states, no matter how inimical the political dogma of each state may be with respect to the American political perspective, should be avoided. In the rare case when a remainder state's external actions pose a bona fide threat to U.S. interests and there is no way to deal with the situation except by military force, that force should be expended only to the extent necessary to defuse

148

the threat and not to mandate changes in the internal affairs of the offending state.

Stress on Infrastructure Building. To the extent that economic aid is given to remainder states, the stress should be on elementary infrastructure building, that is, the means by which a remainder state can become self-sufficient or at least become less dependent on other states for economic survival.

Regional Alliances. Regional groups of remainder states should be encouraged to develop or enhance existing alliances, such as the Organization of the American States and the ASEAN Pact, notwithstanding that for Africa in particular, the conflicts existing between or among many Africa states makes this a dim prospect for the near-term future.

Military Bases. The United States should maintain a sufficient number of military bases in these regions to support bona fide interests but not to support any world policeman role.

Defense Against Invasion. For defense against invasion of any remainder state, the United States should plan either to ally with the affected states in a regional alliance, or in the event of war, not to come to the rescue.

Rationale for Asian and African States

First, the remainder states by definition are outside the global equilibrium, and they have little ability or propensity to coalesce into a united power which could upset it. Therefore the United States should think twice before interfering militarily in any remainder state, and when such intervention does appear to be the only feasible option, it should be done in concert with other affected nations. The interests of those nations are likely to be more severely challenged than those of the United States, given the resiliency of the latter's national resources. As such, while these provisions support self-determination among all nations, they do not and should not support deterrence except by way of alliances. But they do seek to prevent escalation of conflict and thus serve to maintain the equilibrium. And with specific reference to southeast Asia, it would not be in the best interests of the United States to stir up conditions which might impact negatively on the aortic Soviet sea lane of communication skirting southeast Asia unless she intends to put the Soviet Union in a position of economic jeopardy.

Second, the stress on self-determination and infrastructure building is little more than a tacit recognition of the dominant force of nationalism and the simple fact that the United States would not brook interference by foreign powers in its own internal affairs. It also discounts what little influence communism has as a world force beyond a convenient sobriquet and observes that not even the Soviet Union advocates its export anymore. Restated, the United States can well afford to let the forces of nationalism, as may be enhanced by regional alliances and structural aid, serve as the primary means of keeping conflict among the remainder states within bounds.

This is easier said than done. Many remainder states are economic basket cases, capable of absorbing economic aid but incapable of doing much to improve their lot. On the contrary, forms of aid which serve to reduce the tragic death rate in these countries, either through medical assistance or reduction of malnutrition, indirectly increase the drain on scarce resources. Yet if the United States, and perhaps additional salient powers, would shift emphasis to infrastructure building and away from the manipulation of alliances to counter a nonexistent threat of world communism, then some progress in self-reliance could be achieved. This shift in emphasis would also serve as a more effective counter to any resurgence of revolutionary movements.

Third, the concept of regional alliances is worthwhile if the United States expects to disengage itself from a world policeman role, notwithstanding that for Africa at least, the geopolitical cup of obstacles runneth over. If Spanish is the dominant tongue in Latin America, chaos is the dominant language of the African continent. Libya and Chad are not on the best of terms, while most of the Mediterranean countries have little interest in sub–Saharan Africa. South Africa would not likely come to the rescue of the predominantly black nations of middle Africa. The countries in the Horn are inescapably linked to the flash points of the Middle East.

Finally, most African nations wallow in economic destitution, frequently compounded by relentless civil war, though a few evince considerable regional wealth and workable political infrastructure. Added to all of this is the mistrust by many if not most African nations of the United States, if for no other reason than the enormous wealth the latter possesses. Nevertheless, a beginning should be made with the confidence that no matter how many generations it takes to succeed, the internal strife in Africa is not likely to threaten U.S. interests.

Fourth, the issue of deciding what constitutes an adequate number of overseas military bases has been addressed by the Congressional Budget Office, which on occasion publishes geographic regional reviews on just this subject.[1] These documents are near-masterpieces of objective analysis, with due weight given relevant detail. Some of these reports are mandatory reading at the U.S. Army War College. The Department of Defense could do worse than to use them as a model in declaring what is essential and in selecting alternatives if and when the United States should lose its lease on any existing bases. These analyses might prove especially useful in the event the lease on the bases in the Philippines cannot be renewed in 1991.

Fifth, the final implementing policy—that of declaring in advance when and where the United States might intervene in situations not covered by other provisions—arises from the fact that most such situations are not apt to severely threaten U.S. interests. In the event a situation did arise clearly inimical to those interest, the policy could be reversed in that one instance. But where such intervention could be justified, in advance of the contingency, it follows that the intervention should seek to apply itself by way of a regional alliance. The disadvantage of this policy is that it telegraphs exactly what the United States does and doesn't consider to be important. Thus the Soviet Union or another power might feel free to aggrandize a small state America did not consider worth the candle. Yet given the record of Soviet "success" in this arena, the risk seems moot.

Sixth, the United States has grossly exaggerated the importance of its interests in southest Asia. Few problems there pose serious threats. In the case of the Indochina region, one would hope that the world has finally learned a lesson—that it is far and away the biggest international sinkhole in modern history. At one time or another, China, Japan, France, the United States, and perhaps the Soviet Union all trod off to this schoolhouse only to discover it was a woodshed. If some tremendous typhoon tore the entire region away from the Asian mainland, caused it to drift over the Mariana trench and dropped it in, hardly any nation—in the geopolitical, not the personal, sense—would notice the loss.

Seventh, Taiwan no longer represents the interest that it had when it was allied with the United States. The only country apt to invade Taiwan, if at all, would be China on the grounds of Chinese unification. If this did happen, it would not likely upset the equilibrium. Interestingly, *The World Fact Book,* published annually by the Central Intelligence Agency, excludes Taiwan from its alphabetical listing of states and includes it only in as an appendix along with the West Bank/Gaza Strip.

Eighth, though the Philippines are faced with internal turmoil in terms of the elected government and by a long-standing insurgency, the United States has already considered alternate locations for Subic Bay Naval Base and Clark Air Force Base. Hence the importance of these islands for American defense has faded. That doesn't mean America should encourage a Soviet takeover, but short of that event the defense interests here are not what they used to be.

In summary, the United States should assess the relative weakness of each of the Asian and African states and decide whether or not her interests would be harmed if it was invaded, and if so, to what extent would they be harmed. This should be done on a country-by-country basis, because these states evince a much wider divergence than most of the salient powers and buffer states, and range from tiny island kingdoms to poverty-stricken, over-populated lands. This range makes objective analysis difficult. Yet, if America is willing to come to the rescue, the cost of that rescue needs to be assessed. The island states in the Pacific, aside from the Philippines, would be relatively easy to defend. The same is not true for a major war on the Asian or African mainland.

The Special Case of Latin America and the Monroe Doctrine

The Monroe Doctrine was promulgated on December 2, 1823, in President James Monroe's annual message to Congress. The central ideas within this doctrine can be traced to Washington's farewell address, some of Jefferson's speeches, and Monroe's own first inaugural address. Moreover, the critical paragraph on non-colonization was written by Secretary of State John Quincy Adams.[2] In specific terms, the United States did not intend to tolerate Russian occupation of territory in the northwest part of the continent, which by that time America had come to regard as its own, and she did not want Spain and Portugal ro reestablish empires over her former colonies in South America. Thus it might be said the doctrine was the product of the founding fathers, not just Monroe, and its ultimate purpose was self-determination of nations.

In light of this objective, the Monroe Doctrine was largely moot at the time. The United States bought the Alaskan territories from Russia 44 years later for the sum of $7,200,000, a purchase then regarded in some quarters as folly. In the case of South America, Spain and Portugal had no intention of trying to reestablish control of her former colonies. But since about 1898, the doctrine has been used almost with a vengeance in the conduct of U.S. foreign policy in the western hemisphere, more to intervene in the internal affairs of Latin American nations than to enhance self-determination.

Thus notwithstanding its lack of standing in international law, the doctrine is still very much alive and has been used many times in the twentieth century. Unfortunately, the results are becoming increasingly troublesome. The overwhelming national power of the United States permitted her to prevail in most interventions from the Spanish-American war until World War II. In the later case of the Cuban missile crisis, the intervention was limited to the removal of Soviet nuclear-armed missiles from Cuba, which met little objection from other Latin American nations. Three years beyond that crisis, she succeeded in stopping a leftist revolution from gaining power in the Dominican Republic by way of direct military intervention, but as mentioned in Chapter 8, this success had the long-term negative consequence of weakening U.S. influence in Latin America. In recent times, the attempt to support the Nicaraguan contras went nowhere. Only the raid on Grenada and the Panama intervention in late 1989 were successful, and that due to the fact U.S. forces outnumbered the defenders at least 20-to-1 in the former case, and 10-to-1 in the latter. The issue, then, is to determine if the Monroe Doctrine is still needed, and if it is, how it can be entrenched beyond international criticism. The current interpretation is too dog-eared.

It's a safe bet the Soviet Union has been the only significant eastern hemispheric nation that sought to increase its political influence in the western hemisphere in recent times, but for any international doctrine to have permanence it must apply equally to all nations which might be affected by its provisions. Thus the objective of American defense policy should not be just to prevent Soviet influence from gaining an imbalancing foothold in the western hemisphere, but to seek to apply the Monroe doctrine to all nations in both hemispheres. This luxury is affordable because no western hemispheric nation by itself seriously threatens U.S. interests. (Noriega's conduct was petty, and moreover, it seems that at one time he was on the CIA payroll.)

The reason, of course, is that the United States is still the dominant nation in the western hemisphere. The United States GNP is approximately five times larger than the collective GNP of all other states, though the latter have more than twice the land mass and population. Further, very few of these states could remotely be considered objectives for Soviet influence. For the most part, the ambitions of the Soviet Union seem restricted to exploiting civil unrest in a few Central American countries and a few of the Caribbean islands. As such, it would not be too difficult to exert the necessary international leadership to reestablish the Monroe Doctrine as a formal treaty under the aegis of the Organization of the American States (OAS).

By this treaty, no nation would be allowed to intervene or interfere with the internal affairs of any member state without risking war against all other member states of the OAS. This would hold against any interfering state from anywhere in the world, including all members of the OAS itself. Exceptions would be made for French Guiana and those Caribbean islands presently under the protective umbrella of other countries, i.e., Anguilla, Aruba, Cayman Islands, Guadeloupe, Martinique, Montserrat, Netherlands Antilles, the British Virgin Islands, and of course, Puerto Rico and the Virgin Islands (U.S.). In the case of Cuba, which is formally allied with the Soviet Union, special provisions would apply. Cuban intervention in any western hemispheric country would be repelled, but all signatories of the treaty would have to agree to leave Cuba alone.

This restraint would not apply if the Soviet Union again attempted to emplace strategic missiles in Cuba, or elsewhere, reminiscent of the Cuban missile crisis. That form of threat would affect all of Latin America, not just the United States. Moreover, this provisio would apply to any nation which tried to worm its way into western hemispheric equilibrium. Thus the Soviet Union would not be singled out. Finally, the restriction would apply equally to the United States with respect to any Latin American nation as much as it did to the Soviet Union.

The Panama Canal

Although the United States signed a treaty with Panama that will return full sovereignty over the Canal Zone to Panama in the year 2000, she retained the right—by way of a separate Neutrality Treaty—to defend the canal against any attempt by any nation to close or otherwise block free passage through it and to that end has the right to maintain sufficient forces in the zone.[3] In light of the treaty proposal here, it should be asked if this situation could be considered as an exception to a formalized Monroe Doctrine or whether the status of the Panama Canal would need to be renegotiated.

It would not seem so. For starters, the potential for a defensive intervention in the Panama Canal is a right established by treaty and therefore does not constitute intervention in the pejorative sense. Thus it would not contradict the Monroe Doctrine if the latter were enacted as another treaty. But if any nation attempted to emplace threatening weapons in Panama itself, as distinct from the present canal zone, then the proposed treaty provisions, and not the Neutrality Treaty, would apply. Another point is that the Panama Canal is a unique situation. There are only two sea routes between the Atlantic and Pacific oceans, and the passage around the tip of South America is time-consuming and expensive. Clearly, no other terrain in this hemisphere has the international significance of the Panama Canal, an importance rivaled in the eastern hemisphere only by the Suez Canal and Gibraltar.

With respect to military threats to the canal, the most severe would be Soviet destruction of it in the case of a major or global war between the superpowers, but the probability of that scenario grows increasingly dim, and if it did occur, the niceties of a Monroe Doctrine treaty would be moot. More plausible scenarios would be a terrorist attack or the forced closing of the canal by Panama itself. The former would likely be accomplished with a cargo ship ladden with explosives ignited while in the locks, perhaps one at each end of the canal. The latter stretches the imagination, because under the provisions of the Neutrality Treaty that would entail a war with the United States, a war which undoubtedly would have the full support of Congress. At any rate, beyond the obvious sanction to protect the naval base at Guantanamo Bay in Cuba, the Panama Canal is about the only place in Latin America where the United States retains a right to intervene, and that is limited to defense of a specific facility. Elsewhere, the alliance treaty approach might prove more effective.

The Ideological "Threat" in Central America

There remains the supposed threat of communism in Central America, as if: (1) the domino theory had any validity, (2) the combined GNP of all seven Central American states were greater than seven-tenths of 1 percent of the United States GNP, and (3) the Sandinistas—if they come again to power—would charge up through 2,000 miles of Mexico and attack the United States through the soft underbelly of Texas. On the other hand, human nature does not change much with time, and therefore the mindset that once found satisfaction burning heretics at the stake now finds an outlet for ideological purity by selling arms to terrorists and supporting international drug trafficking to fund clandestine support of various anti-leftist movements in Nicaragua and elsewhere in Latin America.

However inane, criminal, or depraved this movement may be—depending on one's point of view—it is a political force with which to reckon, particularly when it emanates from the higher echelons of the executive branch of government.[4] Neither ridicule nor logic has much effect on its tentacles. Yet it is one thing to be concerned over emplacement of Soviet long-range missiles in Latin America—for which there is a remedy—and quite another to get wrapped around the geopolitical axle because of various ideologies. As the problem resides in inadequate perception on the part of U.S. defense planners, not in Latin America, no defense policy can correct it. Unfortunately, as the risk of war in NATO further decreases, the temptation to clean up the geographic backyard, as it were, may become overpowering and lead the United States into foolish and damaging initiatives. In some ways, this temptation may prove to be the most difficult if not the most critical defense problem.

Chapter 19. Defense Against Terrorism

> While it is never possible for a staff officer to feel the full weight of responsibility that rests on the shoulders of his chief, it is feasible for him to gain a degree of insight into the magnitude and intricacies of those of his chief's problems that come before him for study. He learns to live with the frustrating fact that many issues on which he is required to work have no immediate, and sometimes not even a satisfactory future solution.
> —Dwight D. Eisenhower

As discussed at some length in Chapter 9, terrorism actually comprises four different classes, defense against which requires different forms. Moreover, formulation of a consistent defense policy may be impossible due to the psychological nature of the threat *vis-à-vis* different national perspectives on the nature of the threat. Yet because the potential for nuclear terrorism cannot be discounted, some attempt must be made.

This could be accomplished by expanding on principles inherent in international law. International terrorists almost by definition are international renegades beyond the jurisdiction of any sovereignty. This suggests an international tribunal as the criminal counterpart to the civil case–oriented International Court of Justice. By contrast, terrorism sponsored by a sovereign power should be recognized as an act of war and be dealt with accordingly. However, when this form of terrorism is contained solely within the confines of a civil war, there is seldom any justification for international intervention. Finally, the use of terrorist-type tactics in the context of a conventional war should not be regarded as terrorism in the normal sense of that word.

Environment. It should be recognized that a consistent policy for dealing with terrorism in the immediate future is infeasible, but also that apart from nuclear terrorism, the actual damage and number of casualties from terrorist acts, excluding those committed in civil wars, are relatively minor and either self-limiting or subject to countermeasures to effect such limits.

International Jurisdiction. The jurisdiction of international law should be expanded to encompass acts of international terrorism not sponsored by any existing sovereignty, the expansion to include an international criminal tribunal to prosecute such terrorism and its perpetrators.

Interim Right of Retaliation. In the interim, which may consume decades, the right to retaliate against international terrorism, wherever and whenever the perpetrators are located, should be reserved to the offended nation, with the proviso that any country harboring such terrorists must first be notified of their presence. In the event the notified government fails to apprehend and turn over the terrorists immediately, the refusal should be considered after-the-fact sponsorship of the terrorists and thus subject that country to the effects of any retaliation directed at the terrorists. If such delay permits the terrorists to escape retaliation, then any subsequent determination of harboring terrorists would be exempt from the requirement to provide fair warning to the sovereign power.

Permanent Right of Retaliation. The permanent right to retaliate militarily against any nation that sponsors, funds, or otherwise encourages any act or acts of terrorism, provided sufficient proof of the guilt can be demonstrated, should also be reserved to the offended nation, based on the premise that state-sponsored terrorism constitutes an act of war, declared or undeclared, and is therefore subject to retaliation by right of self-defense.

Terrorism as an Instrument of Civil War. Terrorism as an aspect of civil war may be inconsistent with the higher standards of Western civilization, but it exists, will continue to exist, and should not be interdicted or otherwise interfered with in military terms until and unless the civil war itself generates a bona fide and unmistakable threat to national interests.

Terrorism Within the Context of Overt Conflicts. Terrorist-type actions used within overt conflict should be regarded as a form of tactics and not terrorism per se, and accordingly should be addressed as part of the military approach to the conflict, if in fact the United States is in a position and is willing to endure the conflict on its own terms and for the protection of bona fide national interests.

Preemptive Jurisdiction over Nuclear Terrorism. The jurisdiction of the proposed international criminal tribunal should be further expanded to encompass any nation which sponsors or encourages international nuclear terrorism outside of a declared war, the jurisdiction to extend to any plan or attempt to use nuclear weapons in this manner.

Interim Right of Retaliation Against Nuclear Terrorism. In the absence of international authority or ability to prevent international nuclear terrorism, the right to retaliate or conduct preemptive raids on any terrorists or terrorist encampment as necessary must be reserved by any nation that plausibly would be affected by the use of these weapons, in order to punish or preferably to prevent the act. This retaliation, preemptive or otherwise, may be without warning to the nation or nations where located, provided sufficient proof is available on the nature of the threat.

Rationale

These provisions are intended to isolate terrorists from normal international relations and set the stage for an international approach to the problem. At the same time, the United States must reserve the right to defend itself against any form of terrorism inimical to its bona fide national interests in the absence of any international authority or system to prosecute the offenders. The specific provisions regarding nuclear terrorism require additional comment.

If nuclear weapons are used in the course of declared or open warfare, then no international body will be able to exercise jurisdiction over events. Only war itself can resolve such matters. If they are used in the course of a civil war, then the resulting damage might justify military intervention before the long-term effects, e.g. radioactive fallout, begin to mount and affect other nations worldwide. In this instance, however, the United States would encounter little difficulty enlisting a substantial number of other nations in the cause. The consequences of permitting nuclear war to continue more than likely would prove unacceptable to all of the salient powers.

The legal difficulties of dealing with true international nuclear terrorism are more severe. As a matter of self-defense, a nation has the inherent right to prevent or retaliate against any nuclear attack, but the more serious purpose here is to develop an international climate that will serve to deter such acts. The rights of sovereignty do not extend to poisoning the atmosphere to the detriment of any or all other nations. The penalty for doing so in open warfare is instant retaliation and probable yielding of sovereignty to the nation or nations attacked. The penalty for surreptitious nuclear warfare should be no less, though ideally the penalty should serve as a deterrent not a punishment. Thus the onus of instant world-wide condemnation and punishment against any plan for or use of nuclear weapons by terrorists should be developed within the foreseeable future.

The Special Issue of Terrorism
Using Chemical and Biological Agents

If the problem of dealing with nuclear terrorism is a difficult issue, establishing guidelines for defense against chemical and biological warfare is almost insurmountable. First, virtually any country that wants to stockpile these weapons can do so with comparatively little expense.[1] Second, the potential for inflicting severe damage appears to be less than that of nuclear weapons.[2] That is, in the apparent absence of potential damage of a nuclear magnitude, world concern is far less intense. Third, when these weapons were used extensively in the recent Iran-Iraqi war, most of the salient powers registered formal concern but otherwise did not seem too upset. In so many words, the powers that be said it was all right for the remainder states to slaughter each other with such weapons provided they restricted their use to their own environments. Accordingly, a number of remainder states, especially those in the Middle East and adjacent areas, jumped on the stockpile bandwagon. Fourth, the salient powers have been using mild forms of chemical weapons, such as tear gas, for decades without hesitation.

So the issue reduces to: should the potential for chemical or biological weapons terrorism be put on a par with conventional weapons terrorism or with the potential for nuclear terrorism? Or can or should there be two policies, one for relatively low-toxicity chemical weapons, the other for the more deadly chemical weapons, especially the neurotoxic poisons, and for most biological weapons? A differentiation of this kind would require the potential victims to identify the specific stockpiles in advance, not an easy intelligence task.

The resolution of the issue should hinge on the magnitude of the potential casualties. The casualties of specific conventional-weapons terrorism normally range from a few to a few hundred victims, though higher casualties are conceivable. Nuclear terrorism casualties might, in the extreme, reach upward of a million or more if a powerful enough device were emplaced in a major urban area. Now, would the potential casualties from chemical and biological weapons more closely approach those resulting from conventional-weapons or nuclear-weapons terrorism?

That answer is uncertain, but it appears that research in biological agents, at least, has the potential for reintroducing Bubonic Plague, which wiped out a third or more of the population of Europe four centuries ago. If so, and given the difficulty of discerning between the level of toxicity in advance, the answer is plain. The magnitude of potential casualties might reach and possibly exceed that from a nuclear explosion, notwithstanding it would take more than a singular munition to reach those numbers. Hence serious consideration should be given to placing chemical and biological weapons on a par with their nuclear brethern.

True, the United States and the Soviet Union have signed a chemical weapons nonproliferation treaty. However, to be effective it would require the signatures of at least 37 states known to possess these weapons. Unfortunately, most of those states do not possess nuclear weapons and hence would be very reluctant to give up their inexpensive substitute. In short, the need to address the potential use of these weapons will likely remain a valid international concern for the foreseeable future.

Part V
In Perspective

An implicit aspect of the equilibrium argument is that the phenomenon is a more-or-less permanent feature of global politics. On the other hand, there is no presumption that equilibrium will introduce an era of peace except in the sense of preventing a major war among the salient powers. Rather, the competitive antagonisms generated by nationalism, the unlikelihood of an effective supranational authority, the necessity of large standing military forces to maintain the equilibrium, and the competing pressures for domestic spending priorities all suggest the equilibrium will usher in many new problems or at least will exacerbate a number of existing ones.

Though prognostication on these problems is inherently guesswork, certain conclusions seem to warrant serious consideration. Of these, the dilemma of continued armed idleness is the most apparent, coupled with the problem of adequate long-term funding for a decisive deterrent posture in an era of technological revolution and political pressure to reduce and harness the defense budget for reasons not always associated with genuine defense priorities. This is no small matter. If the United States begins to rot from within, either from internal malaise or from inadequate funding of what is really important, then perhaps the equilibrium might begin a long, slow, but steady process of decay.

Beyond this, however, looms an even larger question: Is international peace feasible on a permanent basis? History would suggest that it isn't, at least if peace is defined as the absence of war. That kind of peace depends on the ability to preclude war. The equilibrium may serve as a brake on major war among the salient powers, but it is no guarantee of peace among the remainder states, nor does it foreordain that a salient power will never find itself in a position to intervene in a lesser war or conflict. As such, peace is largely the outcome of another goal, and then only if the circumstances are favorable enough to foster that outcome. The thesis here is that this other goal is justice, not necessarily in the formal sense of international law, but at least in recognition of some of the principles underwriting the jurisprudence that operates within established sovereignties.

Chapter 20. The Dilemma of Armed Idleness

Idleness and pride tax with a heavier hand than kings
and parliaments.
— Benjamin Franklin

The main argument of this book has been that a decisive majority of the world's population, the land that population occupies, and the resources it controls have reached a plateau of geopolitical equilibrium with the concomitant unlikelihood of its nations engaging in sustained armed conflict among themselves. As such, most future wars are apt to be confined to those numerous but mostly weak countries that for any of a number of reasons remain in a state of political flux, at least in terms of international relations and power. Occasionally, one of the salient powers might have a legitimate reason to intervene militarily in a conflict among these remainder states, but the opportunities, apart from the exercise of bad judgment, appear slim.

This is not a bad turn of events, but it brings with it a unique long-term dilemma for defense infrastructure. Among the causes of this equilibrium are thermonuclear weapons and large standing military forces. To do away with or significantly reduce these weapons and forces is to threaten the equilibrium itself; but when large standing forces are idled for long periods from their warrior calling, they begin to rot, a phenomenon harped upon by Clausewitz.[1] How, then, does a nation keep its armed forces honed for war as a prerequisite of effective deterrence with little more than a few wargame simulations to prevent this rot and malaise from setting in? And how does it prevent the misuse of military forces, perhaps itching for action in conflicts that are not amenable to military solution?

Psychologists tend to call this form of malaise *depression,* as when one's energies are suppressed resulting in discordant behavior.[2] For many warriors, the achievements wrought from a deterrent posture, no matter how great the contribution to preserving national interests, are insufficient motivation and reward for services rendered, the situation being analogous to a pro football team sitting out all future seasons on the bench. An occasional raid on a

Grenada or an infrequent air strike against terrorists occupies less than one-tenth of 1 percent of the man-years available among uniformed personnel, yet the very deterrence relies largely on the demonstrated ability of the warriors in such conflicts.

As such, the dilemma is not easy to address. Arms reductions will not resolve it. The elimination of a few missiles can hardly make a dent in the size, scope and mission of the armed forces. Moreover, to the extent the number of missiles are reduced, a plea for increased conventional forces will likely be heard. The doctrine of civil control over the military also fails in this regard. It is often the "civil control" that advocates the imprudent employment of military forces in situations where diplomatic initiatives, if any, would be more appropriate.

To compound the problem, the resolution of the dilemma falls primarily on the secretary of defense, not the president. The latter rarely has the time to become involved in the management and the morale of the defense establishment. Worse, the political clout of the secretary has eroded over the last 20 years at the expense of an increasingly powerful presidential staff, some members of whom have large private agendas and little public responsibility. The person charged with running the world's largest organization and maintaining the means of ensuring international equilibrium has been granted little more than middle management status in the Washington counterpart to Mount Olympus.

Even mild attempts to ameliorate this situation have met with rebuff. For example, the suggestion that Cabinet members maintain alternate offices in the Executive Office Building, to coordinate their work with the president and his staff, has been ignored or rejected on several occasions. Then, too, tales abound of various secretaries attempting to meet with their president only to be rebuffed by some abrasive aide. Other writers claim the Constitutional mechanisms of government are no longer adequate. Some proposals aim at restricting the powers of the president, while others advocate increasing them. But Constitutional amendments are hard to come by, particularly those that tinker with checks and balances among the three branches of government. Hence there is little chance this approach will materialize. In the event, it would not necessarily resolve the long-term dilemma inherent in deterrence.

Thus in the absence of any pedictable change to the structure and authority within the executive branch of government, the resolution falls on the incumbent secretary of defense. The secretary's authority, unfortunately, is even more hemmed in than so far suggested. Congressional pressures, sometimes to force needed reforms on the Pentagon but sometimes to force contracts for unnecessary goods and services, are not to be underestimated. Moreover, congressional committees review defense decisions in increasing detail in what critics call "micro management." But perhaps the most serious impairment is the charge recently leveled by former Secretary of the Navy John

F. Lehman. He concluded that civil control over the military has been fatally impaired, citing that: (a) only the secretary of defense stands between the chairman of the Joint Chiefs of Staff and the White House; (b) the presidency has become surrounded by hundreds of aides; and (c) senior active duty or recently retired military officers occupy positions of influence in the White House sufficient to overrule the secretary without the president's knowledge.[3]

The secretary's influence is further weakened because incumbents are rarely men with extensive military experience, though more than a few have had major responsibility at the corporate level. They lack the necessary know-how to wrestle with essential detail. A major weapons system can incur costs in the billions of dollars and have major consequences on the Defense budget for years to come. A failure to grasp detail or to comprehend the environment in which such systems will be employed can result in de facto abrogating of authority in favor of the separate service officials. The latter will often put the perceived needs of their respective services ahead of defense priorities.

Additionally, secretaries of defense are political appointees. While a few have remained in office for relatively long periods approaching eight years, many of them occupy the chair for only a few years and sometimes for only a few months. Given the long period of time required to effect major changes, particularly if those changes involve Congressional appropriations, the ability to exert influence on behalf of the defense establishment is severely restricted for all but a few incumbents. These restrictions notwithstanding, a number of options are available to address the dilemma and to ameliorate the malaise the dilemma tends to perpetrate.

Resignation Option

If in the considered judgment of the secretary of defense and the deputy secretary of defense, the president or a presidential aide acting with apparent presidential authority orders a military action that is either illegal or extremely imprudent, both officials should tender their resignations simultaneously with concurrent public disclosure of the reasons thereto. Ideally, the chairman of the Joint Chiefs of Staff should also request immediate retirement, but as the Cuban missile crisis demonstrated, senior military officers are likely to have a wider tolerance for imprudent military actions.[4]

This option has ample precedence. First, during the "Saturday Night Massacre" in 1973, both the attorney general and his deputy resigned from office rather than carry out President Nixon's order to fire the special prosecutor investigating the Watergate scandal. That incident marked the culminating point of Nixon's presidency beyond which he fell headlong into abdication. Second, during the recent Iran-Contra hearings, several members of Congress asked Secretary of State George Shultz and Secretary of Defense Casper

Weinberger why they did not resign when the president declined to cease "overlooking" what are now acknowledged as censorable actions.⁵ They both replied resignations would not have done any good. That answer is debatable, especially as Shultz had previously threatened to resign over the issue of polygraph tests to be administered to high officials. The tactic succeeded, a point noted during the hearings.

A third precedent is the resignation of nine senior officials and aides at the Department of Justice to mark the character and behavior of Attorney General Edwin Meese III.⁶ Notwithstanding the self-serving disclaimers that he was "vindicated" by the decision of the special prosecutor not to indict him, it's a safe bet these resignations helped drive Meese from office.

This resignation policy might be considered personal disloyalty to the president, but there are times when integrity and good judgment should prevail over personal loyalties. A critic might counter an incumbent secretary could confuse integrity with personal preference. This is correct, hence the proviso for dual resignations. Secretary of State Cyrus Vance resigned his office in 1980 over disagreement with the planned Iranian rescue mission. That mission failed, but the failure can be attributed more to inadequate planning than to its having been fundamentally imprudent. Thus Vance's resignation differed considerably from that of Attorney General Elliot Richardson during the Watergate scandal. Moreover, Vance's deputy secretary did not resign, while Richardson's did. Finally, in contrast to Nixon's firing of the special prosecutor, the rescue attempt, per se, did not incur public reprobation.

A final argument for the resignation policy is the 1857 letter written by Lord Macaulay to Henry S. Randall, a biographer of Thomas Jefferson, saying in part: "Your Constitution is all sail and no anchor."⁷ Macaulay was referring to the tendency of the "masses" to demand more and more welfare and get it, but his point has a wider significance. The Constitution does lack anchors. It prescribes a system of government, but it does not create or train individuals. The Constitution provides for checks and balances and the means to rid the government of untrustworthy officials, but it cannot prevent them from gaining office. In fine, men and women of capability and integrity are the anchors of government. It is their character, in the final analysis, that makes the government work well or not work well. No system or reorganization of the mechanics of government can substitute for the occasional moral mandate to tender resignations in order to expose wrongdoing and prevent, in this instance, extremely imprudent military initiatives.

Candidness with the Public

As discussed in Chapter 13, the Department of Defense is notorious for disdain toward public opinion when that opinion is at odds with official policy.

This may be a common trait in most large institutions, but it backfires for defense. The Pentagon is too inviting a target to be ignored by the media; the pickings here are anything but slim. A good example was the mini-scandal over the exorbitant price of simple repair parts and unnecessary custom specifications for run-of-the-mill requirements. This culminated with the "revelation" of a custom-made toilet for the C-5A aircraft. The political cartoonist Herbert Block ("Herblock") on several occasions pictured Secretary Weinberger with a toilet seat and high price tag about his neck. In the opinion of this writer, such caricature was beneath the dignity of the *Washington Post,* but it happened and the likes of it will happen again, if not in that paper then in others.

It would be absurd to blame the secretary for instigating these expenditures, but he should have shouldered the blame publicly while initiating and publicizing bona fide corrective actions with some teeth in them. By way of parallel example, Chrysler Chairman Lee Iacocca accepted blame for improprieties in testing Chrysler automobiles, though it is improbable he knew of the abuses beforehand, much less condoned them.[8] This public disclosure option becomes all the more imperative in light of the enormous size of the defense establishment and the increasing political separation of the secretary from the presidency.

Together, then, the dual resignation proviso and a greater willingness to be candid with the public can serve to reduce the risk of imprudent use or abuse of military force. However, these measures would not address the problem of the malaise itself, which accrues from the prolonged inactivity of a large standing military force whose primary utilization is in a deterrent role. Put another way, if this side of the dilemma is to be ameliorated, then in the absence of opportunity for war, a greater focus on the morale and sense of importance within troop units is necessary at the expense of administrative overhead. The means of doing this would be drastic and infeasible in the immediate future, but perhaps discussion of the appropriate measures might force increased recognition of the problem.

Reduction of the Defense Establishment Staff and Economic Incentives

In 1951, General Matthew Ridgway, upon assuming command of UN forces in Korea replacing General MacArthur, requested a clear statement of his mission. MacArthur had made a point of avoiding one. The task was put in queue and finally gained a ten-minute slot within a two-hour briefing, side by side with such other pressing matters as the proposed name for a new training camp.[9] Since that time, the vastly increased size of the defense establishment overhead raises even more serious questions about priorities given to troop units and concerns beyond the usual periodic articles and speeches.

The late Admiral Hyman Rickover was wont to suggest the entire defense establishment staff could be reduced in size to fit on one floor of the Pentagon with no loss and probably a gain to management efficiency. This, of course, is an exaggeration. Half of one floor should suffice. The proposal here is to reduce the entire defense establishment staff and all intermediate, non-deployable commands, agencies and headquarters, to one-half of their present size, diverting funds saved to the enhancement of the training, maintenance and morale of fighting elements.

Concurrent with this proposal, Congress could do worse than realign the distribution of senior general and flag officers. The ideal would be to permit four-star officers only in command of deployable military force (if they retained command once deployed), the chairman and vice chairman of the Joint Chiefs of Staff, and the chief of staff or equivalent for each separate service. Three-star billets would also be reserved for deployable commands plus the five principal staff officers of the Organization of the Joint Chiefs of Staff, the deputy chief of staff (or equivalent) for each separate service, and one other billet per service as selected by the secretary of that service.

These proposals do not gainsay the exponential increase in support functions of modern forces, nor do they deny that more staff support per capita is required now than during World War II. But the defense establishment of the World War II era superintended more than 13,000,000 men and women in uniform, and did so with a much smaller staff than now. Moreover, the increases in logistical requirements and administrative overhead do not require the same senior rank as the commanders of the business end of the armed forces.

Perhaps what would be needed to carry these ideas into practice would be a few economic incentives. Economic incentives could take either of two forms. The first form would penalize a service or the OJCS for excessive administrative overhead. The second form would somewhat reallocate the defense budget among the services based on administrative efficiency. Perhaps both forms could be combined. Briefly, limits would be set on the number of administrative personnel and their budgets, including all of the field operating agencies the services have created to conceal the overhead. As shown in Figure 15 on the next page, the extent to which a service exceeded these limits, based on an independent review, would be the extent to which the total defense budget for that service would be reduced outright or reallocated to the other services. The motivational force of these incentives could be enhanced by setting the number of general or flag officers authorized each service as an inverse function of the administrative overhead.

Granted, these three proposals are what the defense establishment calls *non-starters.* Non-starters are ideas too radical to gain even a toehold within the bureaucracy. But it appears that the mounting national deficit combined with other economic inadequacies may force radical reductions in the defense budget. If so, this would be the appropriate time to invoke these proposals.

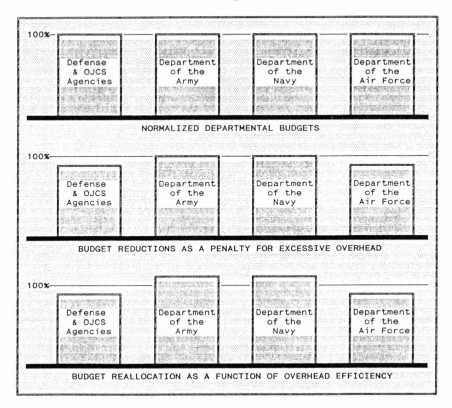

Figure 15. Economic Incentives to Reduce Defense Administrative Overhead. In the hypothetical example where Defense and Air Force departmental budgets were higher than established norms, the budget reduction model would penalize those departments. In the reallocation model, the services that did stay within the limits would gain what the services that did not, lost — what is called a zero-sum game. The theoretical maximum penalty for any one department could be 10 percent, with the actual amount rising exponentially in proportion to an overage, such that minor excesses would not be severely penalized.

Of late, Congress has been sounding warnings that "crunch time" may come sooner rather than later, and President Bush has already initiatied a major defense budget reduction program.

A Final Proposal

The Department of Defense, paralleling its preeminent size, also runs the world's largest educational program. This program culminates, for most officers, in resident attendance at one of the senior service colleges. Each service maintains its own college, while the Organization of the Joint Chiefs of Staff maintains the National Defense University. But none of the colleges requires a comprehensive analysis of the efficacy of war, to include when war has succeeded in achieving national purpose and when war has failed and the reasons therefore. Some of the curricula material covers specific wars, and the Naval War College requires its students to consider the general subject at some length starting with the Peloponnesian War. Yet given the sad record of the employment of United States military force since World War II, it is evident the subject hasn't been pressed home hard enough.

The counterargument is that military officers do not decide to go to war or not go to war; these decisions are a matter of civil control of the military. That truism vastly underestimates the influence senior military officers have on the conduct of international affairs, particularly when the option for military action is a borderline consideration or when officers are serving on the National Security Council. As a minimum, senior officers are almost always asked for their advice on military options. Unfortunately, such advice, when based solely on personal experience and recollections, is often inadequate to the task. A thorough if not exhaustive knowledge of the history of war with respect to national or political purpose, and not just of famous tactical battles, is essential. At any rate, the study of war cannot readily be construed as an irrelevant subject at the senior service college level.[10]

Summing up, the necessity of large standing military forces for deterrence, when combined with inactivity in the arena of actual conflict, generates a two-fold dilemma. That dilemma entails an internal malaise arising from the idleness of deterrence and a propensity to seek conflict in situations not amenable to military solution or where war is inimical to larger national interests. This dilemma is exacerbated by the increasing political distance between the Presidency and the Secretary of Defense, which puts the cutting edge of military force into a lower priority than other concerns of an incumbent administration.

Moreover, there are too many times when civil authority advocates imprudent use of military force to resolve political and diplomatic conflict. All of this places the secretary of defense in an unenviable position, responsible for maintaining a large standing military force while at the same time striving to keep it off the battlefield except as a last resort and then only when such use will serve a bona fide national interest. This he must accomplish without sufficient leverage in the highest echelons of government policy-making.

Chapter 21. Justice as the Moral Equivalent of Peace

Peace is not the absence of war,
it is a virtue, a state of mind,
a disposition for benevolence,
confidence, justice.
— Spinoza

When the treaty negotiations following World War I bogged down, Georges Clemenceau, inverting Clausewitz's most famous dictum, concluded that peace was a method of waging war with less destructive means. Forty years later, Will and Ariel Durant observed that only 268 of the last 3,421 years of history had seen no war.[1] Yet as advanced by Spinoza, it may be an error to think of peace as the opposite of war. The peace that results from an absence of war — if history provides any indicator — is only a breathing spell until the next war. The advent of nuclear weapons may serve to eliminate global war among the salient powers, but a century's worth of wars among the remainder states could run up casualties in excess of the carnage of World War II.

In his address to the graduating class of American University in June 1963, announcing the start of negotiations for a nuclear test ban treaty, President John F. Kennedy said that "peace is a process," though he may have over-simplified the case, a forgivable oversight in light of the momentous nature of the treaty.[2] It would have been more correct to say that peace — in the most profound sense of that word — is the byproduct of other endeavors but that the conduct of mankind and the nations and institutions it creates is probably too competitive and too discordant ever to achieve the ideal. Moreover, this striving has positive qualities and has yielded many good as well as bad results. Justice Oliver Wendell Holmes, Jr., put the case this way:

> I know of no true measure of men except the total of human energy which they embody. . . . The final test of this energy is battle in some form — actual war — the crush of Arctic ice — the fight for mastery in the market or the court. Many of those who are remembered have spared themselves this supreme trial, and have fostered a faculty at the expense of their total life. It is one thing to utter a happy phrase from a protected cloister; another to think under fire — to think

for action upon which great interests depend. The most powerful men are apt to go into the mêlée and fall or come out generals.[3]

Perhaps the preeminence of justice over peace that Holmes hinted at was nowhere better exemplified than by the conduct of Abraham Lincoln during the Civil War. Lincoln was so intrinsically a man of peace he could not bring himself to hunt as a sport—though neither could Grant or Lee—yet he persisted in that war until it claimed 620,000 American lives, more than have been killed in all other American wars combined, before or since. His second inaugural address was a curious mixture of a justification for the continuation of the war irrespective of the bloodshed and a genuine sense of healing and of caring, concluding with a plea for a just and lasting peace. He personified the well-known maxim, "The kindness of kings resides in strength and justice."

But in an era where global war could make the concept of self-defense meaningless, with what attitude should the United States pursue its defense posture? Are Americans to become like the gods of Homer's *Iliad* and manipulate and otherwise intervene in the fighting that does occur among the remainder states? At times, the conduct of government in foreign affairs is not that far removed from our Homeric ancestors, albeit with much less success.

In the nineteenth century Lord Palmerston said, "Great Britain has no permanent friends, she has no permanent enemies, she has only permanent interests." Well, he was wrong on at least two counts. The friendships between Great Britain and the United States, Canada, and Australia are permanent, while her formerly dominant "permanent interest"—the British Empire—no longer exists. Yet today, because of the lethality of most kinds of war and the risk that some of them might escalate to global dimensions, it *is* the permanent interest of the United States to keep these wars from getting out of hand. But peace is not something a state buys at the United Nations. It isn't "bought" at all. Arguably, the only kind of worthwhile peace, given the predilections of men and nations, is that which comes with justice. What, then, is justice?

Four Elements of Justice

The sages have written libraries on the subject of justice, and to do right by that mass of scholarship and analytical thought would probably postpone history indefinitely. Fortunately, the points here can be made without an extensive review of the literature. To begin, then, few scholars would disagree that justice fundamentally comprises four aspects, to wit:

Right of Self-determination. The rock-bottom foundation of justice is the right of an individual—or an individual nation—to pursue what he believes is best to fulfill the promise of his potential, providing the pursuit of that right does not infringe on the same right of other individuals. However, this right in no way presumes intelligence, prudence, or wisdom. On the contrary, the right to self-determination encompasses the right of an individual to make a fool of himself, and certainly many take frequent advantage of this leeway.

Right Against Aggrandizement. This is the obvious reciprocal of the right of self-determination. Justice Holmes once had the opportunity to illustrate this relationship in one sentence to the effect that freedom of speech does not extend to falsely shouting "fire" in a crowded theater.[4] At the extreme, this right extends to inflicting death, if necessary, as a last resort in self-defense, a doctrine which permeates both criminal and international law.[5]

Right to Create or Accept Conditional Sovereignty. Irrespective of the historical debate on the nature of government—of divine right of kings versus the social contract versus whatever—virtually all jurisprudential commentary recognizes the necessity for some form of higher authority to adjudicate the differences arising from the right of self-determination and the right to be free from the untoward effects of the exercise of that right by others, subject to referendum or recall when the authority created or accepted no longer functions to the satisfaction of the members of its jurisdiction.

Right of Sovereignty to Legislate for the Common Weal. As an unavoidable adjunct to the third aspect, the sovereignty created or accepted must also seek to develop a system to facilitate adjudication—due process—and beyond that to both enhance the exercise of self-determination and ameliorate conditions which lead to conflict from that exercise.

Inadequate Foundations of International Justice

The great difference between justice among the citizens of a state and among nations is that for the latter no supranational authority much beyond the largely ineffective power of the United Nations and no real system of law beyond the voluntary acceptance of the provisions of international law really exist. Thus international justice to a major extent has been the product of effective self-defense, an enlightened perspective or at least forbearance among the powers that be, and mutually perceived self-interests. In the absence of an effective supranational authority, the challenge becomes one of international conduct which strives to offset the absence of these legal foundations while at the same time pursuing the right of self-determination—the true and unbiased account of the Civil War from the Confederate viewpoint.

Moreover, even this commendable striving for geopolitical equity is likely to be met with extensive criticism. The war crimes trials following World War II were a good example. No one in his right mind can offer the slightest justification for the Holocaust and the destruction and death rained down on other innocent peoples who stood in the way of the global ambitions of the

Axis powers. Accordingly, the chief perpetrators of these crimes against humanity were brought to trial by the victors and prosecuted in a legal environment where the Allied nations went out of their way to avoid even the appearance of drumhead proceedings. In the end, the most culpable offenders were hanged, and a larger number incarcerated for long prison terms.

And then the judges were "put on trial." The criticisms ranged from a lack of sufficient jurisprudential objectivity, to a failure to observe various niceties of the law, to too much or too little "openness," and so forth and so on.[6] That is, the proceedings were criticized from the perspective of law as it operates within an established sovereignty rather than from the inadequate but unavoidable legal environment in which the jurists found themselves. All things considered, there might have been less criticism if the victors had simply offered the perpetrators the choice of doing themselves in or being summarily shot. This is not to suggest that that course of action should have been taken, but only to indicate the high respect jurists have for established procedure and low tolerance for equity, especially as equity applies mostly civil rather than criminal law and in any event tends to solidify into its own rules and precedents.

The Responsibility for Equity Imposed on the Salient Powers

We thus come to the great challenge imposed on the salient powers, especially the superpowers: (1) to protect their own interests and compete for global influence; (2) to prevent global war, which clearly would be inimical to their best interests; and (3) at least for the United States, to strive to enhance international justice—geopolitical equity—in policies and posture without assuming the role of world policeman or supranational authority. This may not be an ideal posture, but even a cursory review of history suggests that the nations with clout are the ones that make or otherwise influence a disproportionate number of decisions affecting many other nations. Moreover, given the right of self-determination, the United States can speak only for itself, not for the other salient powers. Where, then, lies the correct point to place the fulcrum of its influence? Before attempting the answer, several factors need to be considered.

The Growing Ideological Interdependence. One of the least observed aspects of superpower relationships is the degree to which communism and democracy are edging toward each other in a number of significant aspects. First, the national defense policy of both the United States and the USSR is now defensive in nature. Second, as the Soviet Union strives toward decentralization of economic management, if not quasi-capitalism, the United States seems headed for an increasingly central-funded, if not central-managed, social program which absorbs an increasing share of the gross national product.

Third, Soviet jurisprudence is edging glacially towards the English-American model. At least, there is no comparison with the Stalin era. The overall significance here is that the ratio of complementary to conflicting interests between the superpowers is likely to increase.

The International Power Curve in Light of the Equilibrium. The second factor is more significant. In times past, the dispersion of national power, combined with inadequate technology to make that power felt over great areas except by military or economic aggrandizement, made for effervescent international relations at best. Today that seems to be changing. The bulk of world power is now concentrated in the superpowers and their principal and more-or-less permanent allies, which serves to create and maintain the equilibrium. Thus the superpowers no longer need concern themselves with balance-of-power manipulations. They are in an enviable position in that they have accumulated sufficient resources to act with purpose rather than react with fear to the global problems affecting less favored nations.

The Fortunate Aspect of Superpower Rivalry. Notwithstanding the ideological tendency toward the mean and the fact that the bulk of the world's clout is now subject to geopolitical checks and balances, the prospect of the United States and the Soviet Union becoming permanent allies remains dim and fortunately so. For if the Soviets succeeded in accelerating their economic growth and then joined in alliance with the United States, the two would then own a majority of the world's stock, as it were, and effectively control even more. In this event, the combined superpowers might well become an intolerable power and de facto sovereignty in international relations.

Justice, Judgment and Equity

Dean Acheson, in summing up his tenure as Secretary of State, wrote:

> These eight years engraved on my mind a conviction which I have often heard Winston Churchill express, that the hope of the world lies in the strength and will of the United States. He would not object to my adding — in its good judgment as well.[7]

Given that perspective, justice is not paternalism. It is a sense of fairness and due process. But as the international arena lacks the means to permit disinterested adjudication, each nation must exercise its own judgment. If, however, the United States strives to go beyond protecting its own interests toward justice to improve the world about it, several routes are open. First, she could rely on alliances among various states to counter threats rather than attempt to enforce her will unilaterally. Second, she could work toward the expansion of international law to encompass those problems beyond national resolution, with the understanding that mutually perceived common interests are what make international law work. Third, she could help the poorest nations to improve their infrastructure, knowing that the equilibrium and her vast strength provide an immunity against ever being done in by her largesse.

On the other hand, the nations of the earth will never be equal, nor will their respective resources ever permit approaching that ideal except perhaps in the sense of fair access to the marketplace with whatever goods and services they can produce. Equity is not an equalizer. Moreover, the very equilibrium that permits the luxury of this global jurisprudence, however imperfect it would be, is a paradigm maintained by armed force. Scripture notwithstanding, the sword is not going to be beat into a plowshare. On the contrary, it must be maintained razor sharp. And preferably bloodless.

Appendix A. Military Technology and Behemoths

When an elephant is in trouble,
even a frog will kick him.
                    — Hindu Proverb

   Military technology dates back four or five millennia, but only the last 125 years have yielded dramatic progress. Before that time, about the only significant advance was the discovery of gunpowder, which did not change tactics all that much. At the time of the Civil War, massed troop formations and close-range naval broadsides were still the order of the day. Perhaps the most significant advance in that war was the use of railroads to move troops and supplies between battlefields with what was then perceived as alarming speed. Steam-powered, steel-clad ships may have heralded a new era of naval warfare, but they did not play a major role at the time. Since then, however, progress in military technology has been nonstop.
   This progress has revolutionized tactics several times and promises to continue doing so in the future. There is no shortage of new items such as the particle beam or energy weapons, the computerized battlefield, and "stealth" aircraft. More significantly, this progress evinces a discernable cycle, one which suggests an emphasis for future developments. This cycle is the inevitable consequence of engineering and logistics. In the simplest of terms, most weapon types tend to be enhanced, augmented, or otherwise overdeveloped until they become behemoths and prey to cheaper, dispersed, more maneuverable weapons, which themselves eventually develop into new behemoths. The firepower of dispersed counterweapons can be concentrated on weapons past their prime, inflicting more damage than they sustain. Moreover, this cycle tends to repeat itself with ever-widening physical or geographical dimensions until such time as those dimensions reach global proportions.
   This does not mean each weapon or system will become obsolete. Fortresses are still in vogue as prisons, and the Navy still maintains four World War II battleships in commission. It does mean each weapon will tend to increase in efficiency until it reaches parity with defensive counterweapons and then decline in relative importance to the outcome of battle and war. Many factors serve to expand or contract the period of dominance for any specific weapon type, but the decline seems inevitable. It may not be total, but the opportunities for effective employment shrink to those arenas where the counterweapons have not been introduced in sufficient measure to serve as a foil.

The B-2 Stealth Bomber

The B-2 stealth bomber is perhaps the most appropriate, current example of the cycle of military technology. *Newsweek* magazine put the case this way:

> Miniature missiles like the Stinger, costing about $36,000 each, can bring down a $520 million airplane. Without elaborate electronic countermeasures and other expensive hardware, U.S. bombers have little hope of transiting Soviet airspace in one piece. This triggers a vicious cycle. The more each bomber costs the fewer are built; the fewer bombers, the more Soviet defenses outnumber them. As bombers become vulnerable, even more expensive countermeasures are needed—meaning fewer bombers still. [1]

The supposed justification for continuing with this aircraft is the accuracy it provides, unavailable with missiles—a point refuted by the same article. [2] More to the point, a Soviet field marshal politely told Pentagon officials in July 1989 that if the United States persisted with development of the stealth bomber, the Soviet Union would develop the appropriate defense. In all probability, this would be the Soviet SDI tracking system geared down from 18,000 mph missile targets to 600 mph bombers—child's play in technical warfare.

Naval Warfare as a Case Study

The cycle of military technology applies to all the services, but naval warfare offers the clearest example. This is due to the fact that warfare at sea, with the exception of mines, requires definitive platforms. The application of the cycle for the surface ship, the aircraft, the missile, and the energy-weapon sequence is shown in Figure 16. The surface ship became heavier and heavier in order to provide protection against the increasing effectiveness of aircraft (and submarines), but its tenure was limited. The original purpose of fighting ships was to directly combat other fighting ships, but in World War II, only one daytime photograph was taken showing both Japanese and United States surface ships. [3] Though the speed and armor of the battleship had improved enormously in one generation, the aircraft had become its nemesis.

To be sure, these aircraft, for the most part, were and remain carrier-based. Carriers are surface ships, and moreover, they are ships with comparatively little armor and few guns. But then carriers seldom have been deployed with the same aggressiveness as other surface ships, and today the primary mission of a carrier group, aside from the carrier itself but including some of the aircraft, is to protect the carrier.

Unfortunately, the tactical aircraft itself may have reached the apogee of its effectiveness, to be supplanted by the anti-air missile. Though major naval battles since World War II have been few, and those few between less-than-first-rate naval powers, aircraft have been used extensively in almost all other forms of war. But they have suffered increasingly at the hands of sophisticated missiles, while surface ships have become almost sitting ducks for both aircraft and missiles, for example, the losses sustained by the United Kingdom during the Falkland Islands campaign in 1983. [4] And missiles themselves will undoubtedly eventually yield to energy weapons. The velocity of these weapons is on the order of 300,000 times faster than missiles and the beam is pure warhead. True, they require effective missile detection and "lock on" electronics, but that technology is being developed as part of the Strategic Defense Initiative (SDI) package.

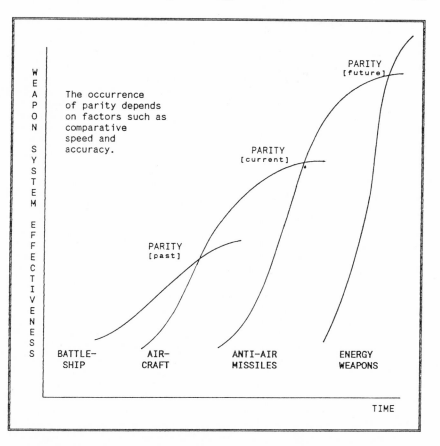

Figure 16. Military Technology Cycles. Each weapon system tends to improve in effectiveness until the counterweapon designed to defeat it reaches parity. Afterwards, the counterweapon gains battlefield ascendency until the new counterweapon designed to defeat *it* gains parity, and so forth. Moreover, in most cases, each new system tends to exert greater geographical significance due to increased speed and lethality per pound of material.

Ground Warfare

The application of the technology cycle to weapons and platforms associated with ground warfare — in the simplest sequence — would include the fortress, the massed-troop formation, massed artillery fire and the machine gun, the tank, the anti-armor missile, and finally, as in naval tactics, the energy weapon. The fortress yielded long before the battleship because it was both ponderous and unmaneuverable. The massed troop formation was probably the ground equivalent of the battleship, but as World War I demonstrated, massed artillery fires and machine guns were too much for it. In the next war, armored forces overcame artillery fire and machine guns, but paralleling the fate of the battleship, the tank is gradually yielding to anti-armor missiles and anti-armor mines.

And both the tank and the missile perforce must eventually succumb to the energy weapon. Armor advocates may disagree with this prognosis, holding to the tenet that the best anti-armor weapon remains another tank. And they may cite technological improvements such as reactive armor, new configurations, and the 135mm gun now found on the new Soviet tank the FST-1.[5] The arguments miss the point. These improvements come with an exponentially increasing price tag, one that should motivate enhanced research in anti-armor missiles, each edition of which may cost only 1 percent of its intended target.

Cause and Effect

The logic underpinning this military technology cycle is straightforward. First, every implement of war can eventually be defeated by concentrating firepower on its platform from a number of dispersed locations. In all fairness, David prevailed over Goliath only with a little luck, but no Goliath could withstand 20 Davids, no more than Butch Cassidy and the Sundance Kid could stave off the Bolivian army.

Second, to defend against these counterweapons, the platform in question must gain speed, maneuverability, and armor. These attributes are in part contradictory, and it takes an exponential increase in weight in order to produce a linear improvement to defense, whereas the counterweapons need only concentrate on speed and explosive power. Associated with this trend is the simple fact that as the platform becomes heavier and more expensive, fewer of them can be built for the same defense dollar. Also, their weight taxes logistical support and strategic lift at an exponential rate. Finally, they become more technical in nature and increasingly subject to breakdowns.

Third, the necessity for increased explosive power and speed in the counterweapons does not come free. Once they come to dominate the original behemoth targets, they themselves become the offensive weapon of choice and evolve into platforms in their own right. The tank was used originally to support massed infantry attacks, as it was impractical to armor-plate infantry personnel sufficient to withstand machine gun and artillery fire. But when the tank became an offensive weapon in its own right, the demands for more speed, armor plate, and firepower increased exponentially. By contrast the cost of field artillery, adjusted for inflation, has not changed much since World War I except for the self-propelled feature, and that feature replaces the means formerly required to move the tube. By avoiding the behemoth syndrome, field artillery remains one of the most devastating and not easily supplanted conventional weapons in the army's arsenal.

The Factors of Parity

Though it appears that every weapon eventually encounters its nemesis, the process of obsolescence — that is, the reaching of parity between behemoth and counterweapon — can consume a variable length of time. It is rarely, if ever, instantaneous, though the sudden realization of it in a war after many years of peace can create an appearance to that effect. At least seven factors contribute to the process of reaching parity: (1) the relative velocity of the two weapons, (2) maneuverability, (3) synergistic or deprecating effects from a combination of behemoths in proximity to one another, (4) countermeasures, active and passive, (5) relative cost, (6) the priorities and rate of technological development, and (7) the national outlook on the purpose of war.

Velocity and Maneuverability. These two factors are tightly interwoven. To the extent a counterweapon can quickly overtake and outmaneuver a behemoth, the latter's obsolescence is hastened. The airplane demonstrated much greater speed and maneuverability than the battleship and thus proved its dominance less than 25 years after it was introduced on the battlefield. By contrast, missiles, while faster than aircraft, are not generally as maneuverable, and therefore the period of takeover is taking much longer.

Synergism. Multiple behemoths may add or detract from the rate of decline depending on whether they compensate for each other's weaknesses or exacerbate those weaknesses. Surface ships in a task group protecting a carrier have served to extend the life of the carrier against all forms of counterweapons. By contrast, the armored personnel carrier (the infantry "fighting machine") and the tank may prove to be detrimental to each other. The personnel carrier affords little protection to the tank — isolated circumstances excepted. The tank by contrast does offer excellent protection to the carrier, but carriers inherently concentrate infantry into far fewer targets more susceptible to missile attack than infantry on foot. That is, the enemy would have fewer targets at which to strike. Also, once a sufficient number of tanks are destroyed, the utility of personnel carriers drops considerably.

Countermeasures. Countermeasures are a favorite means of prolonging the usefulness of many weapons. The submarine is particularly fortunate in being able to stay deeply submerged for prolonged periods in a medium where any kind of detection is difficult, but once a submarine engages in tactical warfare its location can be fixed and the increasingly sophisticated implements of anti-submarine warfare put to work. Aircraft utilize chaff to disorient radar fixes and missiles. Tanks employ unique configurations, reactive armor, and hull defilade tactics to offset the firepower of the opponent's tanks and some missiles. But most countermeasures either add weight to the weapon or force it to expend time that otherwise would be better employed for the principal order of business. Eventually the accumulation of the countermeasures takes its toll and contributes to the decline of the weapon.

Cost and Rate of Technological Development. Cost is a major factor, particularly when counterweapons are prohibitively expensive. High cost can prevent a nation from fielding a sufficient number of them to be effective. Closely related to cost is the rate of technological development, or at least the priorities given to technology. Few countries can afford all the technological research they would prefer. Priorities must be selected, and if selected incorrectly, the opponent's behemoths may prevail for a longer time than necessary. The history of inept anti-armor missiles is a good cause in point.[6] Also, technological advances may take years to develop irrespective of how much money is invested. For example, the development of an effective Strategic Defense Initiative might take at least a decade even if the entire defense budget for weapons were given over to it.

National Perspective on Warfare. This last factor is perhaps the most significant. If a nation is primarily defense oriented, then its main interest should be in counterweapons, whereas if it is an aggressive nation, then it must depend on extending the life of its offensive behemoths. To be sure, a defensive orientation may require offensive tactics on the battlefield, but considering the lethality of modern weapons, deterrence takes on a much higher priority than in the past. Deterrence has two variants. The first tries to convince the potential opponent that if he attacks, he will be eventually defeated by the offensive means of warfare that will be thrown against his attack. The second stresses that the opponent's offensive means of warfare will be decimated *before* he can engage in decisive warfare, and in that event, the defender will decide the war for him. The latter is preferable and is a form that is enhanced by first-rate counterweapons that make offensive behemoths increasingly obsolete.

Exceptions to the Cycle

Two possible exceptions to the cycle occur. The first is when a weapon becomes so deadly that counterweapon tactics are moot. The thermonuclear warhead and chemical or biological warfare fit into this category, though in time the Strategic Defense Initiative technology might be able to defend against missile delivery of either form of warfare. And in theory, counteragents to all known forms of nerve gas and biological agents may be possible. But to the extent counterweapons cannot be developed, the virtual counterweapon is the weapon itself. The threat of retaliation induces so much fear that its employment is not likely. Put another way, this phenomenon could be thought of as an endpoint in an application of the cycle.

The second exception is when the counterweapon is not transformed into an offensive weapon, at least not in the sense of fighter aircraft and tanks. As mentioned, field artillery is a good example. When the artillery gun was transformed into the tank — armored, mechanized artillery — it subjected itself to the cycle. Yet in its original form, field artillery remains tactically dispersed and very effective without exponential increases to its weight and required logistical support. And though artillery can be and is used in offensive as well as defensive tactics, in the former case its primary role is preparatory or interdictory fire. Field artillery platforms are not hurled into battle in the same sense as armor and infantry.

Implications for the Global Equilibrium

Though the cycle of military technology is important to tactics, it is critical with respect to operations and even entire wars. As such, the behemoth syndrome plays a major role in maintaining the equilibrium, because the reach of new weapons and systems takes on ever-widening geographic dimensions. For example, the Strategic Defense Initiative is global in scope, with some of its weapons components traveling at the speed of light. As the earth is not growing larger and the speed of light is the ultimate speed limit, there is no way to envelop or bypass SDI except by an increasing number of missiles — missiles that will eventually prove to be more expensive than improvements to SDI.

At the other end of the spectrum, the tank may be reaching its practical limit in size and weight if for no other reason than that the cost of transporting and maintaining even larger and heavier models might well prove prohibitive. Hence the era of anti-armor weapons should shortly be in the ascendency and make the offensive use of armor as the means of operational breakthroughs in combat increasingly a losing proposition. The same analysis could be applied to a number of other weapons, though undoubtedly the submarine, due to its resistance to detection underwater, may enjoy a longer offensive-war lifespan than others.

However, there is a lesson to be learned here with respect to the Strategic Defense Initiative. To avoid reaching parity with countermeasures, it should be more physically defensive in nature, meaning that it should not be primarily space-based. Unfortunately, it appears compromises are being made in this direction to hold costs down.[7] Anything stationed in space would be more subject to counterattack than if it was ground-based. Understandably, the safer alternative would be more expensive and time-consuming to build and would present technological challenges that seem insurmountable at the present time. Yet what is the use of an expensive system that could be easily overcome?

Summing up, in terms of the overall argument of this book, once relatively inexpensive technology is put in the hands of even ragtag forces, those forces can keep highly sophisticated and much larger forces at bay, e.g. the Afghani *mujahedin* versus the Soviet Union 1980–1988. To overcome this defensive advantage, the would-be invader must expend an exponentially increasing amount of force or resort to genocide or both. That is, while the remainder states will never be in a position to take on the salient powers, many of the former will eventually be able to resist invasion by the latter.

Appendix B. Wars, Operations and Tactics

Eagerness for battle is appropriate for the soldier, but generals serve the cause by forethought, by counsel, and by delay more often than by temerity.

— Tacitus

I beat the Russians every time,
but that does not get me anywhere.
— Napoleon, 1812, on the eve
of his retreat from Moscow

Wars are not the same thing as military operations, and operations, at least in the largest sense of that word, are not the same thing as tactics. An act of war is a political act, normally initiated by a head of state, be it for offensive or defensive purposes. The implementation of that policy decision is usually by way of one or more military operations, which in turn comprise one or more tactical engagements. Chapters 6, 7 and 8 of this book dwelled on the differences between war and operations. This appendix concentrates on the differences between operations and tactics, albeit with a final section that reexamines the relationship of wars and operations.

Military Operations Versus Tactics

Over the past few years the military has elevated the concept of operations to a major field of study. Some writers have pointed out that wars and operations have been lost in spite of continued tactical success and vice-versa.[1] Others concluded operations and tactics are fundamentally different from one another.[2] Still others claim that while the differences have been recognized, they have not been dealt with.[3] This raises the issue if the principles of war, as stated, are as applicable to operations as they are to tactics.

Conceptually, a case can be made that the principles apply equally to both levels of command, but for operations the explanations can occupy major portions of entire books.[4] These extended ruminations suggest that the principles could be profitably reworked for use in operations, preserving their generic value but restating them in terms more encompassing of the factors which come into play only at the operational level. The existing statements would be retained for tactics, and both sets could be presented in parallel. To this end, the discussion (1) addresses the substantive differences between tactics and operations; (2) briefly outlines why these differences have gained currency in the last 50 years; and (3) proposes the operational-level restatement of the principles based on these differences.

Perhaps the root of the problem is the lack of a clear dividing line between operations and tactics. In some cases an operation may consist of a closely knit series of tactical engagements, such as *Operation Market Garden* during World War II. In other cases, an operation can obviously go beyond tactical considerations, for example the European Theater of Operations during the same war. One way out of this taxonomic slurry is to recognize that to the extent to which a specific operation evinces the major differences between tactical engagements and definitive operations is the extent to which the operation should be managed on operational principles. And conversely, to the extent that the differences are not prevalent, the "operation" should be considered primarily in tactical terms. A specific operation should be managed by the appropriate mixture of rules applicable to the polemics, much like the adjustments available in a stereo set graphic equalizer.

Figure 17 outlines the polemics of tactics versus operations in terms of seven factors plus the ideal mindset and hallmarks of the respective commanders. Most of the factors are self-explanatory, but several points rate emphasis. The combined effect of the dominating influence of logistics at the operational level, the sustained period of time, the relative diffusion of the chains of command, and the not-so-occasional conflict of political purpose with military attributes suggests that the operational commander's management skills will be more heavily taxed than those of his tactical subordinates. It is interesting to note that General Eisenhower, who commanded the largest military operation in U.S. history, had never seen war until a year earlier and then as a commander of another, smaller operation.

To restate the argument, an operation is something more than the sum of the results of tactical encounters. A synergistic effect operates which can improve tactical efficiency, or conversely, result in operational defeat notwithstanding repeated tactical success. Thus brilliant tactics and bold moves are not necessarily the arbiters of operational success. The mass of resources and how those resources are organized and managed can play a role just as important as—or perhaps greater than—warrior ability. In lieu of this warrior ability, the operational commander should have a sense of perspective over a time—the motivation to prevail in the long run rather than a concentration on making every sale.

This requisite dates back at least to the battle for Troy. According to Homer's *Iliad*, Achilles was the hero of that war, albeit a spoiled brat. But it was Agamemnon that persevered for nine years notwithstanding untoward interventions by the gods richly portrayed by Homer. On the other hand, he might have accelerated the course of the war by exercising a little more management. That is, as pointed out by other writers, he should have boxed Achilles' ears.

Historical Background

In ancient times, the head of state, the operational commander, and the chief battle fighter were often the same person. Agamemnon, Alexander of Macedonia, Caesar Augustus, and Marcus Aurelius all assumed this trinitarian status. As late as 1815, Napoleon wore all three hats, and to this day the pagoda-hat phenomenon continues in some Third World countries. But for the United States and most other developed nations, this consolidation of functions no longer prevails. The head of state is rarely if ever an operational commander. The complexities of running modern nations bar the practice. Similarly, the operational commander is seldom the chief battle

Factor	TACTICAL ENGAGEMENTS	OPERATIONS
NATURE and SCOPE of OBJECTIVES	Objectives tend to be physical, either singular or a closely linked or sequenced set. Most physical objectives stress inflicting damage/casualties on enemy forces or securing/denying terrain, or both.	Operations have one or more overarching objectives supported by a sequence of tactical objectives. To the extent the war is limited, overarching objectives will tend to be political or economic in nature.
INTENSITY and DURATION	Tactical engagements tend to be brief—usually less than a week —marked by intensity, heavy damage, high casualties, and considerable maneuver.	Operations tend to be of longer duration; six months to a year or more is not uncommon. The periods of tactical intensity normally alternate with lulls.
SINGLE vs. JOINT SERVICE	Most tactical engagements are single-service based, though often with joint fire support.	Most operations are joint in nature, under a unified command or joint task force commander.
The use of STANDARD OPERATING PROCEDURES	Most tactics tend to adhere to standard operating procedures for almost all levels of command engaged in the fighting.	Operations are usually too diverse for SOPs, except in the administrative sense, that is, staff procedures, reports, etc.
SPACE and TIMING CONSIDERATIONS	Most tactics emphasize either a mobile force or specific piece of terrain where timing is more important than duration per se.	Most operations occur in relatively fixed geographical areas with scheduling/sequencing usually more critical than timing
LINEARITY versus DIVERSITY	Tactics are characterized by straightforward chains of command, with liaison coordination as appropriate.	Operations crosshatch service command channels with joint control of tactical units, exacerbated in coalition warfare.
LOGISTICS versus WARRIOR ABILITY	Normally, logistics yields to fighting considerations among the commander's priorities, except for extended engagements which are micro operations.	Logistics are increasingly the dominating or limiting factor in operational warfare, due primarily to increasing pounds-per-man-per-day requirements.
IDEAL MINDSET of the COMMANDER	TO WIN. Irrespective of the context or scope of the war, in a tactical engagement two warrior commanders will slug it out both seeking to be the victor of the moment.	TO PREVAIL. The operational commander knows that fleeting tactical success will amount to little if his opponent has the wherewithal and perseverance to prevail against him.
HALLMARKS	Willfulness and courage.	Perseverance and perspective.

Figure 17. Comparison of Tactical Engagements and Military Operations

fighter though he might have a lot to say about tactics and on occasion might find himself directing a number of concurrent major battles. The reasons, of course, comprise the factors differentiating operations from tactics, but most of the factors which force the issue have risen to prominence only recently.

Before World War II, the responsibilities of the army and navy rarely overlapped on the battlefield, and airpower was little more than a novelty. Today airpower is the common denominator among the services, a factor which puts all of them on the same tactical map. Then, too, the exponentially increasing logistical support requirements of war, as discussed in Chapter 6, mandate a much greater attention to management over a sustained period of time, often at the price of warrior skills. Finally, many wars are now fought over ideological perspectives without an intent to inflict as many casualties as possible on an opponent. As a corollary to this, the very existence and lethality of thermonuclear weapons causes the more powerful nations to sometimes "pull punches" lest the conflict erupt into far more war than they bargained for.

TACTICAL LEVEL DOMINANT PRINCIPLES	OPERATIONAL LEVEL
Objective. Direct every [tactical engagement] towards a clearly defined, decisive, attainable objective.	Translate the operational mission into a series of clearly defined, attainable military objectives which collectively will ensure success of the mission.
Mass. Concentrate combat power at the effective place and time.	Control and direct resources to ensure sustained success for the tactical objectives of the operation.
Maneuver. Place the enemy in a position of disadvantage through the flexible application of combat power.	Schedule and sequence objectives, prioritize military allocations, and galvanize logistical push to keep the enemy off balance.
Offensive. Seize, maintain and exploit the initiative.	Maintain the initiative during the conduct of an operation by a resilient sustainment of tactical objectives.

SUPPORTING PRINCIPLES

Economy of Force. Allocate minimal essential combat power to secondary efforts.	Allocate minimum essential combat power to tactical engagements not directly essential to accomplishment of the operational mission.
Simplicity. Prepare clear, uncomplicated plans and clear, concise orders to ensure thorough understanding.	Prepare a clear, concise operational plan and encourage the maximum consistency possible among tactical plans without sacrificing security.
Security. Never permit the enemy to acquire an unexpected advantage.	Prevent the enemy's acquiring of military advantages above that threshold that would permit him to regain the initiative permanently.
Surprise. Strike the enemy at a time or place, or in a manner for which he is unprepared.	Commence an operation at a time or place for which the opposing commander is least prepared and insofar as possible, plan the sequence of tactical engagements to continue doing so.
Unity of Command. For every objective, ensure unity of command under one responsible commander.	Assign responsibility for the operational mission to one commander with the necessary authority over the resources required to prevail.

Figure 18. Principles of War at the Tactical versus Operational Level. Source: Army Field Manual 100-5 *Operations,* for the tactical principles.

The Principles of War

More often than not, the principles of war are considered coequal, but upon reflection a definite hierarchy and priority of relationship appears among them. In more specific terms, the four dominant principles of war are those of *objective, mass, maneuver,* and *offensive.* Without an objective, war is senseless. Without the necessary mass or sufficient maneuver to apply that mass, it is futile. And all three must be encompassed by the spirit of the offensive — to seize, retain, and exploit the initiative. The remaining five principles are supportive or enhancing in nature. *Economy of force* is an unavoidable adjunct of mass, and *security* is essentially the inverse of the offensive. One cannot readily maintain the initiative if the opponent gains an unexpected advantage over him. *Surprise* is an enhancer of the offensive spirit, while *simplicity* is largely

an enhancer of maneuver. This leaves *unity of command,* perhaps the most independent of the principles because it is something that needs to be established before battles
and wars are initiated and is the one thing a commander at any level must depend upon
his seniors to ensure. The significance of this apparent hierarchy is that the four dominant principles—indicated in Figure 18—seem to benefit the most from rewording.

Objective. An operational mission is rarely directly attainable. Rather, its attainment is usually the result of the collective success of tactical objectives. In absolute wars,
where the destruction of the enemy's ability to wage war is the operational objective,
operational success may nearly be equated with the sum total of tactical successes provided those successes sufficiently decimate the opponent's ability to wage war. But most
wars are limited in nature and more often than not have a political, economic, or
ideological purpose. Thus the restatement of this principle for use at the operational
level should encompass both the breakdown of the mission into tactical objectives and
the potential for those tactical objectives to yield attainment of the mission. This
presumes that an operation has a clearly stated mission, but where the mission statement waffles ambiguously, translating it into appropriate tactical objectives may be an
exercise in wishful thinking.

Mass. The present wording of the principle of mass lacks the eloquence of its
former version—achieve superiority in combat power at the decisive place and time—
but the revision is more specific.[5] Superiority is often achieved by concentrating
firepower that by itself might prove inferior if committed piecemeal. But both versions
stress singularity, whereas operations almost always encompass a series of tactical
engagements. The operational commander must allocate his resources accordingly. If
he believes they will be expended at too great a rate, he must slow down the pace, albeit
without yielding an advantage to his opponent fatal to himself.

Maneuver. The current wording for this principle evinces the greatest revision from
an older form, which was: "position your military resources to favor the accomplishment
of your mission." The older version stressed vectoring resources to enhance the principle
of mass; the newer, to keep the opponent off-balance, which tends to overlap with the
principle of security. Also the choice of the word "flexible" implies a series of tactical
engagements. This rewording makes explicit the implicit intent of the tactical-level
wording, which of necessity could not stress multiple objectives.

Offensive. The wording of this principle has not changed an iota for at least 35
years, but contrary to popular belief, the principle of the offensive stresses maintaining
the *initiative,* not the attack per se. For example, when a defender momentarily
withdraws or otherwise gives ground in a classic "trading space for time" tactic, he is
preventing his opponent from engaging in decisive war until such time as *he* chooses
to engage in it. By definition this tactic maintains the initiative even though it is not
an attack. Also, maintaining the initiative in an operation is less a matter of seizing it
than maintaining it by flexibility—or more precisely, by resiliency. The former con-
notes a lack of rigidity; the latter, a more positive attribute that employs flexibility to
keep the pressure up and prevent the opponent from gaining the initiative.

Turning now to the five supporting principles, the suggested revisions involve less
change than the dominant principles. This arises from the fact that, as mentioned, most
of them are enhancers of several principles and are thus already stated in somewhat
more general terms.

Economy of Force. This principle is the obvious inverse of the principle of mass.
The proposed rewording is intended only to make the expression "secondary efforts"
more explicit from the perspective of an operation. This wording raises the issue that
if a tactical engagement is not essential, why include it in the first place? The key word
is *directly.* A feint is a frequently used tactic to put the opponent off guard as to the

real objective. These indirect tactics do not require locally superior force. On the contrary, the idea is to use the absolute minimum resources possible in order to invest the balance in the "critical path" of tactical engagements, as it were.

Simplicity. Of all the principles of war, this one is the most self-explanatory. But in an operation inconsistency among tactical plans can introduce a form of confusion in its own right. The ideal, therefore, is to encourage consistency among tactical plans short of violating the principle of security, that is, it should avoid "telegraphing" punches.

Security. The principle of security, as stated, is probably impossible. A resourceful opponent can and will acquire unanticipated advantages. A more realistic goal, particularly in a sustained operation, would be to minimize the opponent's acquiring of advantages, with the ultimate criterion being the principle of the initiative. The only way an operational commander can fail without relinquishing the initiative is when the political purpose is beyond military solution, in which case he hasn't really failed in military terms.

Surprise. The clarity of this principle is second only to simplicity, but it is difficult to achieve in practice, particularly in very large operations. The deception plan as to beachheads at the beginning of *Operation Overlord* in World War II was a master stroke, but one that took extraordinary effort. Once an operation begins in earnest, it is even more difficult to employ this principle. Therefore the suggested revision adds a little modesty to the ambition of the tactical statement.

Unity of Command. This brings the discussion to the last of the principles, one that in concept requires the least change. About the only point to note is that some operations require a change of commanders. For example, an amphibious operation is under command of the navy task force command until such time as the beachhead is secured, at which time command reverts to the ground commander. This sequence could be considered as two back-to-back operations, but in reality a more senior unified command commander will usually retain control over the entire effort. The restatement focuses on that higher level.

National Policy versus Military Operations

If the difference between tactics and operations is significant, the difference between operations and national policy is profound. Clausewitz rose to historical fame precisely because he understood this profundity. This prevails even in the case of absolute wars fought on the defensive. For example, a superficial view of World War II might hold that for the United States, the military objective of eliminating the Axis ability to wage war—the demand for unconditional surrender—*was* the national policy and that the only additional consideration was the relative priority for each theater. But war, as Clausewitz observed, is never the end of matters. As World War II wound down, the political concern for the United States, and Great Britain, was the Soviet Union. Neither wanted Russia to grab too much of Europe, especially Berlin. General Eisenhower understood this, but he declined to adopt that outlook in the absence of a written directive. He stated that Germany, not Russia, was the enemy, even though the former was on her military deathbed.[6] Ike cannot be faulted for his view, but the decision not to push the linkup eastward haunted the western powers for more than 40 years and perhaps even Eisenhower, as President, came to rue the day.

The difference can be made clearer by an analogy from the business sector. A business operation might comprise an attempt to market a new line of goods or services and to gain as large a share of the market as possible. But a corporate-level interest—

read *national policy*—would be to remain profitable if not increase profitability. Operational failures seldom result in bankruptcy; a failure to maintain profitability usually does. Similarly, a military operation fails when it can no longer prevail in its theater, but national failure occurs when the reservoir of national power can no longer sustain operations, be it by logistical shortfall or a "thinning" of the national ethos. If the objective of the operations equates to national survival, the failure will result in national bankruptcy.

Restated, a military operation must perforce concentrate on a semifixed geographical region, for a sustained but nevertheless limited period of time, under a single individual in command, ideally with sufficient authority and logistical support to see his way clear to prevail in a sequence of tactical engagements. By contrast, national policy is much more concerned with the advancement of national interests and other abstractions. In extreme cases this may equate with defense of homeland, but the interest is not to regain or maintain the territory so much as to survive and to continue advancing the cause of the nation's interests. Military operations are a means to that end. A military commander seeks to prevail; a nation, to endure.

Thus it follows that when military operations do not readily lend themselves to fulfillment of national interests, the operations will fail of their purpose even if the military commander prevails on the battlefield. Recalling the lexicon in Chapter 6, defensive wars tend to have a high degree of definition and controllability. The war is fought to maintain or restore the status quo. Military objectives usually lend themselves to that national policy. This is seldom true in offensive wars when the intent is to go beyond the status quo.

In perspective, Rudyard Kipling, who understood things military, regarded triumph as an impostor. He understood the difference between the battlefield and wars. Others would also come to understand this difference. When Colonel Harry G. Summers, Jr., was negotiating with the U.S. team in North Vietnam, he said to one of his counterparts, "You know, you never defeated us on the battlefield." The North Vietnamese colonel replied "That may be so, but it is also irrelevant."[7]

Appendix C. Mobilization as an Instrument of Deterrence

Not to promote war, but to preserve peace.
  —Elihu Root
  Motto of the U.S. Army War College

Mobilization is commonly regarded as a transition between peace and war—the necessary mechanics to refocus diverse elements of national power into sustainable military force to protect national interests in the face of actual or impending war. That perception is inadequate on two counts. First, in the course of history, aggressive nations have launched major offensives against stronger opponents partly due to a perceived lack of resolve within the opponent's ethos as evinced by rusty mobilization mechanics. For example, in 1941 the Japanese presumed the United States would withdraw militarily from the Pacific basin, in part because the draft had been passed by only one vote and because some of the draftees were training with mock weapons.

Second, in an era of potential mass destruction from even conventional weapons, *deterrence takes precedence over actual conflict.* Because mobilization is the forerunner of the posture necessary to convince potential opponents to stay within bounds, it too should be considered a major element of deterrence. This requires that a nation be able to quickly refocus the elements of its national strength to project military power wherever necessary. More importantly, that nation must also ensure that potential opponents fully recognize the speed and efficiency of that process. However, this should be accomplished without provoking war, without entailing major expense, without generating fear and concern in the civil population, and without raising the ire of the national legislature. That is not an easy task and suggests the enhancement of the mobilization process would concentrate on existing resources, primarily those which could readily be transformed into military force, and on the ability to rapidly project and support that force. Then, too, it would be limited to contingencies where deterrence itself already plays a decisive role, e.g. NATO, Korea, and possibly a few other regions. Moreover, if NATO eventually disbands as a result of German reunification, it would be all the more important for the United States to demonstrate an efficient mobilization capability.

In practical terms, the process of harnessing mobilization as an instrument of deterrence entails four general tasks: (1) understanding the radical changes to the factors affecting mobilization preparedness accruing since 1941; (2) phasing the mobilization process to make the best deterrent use of existing resources; (3) overcoming the mistrust between the legislative and executive branches on issues of employing military force; and (4) developing the administrative mechanics to make the phases of mobilization work well.

Changes to the Mobilization Perspective

A substantial number of differences between the World War II mobilization experience versus current requirements exist, though most of them are facets of the
generic problem of attempting to meet more complex and long-leadtime requirements
with limited time and resources. The more significant ones are:

Funding. During the World War II era, once war was declared, the defense effort
was given a virtual blank check. The country had no national debt to speak of, while
massive numbers of skilled individuals remained unemployed at the time. Today, the
national debt is astronomical; unemployment, in the 5 to 6 percent range. And most
of the unemployed are unskilled and located in inner cities far from points where the
individuals might best be put to work, and then only after extensive training to meet
the incomparably more complex technical aspects of current military logistical
requirements.

Statutory Restrictions. These have increased exponentially since 1941, not only in
the environmental arena but in budgeting and funding. Various mobilization exercises
conducted since 1976 have recognized this obstacle.

Strategic Lift. The United States does not own, control, or exercise influence over
the necessary air and sealift capacity to project and sustain massive military force
overseas.[1] Military surge requirements, at peak, could multiple peacetime military
shipments by a factor of a 50 or more, and this presumes no enemy interdiction en route
and no natural disasters, such as a major earthquake in California, competing for
transportation resources. To some extent, this deficiency is offset by the prepositioning
of war material (POMCUS) in NATO and elsewhere.

Ammunition Reserves. In order to maintain large standing forces to effect deterrence, ammunition reserves have been cut back to a minimum with the result that it
is exceedingly difficult to implement some critical surge requirements. Munitions
manufacturers cannot maintain such facilities with only ongoing production to pay for
them. Moreover, the so-called "smart weapons" or "preferred munitions" of today's
defense are far more complex, expensive, and time-consuming to produce.

Mobilization Rate. During World War II, the United States made the intentional
decision to mobilize at a rate that would not generate permanent danger to the
economy.[2] The invasion of Europe was therefore postponed to 1944 rather than 1943.
In the current era she no longer has this option.

Infrastructure. The present mass of the defense establishment, combined with
overlapping responsibilities of the Federal Emergency Management Agency (FEMA) and
other agencies, makes for a complex and somnambulistic decision-making process in
time of mobilization. There is little satisfactory mechanism in place for the expeditious
adjudication of the competing demands for limited funds and for the reallocation of
funds and resources under a rapidly developing but uncertain contingency.[3] This competition exists: (a) within each separate service, (b) within the defense establishment,
and (c) between defense and civil sector requirements, even when those requirements
are all intended to support defense.

Phasing Mobilization for Deterrence

At present, mobilization begins only when a potential threat has materialized to
the point where military force might be required significantly beyond the capabilities
of standing military force, supplies on hand, and available strategic lift and transport.
Until a threat becomes this ominous, mobilization would be regarded as too pro-

INFRASTRUCTURAL PHASES

PHASE I.   Preliminary Warning

Indirect diplomatic warning of concern by way of Congressional authorization to set in motion the activation of the legal and economic infrastructure necessary to mobilize military force. Military activity, per se, would not substantially increase.

PHASE II.   Definitive Warning

Direct diplomatic warning coupled with Congressional authorization for the full implementation of all legal, economic and industrial infrastructure required to implement mobilization. Activation of the Selective Service infrastructure.

MILITARY PREPAREDNESS PHASES

PHASE III.   Cadre Mobilization

Mobilization of cadre strength of reserve units and deployment of advance parties of active units to or near the anticipated theaters of operation. However, the draft itself would not yet be implemented, though that option might be reconsidered.

PHASE IV.   Full Mobilization

Full mobilization of all reserve units and personnel. Maximum deployment of forces. Implementation of the draft. Peak industrial production activated, with high priority for defense transportation requirements. The draft would be implemented.

WAR

PHASE V.   Declaration of War

This phase is to be avoided. A declaration of war would be tantamount to global war. The mobilization process itself under this concept would be intended as a means of deterrence. But if war must come, then the U.S. would be fully prepared.

Figure 19. Phases of Mobilization as an Instrument of Deterrence

vocative and thus politically unacceptable. The inadequacies with this posture, to expand on the preceding discussion, are threefold. First, it does not make the most of deterrence. Second, the requirements of the mobilization process, which are far more complex than the general mobilization during World War II, will consume more time than available once the threat becomes obvious.

Third, a hurried mobilization is likely to overreact and denigrate many of the environmental protection laws so laboriously implemented over the last 15 years, be it by Congressional relief or by senior military commanders overlooking the violations to accommodate the exigencies of the situation. Thus as shown in Figure 19, a phased mobilization process with five phases would be appropriate. The first two phases would be structured to overcome the deficiencies cited by concentrating on the inadequacies of infrastructure, while the last three comprise a major modification to the existing phases of partial, full, and total mobilization.

Phase I. The first phase would comprise a resolution on the part of Congress that an unmistakable threat to U.S. interests had materialized or intensified to the point where it was necessary to convey concern to the potential opponent without exacerbating international tensions or provoking war. This concern would not consist so much in a diplomatically worded statement as in the activation of the infrastructure necessary to mobilize force. But no reserve component units or personnel would be recalled with the possible exception of a few key individuals with mobilization assignments to major headquarters and directorates. Neither would active units be deployed or redeployed. The manufacture of munitions would not be increased, though long-leadtime capacity to do so might be implemented. The mobilization infrastructure would consist largely of authority to "clear the road" for the tens of thousands of contracts and other provisions necessary to effect mobilization. Few of these contracts would be executed, but they would be drawn up or brought up to date as appropriate contingent upon implementation of later phases of mobilization.

Phase II. The second phase of this mobilization process would bring on line the specific contracts negotiated or brought up to date in phase I. But as in the first phase, no reserve component units or personnel would be called up, and no active units would be deployed with the possible exception of security for critical points in the physical infrastructure against sabotage, such as power stations and communications networks. This phase would also include activation of the Selective Service, but the draft itself would remain on the shelf. Summing up on these two phases, the result would be to put the infrastructure essential for actual mobilization in high gear without provoking war or unnecessarily exacerbating international tensions.

Phase III. This phase would equate with the existing concept of partial mobilization, but the intent and mechanics would be different. In this proposal, partial mobilization would not be intended for partial war fighting capability, but for the means to make the full mobilization — phase IV — more efficient. As such, this phase would be considered as military preparation. Reserve component personnel might be called up, but they would more likely be cadre elements of most if not all troop units rather than a complete mobilization of a few selected units. Active units might be deployed, but most of them would be support units intended to facilitate deployment of the "warrior" units. Civil-sector support contracts would go into effect but at a reduced level of consumption or work, the intent being to iron out problems before the mobilization process was put into high gear.

Phase IV. This phase would equate roughly with full mobilization and would activate essentially all reserve component units and personnel and increase call-up of the industrial base to maximum armament and munitions production, relying on either mothballed facilities (or additional production lines) or additional shifts. The draft would be implemented. Major units would be deployed to the area of potential war insofar as practical or at least to staging areas, but war itself still would not be declared. The intent would be to give the opponent one final warning under conditions where the political situation is precipitous but not foregone.

Phase V. The beginning of this phase would coincide with a formal declaration of war and in all probability immediate commencement of hostilities. Every national resource necessary for the successful prosecution of the war would be tapped, with the advantage that the bottlenecks associated with direct military mobilization would have been overcome in the earlier phases. *In point of fact, however, the United States would never want to reach this phase.* Any armed conflict today that required a Congressional declaration of war would inevitably incur intolerable casualties, massive devastation, and a definitive risk of escalation to thermonuclear warfare. The central idea remains to make mobilization an instrument of deterrence, with the advantage that if this well-honed deterrence still failed the nation would be better prepared to fight than it would under existing procedures.

The Difficult Issue of Implementation Authority

Although the president has the authority to implement partial and full mobilization without prior Congressional approval and certainly without a declaration of war, this authority is limited both in numbers and time. Congress retains an effective veto by way of its funding authority. Given the record of discord between these two branches of government, it is not likely Congress would give the president further authority to put the nation on heightened preparedness prior to a call-up or major deployment of troops.

The only practical solution, politically and legally, would be to leave the authority for implementing all the proposed phases with Congress. This may seem to be at odds with existing presidential authority, but if the threat is severe enough for the potential of a formal declaration of war, then it follows that only Congress should be authorized to implement the preparatory phases. The president, of course, could always request implementation, but that is not the same thing as the authority to implement. On the other hand, the existing legislation could remain on the books. That is, the president would retain his existing authority to address contingencies without initial Congressional approval with the proviso that if the five-phase process were implemented, the authority to use the existing legislation would be held in abeyance until a complete stand-down had occurred.

Administrative Mechanics

The administrative mechanics of this proposal would need to take cognizance of many changes in the defense infrastructure implemented since World War II. For starters the Department of Defense did not exist in 1941, and the secretariats of the Army and the Navy were small. Further, the two military departments perforce had to concentrate on direct war-fighting capability. Aside from the civil works functions of the Corps of Engineers, the services had little experience with managing elements of the civil sector. Moreover, by the time mobilization really got underway, the Axis forces had reached the extreme limits of their short-lived conquests. The number of Americans in uniform would increase by a factor of at least 25, with up to half that number in war zones at any given time. In short, the military departments could not give much priority to the mobilization process in the civil sector, with the notable exception of the secret atomic bomb project.

Those conditions do not prevail today. First, the number of individuals in uniform is in excess of 2,000,000, while reserve component units are larger and in far better condition than similar units before the outbreak of World War II. Second, the Department of Defense exercises an increasingly effective control over the separate services and is essentially a civilian-staffed department. Third, DOD has developed an enormous logistics capability. This includes the Defense Logistics Agency and the designation of separate services as the sole "proprietor" of defense-wide distribution of many other goods and services. The separate services today handle only a fraction of their own wholesale logistical requirements. Fourth, the Organization of the Joint Chiefs of Staff (OJCS) maintains the Industrial College of the Armed Forces (as part of the National Defense University), a program which includes many nonmilitary graduates. Restating these points, the Department of Defense now possesses the raw infrastructure for management of mobilization although it has never been tasked to that end.

The proposal here is to harness that capability, notwithstanding it would incur an instant turf battle with FEMA. In specific terms, the Civil Works Directorate of the U.S. Army Corps of Engineers would assume responsibility for the infrastructure of mobilization management, with provisos that in time of peace (1) only a small part of that directorate would be involved; (2) the mobilization management function would come under the operational control of the Secretary of Defense; and (3) it would be subject to direct Congressional Oversight.[4] The precedence for this is the existing standard procedure of designating a joint-service responsibility as a *specified* rather than a *unified* command when a single service is tasked to perform all or most all of the associated missions. In time of mobilization the bulk of the directorate would be transferred to the Department of Defense.

Rationale for Using the Civil Works Directorate

The rationale for using the civil works arm of the Corps of Engineers (COE) has ten parts, most of which relate to existing COE functions and expertise:

Existing Structure. The approximately 10 divisions and 40 districts of the COE have been in existence, with some changes, since before World War II and therefore offer an established infrastructure for mobilization administration.

Relevant Experience. This infrastructure has managed construction and maintenance of civil as well as military construction for the same length of time. No other agency, civil or military, has a comparable record.

Real Estate Functions. Virtually all mobilization requirements are tied to real estate or improvements thereon, a prospect for which COE has considerable experience and expertise. On the negative side the COE is not equally strong in mechanical and industrial engineering except what may be gained by osmosis. However, it has more than a thousand reserve officers on tap, many of whom have this experience and the appropriate professional engineer registration. In time of mobilization, under present authority, these officers would be called to active duty.

Congressional Relationships. Congressional relationships with COE are long-standing and generally in good repair. It should be noted the allegations of COE pork barreling are based on occasional Congressional mandates to build structures and facilities of debatable merit. These projects are neither illegal nor immoral and hence COE is guilty of nothing more than carrying out aboveboard Congressional orders.

COE Organization. The COE is easily subdivided, having two primary directorates, one for civil works, the other for engineer and operations, both of which are supported by a sizable real estate division. In time of mobilization, cross-filling of specific expertise could be initiated if necessary.

Civilian-Military Relationships. At most COE levels, career civil servants and military officers work with remarkable cooperation based primarily on common professional preparation, experience, and duties.

Troop Unit Experience. Most COE officers have had considerable troop duty assignments. They understand the bottom line of military force, yet most of them remain sufficiently detached from this experience to gain the larger national perspective. The engineering rather than military troop unit experience takes precedence in career advancement as rank increases, though a few Engineer officers continue to alternate assignments in senior troop command or staff positions or even to revert to such command entirely. In the latter regard, the most notable example was General MacArthur.

Colocation. It appears that the COE as well as the Army Matériel Command will be relocated to Fort Belvoir, Virginia, a post which is evolving into the logistical counterpart of the Pentagon. The Defense Logistics Agency remains at nearby Cameron Station, but it too could be relocated to Fort Belvoir as Cameron is one of the facilities slated for closure. If that occurs, then all of the elements essential for mobilization management of the sustaining base would be colocated on one post. Also, the burden of mobilization tends to fall on the Army rather than the other services. The Air Force and the Navy are largely self-deploying, and the long leadtimes for increasing ships and major aircraft lower the need for increased personnel on a par with the Army. Also, COE at present manages Air Force construction.

Civil Disaster Relief Experience. The COE has extensive experience in civil disaster relief, a mission which closely parallels surge mobilization requirements, both in the technical sense and in working relationships with civil sector agencies. Also, the working relationships between COE and FEMA are probably the most extensive of any similar relationships with other defense agencies.

Public Scrutiny. The final part of the rationale is subjective but perhaps the most important. The COE works openly with Congress and the public and is under the continuing scrutiny of both. For deterrence to be effective, the mechanics must be well publicized. It is not a matter of having a secret plan under the carpet for assuming control when a threat is imminent. On the contrary, the requirement is for total openness. For example, mobilization preparedness should work to find means of maintaining environmental protection laws in time of emergency and not ways of bypassing them.

Command and Direction of the Mobilization Function

The Chief of Engineers, a three-star billet, could be elevated to four-star rank with precedence equal to the vice chairman of the Joint Chiefs of Staff. This promotion would be temporary and moreover the incumbent could be explicitly prohibited from wearing the uniform at any time during the contingency. Furthermore, he would serve as the executive officer of a governing board which included the Secretary of Defense, the Secretary of the Interior, the Secretary of Transportation, the Director of FEMA, and other officials with responsibility for oversight of national resources in time of national emergency. The elevation in rank combined with not wearing the uniform is meant to provide the necessary authority to carry out the mission while recognizing that such authority would be exercised primarily over the civil sector. The fear of "the man on the white horse," however ill-founded it may be, is nevertheless a political reality.

A Case Study Example

The preceding discussion provides an overview of some of the problems that confront mobilization effectiveness, but it is short on detail. Perhaps the single most intriguing problem demanding attention to detail is the provision of hospital space for anticipated casualties. For a nonnuclear war in NATO, the projected *nonfatal* casualties for U.S. military forces would be approximately 275,000 for the first 90 days, of which nearly 190,000 would require acute-care or rehabilitative-care beds at the peak on the ninetieth day. This does not include allied force casualties which might require evacuation to the United States due to the destruction in Europe. Many of these facilities would be provided by agreements with existing civil sector and Veterans Administration hospitals, but this would still leave a shortfall of 50,000 beds for the Army and perhaps 20,000 or more for the other services.

Now it is certain the government would provide for the care of wounds sustained in any war. On the other hand, constructing 70,000 hospital beds on short notice is impractical. The quick-fix solution would be to use expedient alternatives, such as vacated barracks space in the vicinity of existing military hospitals, but this generates new problems. Ask any nurse why. Further, any solution depends on the funds and the time available. Thus a variable range of solutions should be worked out in advance. Moreover, this issue begs a higher perspective. If the United States intends to participate in a conflict generating casualties at the aforementioned rate, Congress could exercise the right of eminent domain and secure additional civil sector facilities to meet the need. This alternative would shift funds to the primary mission of surge projection of military power. The stronger this capability, the more likely deterrence will be effective and possibly *prevent* the hostilities that would generate the casualties in the first place.

There are no easy answers to problems of this kind, but there is little doubt that attempting to solve them after a threat becomes imminent is less likely to produce good solutions. However, as long as mobilization is considered tantamount to war, rather than as an instrument of deterrence, defense officials and Congress will tend to avoid many of the issues.

Summing up, a war in which the United States might have to mobilize its national resources on a substantial scale will more than likely entail intolerable numbers of casualties and damage and the risk of escalation to thermonuclear warfare. This being the case, it would be in the national interest to deter such war, not only with large standing military forces as now exist, but by turning the mobilization process itself into an instrument of deterrence. This would not entail major additional expense, but it would mean coming to grips with the legal, administrative, and infrastructural tasks associated with this concept. The resources to do this are largely in place but hitherto have not been tasked to this end. Given the price of war today, it would behoove Congress and the Department of Defense to reconsider the ground rules.

Appendix D. Long-Range Defense Programming

Complex problems have simple, easy-to-understand
wrong answers.
                    —"Murphy's Law" graffiti

As discussed in Chapters 13 and 20, one of the more serious systemic problems
within the defense posture of the United States is that of stabilized long-term funding
of military force in the face of (1) the massive national deficit; (2) the political pen-
dulum on controversial programs such as the Strategic Defense Initiative; (3) the competition for funding of domestic programs; (4) the annual funding process, which is
at odds with the fact that most defense expenditures are long-term programs; and (5)
defense funding beyond certain mandatory or inevitable expenses being largely a subjective and political process.

Between 1961 and 1967, Secretary of Defense Robert McNamara imposed an objective system on the Defense budget process—an application of systems analysis and
operations research. To this day, the mechanism of his Planning, Programming and
Budgeting System (PPBS) remains in use. But as the recent Defense contracting scandal
revealed, it is fairly easy to circumvent the system, be it by outright fraud or by Congressional pressure to force the Pentagon to buy systems it doesn't want in order to direct
business toward various Congressional districts. The question, then, is whether it is
feasible to institute a system which could nudge the defense programming and funding
system back towards more objectivity. The answer is itself subjective. The political environment must be willing to tolerate more objectivity, but the yin and yang of that
toleration is difficult to gage in advance.

Under these circumstances, the ideal system would give the Secretary of Defense
the necessary means to enforce greater objectivity when it was tolerable to do so but
would survive latently intact when conditions were otherwise. The latent nature of the
system must also accommodate the fact that half or more of the incumbent secretaries
of defense stay for less than three years. Thus a new secretary must be able to activate
the system almost instantly. That, of course, is impossible in any direct sense. The PPBS
cycle itself runs approximately 18 months with a six-months overlap between successive
years.

Moreover, most defense commitments, notwithstanding the annual budgeting
process, possess considerable inertial momentum. Once systems are in development,
they cannot easily be eliminated, and once in the field, they must be maintained. And
many defense budget commitments defy significant change in anything less than one
or two decades, for example, retirement benefits. That is, while Congress may enact
major changes to the calculation of benefits, as they did recently, it will be roughly

199

20 years before the impact of that change begins to significantly affect the defense budget.[1] In fine, even if the supposed "instant response" system were feasible, the impact of any activation would be years in coming. But at least it would come, and that would be an improvement over nothing.

An Approach

About the only way to remotely approach the ideal would be to fully automate the current PPBS in the form of a decision support system. A decision support system has a vast amount of "what if" computing power built into it. In the case of Defense, that "what if" metholodology would have to extend into the future for at least ten years and do so with high speed, drawing on banks of contingency, resource, and funding data. Unfortunately, obtaining that data would itself be a monumental task. The defense establishment, as in most large corporations and institutions, developed data processing (ADP) systems piecemeal and then later attempted to integrate them without much success. The horror stories abound.[2]

The underlying difficulties in the endeavor to integrate disparate systems are manifold and range from incompatible data bases, to hardware and operating systems never designed with interfaces in mind, to differences in the accuracy and timeliness of data among various systems. As the number of systems to be integrated increases, the difficulties expand exponentially. The Organization of the Joint Chiefs of Staff is spending enormous sums in an attempt to provide a comprehensive data processing system to facilitate the management of war, while the separate services have also invested considerable funds in other attempts to integrate existing systems. In the former case, the project is called the Joint Operations, Planning, and Execution System (JOPES) and encompasses about 80 existing systems. To date, the progress has not lived up to the promise.[3]

On the other hand, integration of existing systems to support macro-level decision-making, for Defense or anyone for that matter, may not be necessary. Macro-level decisions are rarely based on exact quantities and relationships found in most functional or operational data bases. This is due to the fact that such data change daily and that for predictions and projections over a period of years, extreme accuracy of raw data is meaningless. The so-called law of averages tends to overcome the inaccuracies with compensating pluses and minuses. Moreover, projections of contingency requirements beyond a few years are themselves somewhat fuzzy. Thus an organization could base its macro decision-making on generalized data. This type of data is readily available from existing systems and obtainable on a periodic basis without any attempt to integrate those systems, logically or electronically.

The Two Critical Classes of Defense Decision-making

Decisions to use or not use military force in various potential conflicts and contingencies are beyond doubt the most critical decisions made in the Defense arena, but those decisions are inevitably made by the President or Congress and rarely depend on automated analysis. Moreover, such decisions are not made very often, though the consequences can linger for generations. The types of critical decisions that are made periodically arise from two questions:

• What are the short-range and long-range impacts of including a specific line item (and dollar amount or quantity thereof) in the current Planning, Programming, and Budget System (PPBS) cycle?

- How well will the resources projected to be on hand or readily available by such-and-such a date enable the United States to sustain armed conflict in such-and-such a contingency under such-and-such conditions?

These two questions consume untold man-years of intense effort in the Pentagon. Further, because the complexities of the calculations tend to defy human ingenuity, the planning decisions are often resolved by compromise, personal influence, politically inspired trade-offs, and a host of other subjective factors. By the time the secretary of defense issues guidance, or reviews recommendations, or forwards the proposed annual defense budget to the Office of Management and Budget, the opportunity for comprehensive evaluation has evaporated. No system of any kind can eliminate the subjective factors, but first-rate ADP support could give the secretary the option and capability of putting those subjective factors in perspective.

That is to say, to the extent subjective factors encompass quantitative aspects or logical relationships with other objective factors, that "extent" can be compressed into high speed data processing and analysis. This analysis would reduce the subjective factors to a minimum and provide a more objective perspective from which to evaluate them. For example, the Navy has a goal of 600 ships, a goal which of course has been reduced or postponed with the current Defense budget cuts. But what is the impact of 600 ships on the Navy budget for the next ten years, and would the Defense department be able to sustain those ships in times of various contingencies? Some of those ships depend on high-technology weapons, which may or may not be kept in sufficient reserve to sustain warfare in some contingencies. If the budget has been strained to provide the ships, there may not be sufficient money to fund manufacturing mobilization capacity to produce those weapons in sufficient quantities. As this is but one of several thousand conflicts that underlie the annual defense budget process, it should be obvious the secretary of defense could benefit from marco-level data processing support.

Concept of the Model

The proposed model would have two parts. The first part would fully automate the Planning, Programming, and Budgeting System on a Defense-wide integrated basis. The main feature of this part would be the "what if" computer programming that evaluates the long-term and short-term funding consequences of budgeting decisions under various user-specified control parameters, for example: projected defense budgets, inflation, changes to alliance commitments and surge funding under various mobilization contingencies. The second part of the system would use data projected by the first part (which would normally be stated in terms of quantities or resources available in different years) and then compare the resources available with the time-phased requirements for any war plan or any contingency plan or any combination thereof initiated concurrently or in any sequence. Figure 20 illustrates the two parts and their principal relationships, while Figure 21 provides a greatly simplified picture of how the system might operate.

The PPBS part of the model, even without the forecasting and evaluation features, would replace the current semi-automated, disjointed word processing system in use. The separate services, however, would not exactly welcome an automated process of this type with open arms. Service parochialism comes with a certain amount of competitiveness in the budgeting process, and the players sometimes play their cards close to the vest. Hence, this part of the system would have to be imposed by the Department of Defense. The contingency part of the model would encounter much less resistance. A number of budding systems are already reaching for this goal. The obstacles are

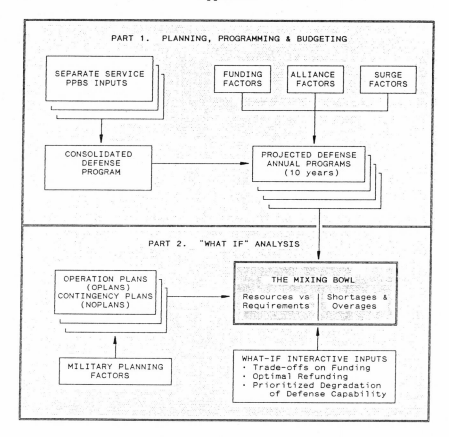

Figure 20. A Conceptual Model for Long-Range Defense Budget Planning. This decision support system would automate the existing PPBS and use maximum "what if" processing based on user-specified factors affecting funding and resources over a ten-year period. The files thus generated could then be compared with various summations of war and contingency requirements. The system can be run from both ends, that is, to determine the adequacy of present funding for various requirements *and* to determine the funding required to adequately provide for various contingencies.

largely technical, e.g. obtaining data from separate systems and developing the hardware and software necessary to process that magnitude of data and algorithms.

Implementation Obstacles

In the process of implementing this model, a number of de facto obstacles would arise from the usual method of government contracting for systems and the documentation required, even in the absence of any fraudulent conduct. To bypass these problems

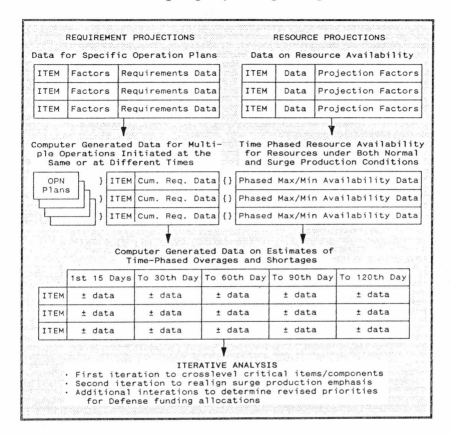

Figure 21. Application of the Technique

the system could be developed on a stand-alone basis and use only generalized data. In this way the technical problems could be reduced to more manageable proportions. In theory at least, that would permit a modification to the way systems are normally developed. In practical terms, this means using the basic research and development route rather than the operating system contracting procedure.

A Caveat

The proposed model would not by itself reduce the political and subjective factors impacting on the Defense funding process. At best it would provide the secretary of defense with a means of instantly evaluating various funding alternatives in light of various contingencies and factors. That is, it could provide an objectively oriented incumbent secretary with the necessity analytical wherewithal to hold his own against occasional outbursts of service parochialism and Congressional "mandates" to buy such-and-such items. It would be naive, of course, to presume that this advantage will eliminate the trade-offs that are a fact of life in the government funding process, but what is traded could be the least detrimental to the long-term defense posture of the United States.

Appendix E. Comparative Chronological Data

This brief appendix compares data for the years in the period 1985–1990, obtained from the yearbooks published by the *Encyclopaedia Britannica*. Table 11 lists the comparative data on area; Table 12, on population; Table 13 on gross national product (GNP), and Table 14 on military spending. Figure 22 graphs the comparative data for GNP, both in terms of dollars and percentiles, and Figure 23 does the same for military spending.

Area

The total land surface reported increased about three one-hundredths of 1 percent over the six years. Within the groups (superpowers, major powers, buffer states, and remainder states), no group changed its percentage share by more than six one-hundredths of one percent. Most of this small amount was due presumably to more accurate surveying, as most of the increase is attributable to changes in data for only a few countries. In a few cases, land mass does increase slightly due to alluvial deposits and other natural phenomena.

Population

During this period, the reported population increased from 4,852,281,000 to 5,209,960,000, an increase of approximately 358 million—about 7.4 percent. Yet the proportionality among groups remained nearly constant. The remainder states increased slightly over 1 percent at the "expense" of the salient powers. The buffer states increased only about one-tenth of 1 percent. Most of the salient power gain, of course, occurred in China and India.

Gross National Product

The *Britannica* yearbooks did not include dollar-equivalent GNPs in 1985. For the 1986–1990 period, reported GNP increased dramatically (representing the period from 1983 to 1987). The increase between 1986 and 1987 is attributable almost solely to the change in reported data on the Soviet Union and the eastern European nations. Thus the *proportionality* among groups evinced a major change between those two years. After that, the proportionality remained steadier. The buffer states showed the strongest increase, with Japan accounting for the lion's share, but the combination of

Year	SUPERPOWERS	MAJOR POWERS	BUFFER STATES	REMAINDER STATES	MIDDLE EAST	WORLD TOTAL
1985	12,268,270	15,668,643	8,877,336	13,130,588	2,388,390	52,333,227
	23.44%	29.94%	16.96%	25.09%	4.56%	100.00%
1986	12,272,961	15,668,631	8,878,336	13,133,317	2,386,617	52,339,862
	23.45%	29.94%	16.96%	25.09%	4.56%	100.00%
1987	12,272,961	15,708,159	8,879,238	13,133,271	2,386,622	52,380,251
	23.43%	29.99%	16.95%	25.07%	4.56%	100.00%
1988	12,328,692	15,708,282	8,869,115	13,138,413	2,409,638	52,454,140
	23.50%	29.95%	16.91%	25.05%	4.59%	100.00%
1989	12,328,692	15,708,282	8,902,226	13,141,620	2,409,638	52,490,458
	23.49%	29.93%	16.96%	25.04%	4.59%	100.00%
1990	12,328,992	15,708,283	8,902,577	13,135,662	2,408,255	52,483,769
	23.49%	29.93%	16.96%	25.03%	4.59%	100.00%

Table 11. Chronological Data on Area. The data shown (in square miles) are from sources considered applicable as of one year before the publication data. Source: Yearbooks of the *Encyclopaedia Britannica* for the years 1985–1990.

Year	SUPERPOWERS	MAJOR POWERS	BUFFER STATES	REMAINDER STATES	MIDDLE EAST	WORLD TOTAL
1985	510,316	2,260,435	967,321	940,196	120,548	4,852,281
	10.63%	46.40%	20.16%	19.59%	2.51%	100.00%
1986	516,316	2,251,631	989,059	970,425	124,850	4,920,581
	10.64%	46.24%	20.38%	20.00%	2.57%	100.00%
1987	521,527	2,275,215	1,003,684	992,819	127,336	4,920,581
	10.60%	46.24%	20.40%	20.18%	2.59%	100.00%
1988	526,584	2,303,548	1,019,023	1,016,440	132,124	4,997,719
	10.54%	46.09%	20.39%	20.34%	2.64%	100.00%
1989	531,909	2,341,977	1,036,240	1,052,870	135,291	5,098,287
	10.43%	45.94%	20.33%	20.65%	2.65%	100.00%
1990	536,577	2,396,840	1,056,465	1 078,949	141,129	5,209,960
	10.30%	46.00%	20.28%	20.71%	2.71%	100.00%

Table 12. Chronological Data on Population. The data (in millions) are from sources considered applicable as of one year before the publication date. Source: Yearbooks of the *Encyclopaedia Britannica* for the years 1985–1990.

Year	SUPERPOWERS	MAJOR POWERS	BUFFER STATES	REMAINDER STATES	MIDDLE EAST	WORLD TOTAL
1986	$3,998,444 34.07%	$3,620,661 30.85%	$3,050,433 25.99%	$620,893 5.29%	$446,678 3.81%	$11,737,109 100.00%
1987	$5,595,490 41.70%	$3,666,870 27.32%	$3,085,606 22.99%	$628,524 4.68%	$443,121 3.30%	$13,419,611 100.00%
1988	$5,840,350 42.62%	$3,630,080 26.49%	$3,169,420 23.13%	$642,288 4.69%	$421,954 3.08%	$13,704,092 100.00%
1989	$6,578.450 41.87%	$4,023,890 25.61%	$4,024,634 25.62%	$654,498 4.17%	$429,442 2.73%	$15,710,914 100.00%
1990	$6,986,176 40.34%	$4,665,876 26.94%	$4,659,261 26.90%	$671,910 3.88%	$334,758 1.93%	$17,317,981 100.00%

Table 13. Chronological Data on Gross National Product. The data (in millions of dollars) are applicable as of three years before the publication date. Source: Yearbooks of the *Encyclopaedia Britannica* for the years 1986–1990.

Year	SUPERPOWERS	MAJOR POWERS	BUFFER STATES	REMAINDER STATES	MIDDLE EAST	WORLD TOTAL
1986	$453,345 55.83%	$166,932 20.56%	$103,646 12.76%	$27,639 3.40%	$60,507 7.45%	$812,069 100.00%
1987	$475,154 58.54%	$149,228 18.38%	$96,214 11.85%	$30,348 3.74%	$60,507 7.49%	$811,737 100.00%
1988	$497,100 59.51%	$136,165 16.30%	$101,133 12.11%	$32,703 3.92%	$68,172 8.16%	$835,273 100.00%
1989	$540,800 61.42%	$133,113 15.12%	$103,987 11.81%	$34,393 3.92%	$68,266 7.75%	$880,599 100.00%
1990	$599,200 58.69%	$181,198 17.75%	$137,722 13.49%	$38,540 3.77%	$64,296 6.30%	$1,020,956 100.00%

Table 14. Chronological Data on Military Spending. The data (in millions of dollars) are applicable as of three years before the publication date. Source: Yearbooks of the *Encyclopaedia Britannica* for the years 1986–1990.

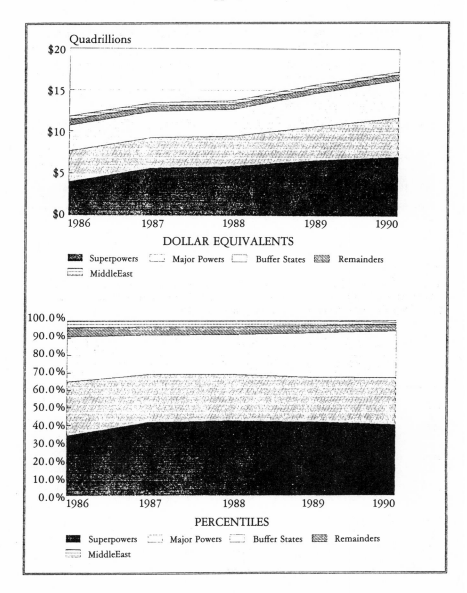

Figure 22. Chronological Distribution of Gross National Product. Source: Yearbooks of the *Encyclopaedia Britannica* for the years 1986–1990.

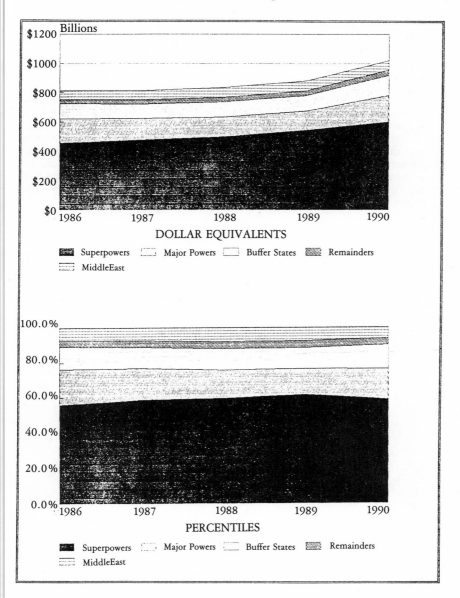

DOLLAR EQUIVALENTS

Superpowers   Major Powers   Buffer States   Remainders
MiddleEast

PERCENTILES

Superpowers   Major Powers   Buffer States   Remainders
MiddleEast

Figure 23. Chronological Distribution of Military Spending. Source: Yearbooks of the *Encyclopaedia Britannica* for the years 1985–1990.

the salient powers and buffers increased only about 1 percent, corresponding to a similar decrease for the remainder states.

Military Spending

The reported data on military spending (also representing conditions three years earlier than the publication data) show some fluctuation during this period, probably more due to the reporting criteria than to actual spending. Still, for the remainder states, it remained in the 10 to 11 percent range, with seven-tenths or so of that being spent in the Middle East. And it must be noted that three major wars occurred in that region during the period covered by the data: the Soviet occupation of Afghanistan, the Iran-Iraqi war, and the Israeli invasion of Lebanon. In all, the salient powers have even less to worry about as time progresses. Their clout continues to mount, yet seems to remain in geopolitical equilibrium.

Notes

Chapter 1. The Argument

1. Because of the variable spending of the dollar or its equivalent in local currency, it is impossible to establish a specific value that would be useful for all countries. However, even where the cost of living is inexpensive, $500 per year per person of a nation's GNP doesn't go very far. Among the buffer states only Bolivia, Indonesia, Nepal, Pakistan, and Tokelau have GNPs lower than $500 per person (as do China and India), and most of those are borderline cases of buffer states. But among the remainder states, beyond the Middle East, GNPs below $500 are the rule more than the exception.

2. Ruth Leger Sivard, ed., *World Military and Social Expenditures 1987–1988* (Washington, D.C.: World Priorities, 1987), pp. 29–31.

3. *Ibid.* The closest thing to a war among the salient powers and buffer states in the last 30 years, excluding the Falkland Islands campaign in 1983, was the Sino-Soviet border clash in 1969, which resulted in approximately 1,000 fatalities. The current border despute between India and Pakistan could erupt into war and in theory bring the long period of stability to an end. But such a war would remain local and not effect the other salient powers and buffer states significantly.

4. *Ibid.,* p. 28.

Chapter 2. Geopolitics as Science and Art

1. Paul Kennedy, *The Rise and Fall of the Great Powers* (New York: Random House, 1987), pp. 515.

2. Book review by Lee D. Olvey, *Parameters,* June 1988, pp. 111–113. In the review, trading on Paul Kennedy's expression "imperial overstretch," Olvey suggested that Kennedy might have fallen into the trap of "historical overstretch." That is, the current parameters operating in international relations do not necessarily portend a replay of the fatal errors of previous world powers.

3. The *World Factbook 1987* (Washington, D.C.: Central Intelligence Agency, 1987). There are no tables in this book. Data must be extracted from the narrative text accorded each country. The percentages for the four groups on all five statistics did not vary by more than two percentage points compared to the *1987 Britannica Book of the Year,* and much of that minor difference can be attributed to different effective dates of the source data.

Chapter 3. The Elements of National Power

1. Alfred T. Mahan, *The Influence of Sea Power Upon History 1660–1783* (Boston: Little, Brown, 1890), pp. 28–88.

2. Frederick H. Hartmann, *The Relations of Nations,* Sixth Edition (New York: Macmillan, 1983), pp. 43–64. Hartmann occupies the Alfred Thayer Mahan chair at the U.S. Naval War College, Newport, Rhode Island. Mahan's elements were: (1) geographical position, (2) physical conformation, (3) extent of territory, (4) number of population, (5) national character, and (6) character of government. Mahan portrayed military power, at least the seapower facet of military power, as the product or result of his six elements. Beyond this, the only major difference in the two lists is the addition of technology.

3. Richard W. Turk, *The Ambiguous Relationship: Theodore Roosevelt and Alfred Thayer Mahan* (Westport, Connecticut: Greenwood, 1987), pp. 7–8 and elsewhere.

4. Letter to J.K. Bluntschli, December 11, 1880.

5. Ross Terrill, "China and the World: Self Reliance or Interdependence?" *Foreign Affairs,* January 1977, pp. 295–305. In general, China has demonstrated a history of absorbing her conquerors over a period of many generations, a trend which reappears today as so-called "Chinese Communism" gradually fades into a run-of-the-mill, quasi-dictatorial government insofar as any government can exercise control over more than a billion people.

6. U.S. Department of Commerce, *International Economic Indicators* (Washington, D.C.: Department of Commerce, June 1983), pp. 19, 21–22. From 1970 to 1982, U.S. exports rose from 42.1 to 212.2 billion dollars; imports, 40.4 to 224.0 billion, a sixfold increase in 12 years.

7. *Facts on File,* December 2–8, 1973, p. 1001, and January 1–12, 1974, p. 1. Kissinger's veiled warning in late 1973 was followed by an explicit warning by Schlesinger early in 1974.

8. To be fair, an investigative report published in Norway cited that machine tool companies in France, West Germany, Italy, Japan, Great Britain, Norway, and possibly the United States, all sold similar technology to the Soviet Union and China and have been doing so for at least ten years. *The New York Times,* October 22, 1987, p. D2.

9. Richard F. Starr, ed., *Yearbook on International Communist Affairs 1988* (Stanford University, Stanford, California: Hoover Institute Press, 1988), pp. xii–xxix.

Chapter 4. Anvils, Swords and the Pen

1. A number of references are available on this point, among them: Donald L. Davidson, *Nuclear Weapons and the American Culture* (Boulder, Colorado: Westview, 1984); Daniel Ford [Executive Director of the Union of Concerned Scientists], *The Button* (New York: Simon & Schuster, 1985); Joseph Nye, Jr., *Nuclear Ethics* (New York: Free Press, 1986); and William V. O'Brien and John Langan, *The Nuclear Dilemma: The Just War Tradition* (Lexington, Massachusetts: Heath, 1986). The point is also addressed in the orthodox military literature, for example James L. Carney, "Is It Ever Moral to Push the Button?" *Parameters,* March 1988, pp. 73–87.

2. The books (but not the article) cited in the previous note all touch on this subject. The essays in *The Nuclear Dilemma* are the strongest.

3. *The History of Herodotus,* Volume 6, *Great Books of the Western World* (Chicago: Encyclopaedia Britannica, Inc., 1952), pp. 281–282.

4. Theodore H. White, *Breach of Faith: The Fall of Richard Nixon* (New York: Atheneum, 1975), pp. 22–23.

5. See "Who Has the Bomb?" *Newsweek,* December 5, 1983, pp. 56–57, and Rod Nordland, "The Bombs in the Basement," *Newsweek,* July 11, 1988. The first article lists the known possessors of thermonuclear weapons and those likely to obtain it by 1989. The second article confirms the predictions. The known nuclear powers: United States, USSR, United Kingdom, France, China, India, Israel, South Africa, and Pakistan. Ten others may have the capability.

6. *New World Dictionary of the American Language* (Englewood Cliffs, New Jersey: Prentice Hall, 1987), p. 491.

7. Robert B. Downs, *Books That Changed the World* (New York: New American Library, 1956), especially pp. 7–16. This book has been revised and expanded.

8. Hans Kohn, *American Nationalism* (New York: Collier, 1961), pp. 19–20.

9. Carl Sandburg, *Abraham Lincoln: The War Years,* Volume II (New York: Harcourt, Brace & World, 1939), p. 201.

10. See Mao Tse-tung, *Selected Works,* 4 volumes (New York: International, 1954).

Chapter 5. The Powers That Be

1. The custom was always preceded by a vote, not always in the affirmative. This particular desert was served only at lunch, a meal that the plebes (freshmen) rarely ate at other than a sitting position of attention. Yet if a plebe won the contest, he was allowed to eat his winnings in peace, so to speak, and was never given any cause to later regret the turn of fortune.

Chapter 6. The Anatomy of War

1. Carl Von Clausewitz, *On War,* edited and translated by Michael Howard and Peter Paret (Princeton, New Jersey: Princeton University Press, 1976), pp. 77, 93–94.

2. Based on correspondence with Colonel Harry G. Summers, Jr., while he was assigned as a professor at the U.S. Army War College. The proposed addition made it as far as the secretary of the Army's desk. Summers is now retired and is presently the military editor for the *Los Angeles Times.*

3. Clausewitz, *On War,* pp. 105, 139.

4. Perhaps the best-known writer in this regard is the late Barbara Tuchmann. See "An Inquiry into the Persistence of Unwisdom in Government," *Parameters,* March 1980, pp. 1–9. The article was based on the Sol Feinstone Lecture given at the United States Military Academy by Mrs. Tuchmann, October 24, 1979. The central idea of the lecture was one of the main themes in her subsequent book *The Praise of Folly.* A related essay is her "The Decline of a Nation," *New York Times Magazine,* September 20, 1987, pp. 52–54.

5. Thucydides, *The History of the Peloponnesian War,* Volume 6, *Great Books of the Western World,* p. 403. This speech, according to Thucydides, was given by Pericles after the Athenians had twice suffered severe reverses.

6. The Naval War College. Army veteran and noted author Josiah Bunting III was instrumental in adding it to the curriculum.

7. "The 'Winds of Death,'" *Newsweek,* January 16, 1989, pp. 22–25.

8. *Ibid.,* pp. 24–25.

9. For example, see Harry G. Summers, Jr., *On Strategy: The Vietnam War in Context* (Carlisle Barracks, Pennsylvania: Strategic Studies Institute, 1981), especially pp. 53–56. The United States completely misread the guerrilla tactics used by the insurgents as a form of ideological "warfare," rather than just what they were—a means of wearing down the insurgents' opponents until more conventional tactics could be employed decisively.

Chapter 7. Culminating Points: When Reach Exceeds Grasp

1. U.S. Army Field Manual 100-5 *Operations*, May 1977, p. 181.

2. *Ibid.*, p. 182.

3. Clausewitz, *On War*, p. 572.

4. *Ibid.*, p. 570. Emphasis is in the original.

5. Bruce Catton, *Never Call Retreat*, Volume II of the *Centennial History of the Civil War* (Garden City, New York: Doubleday, 1974), p. 108.

6. Henry Steele Commanger, ed., *The Blue and the Grey: The Story of the Civil War as Told by Participants* (New York: Fairfax, 1982), p. 637.

7. Bruce Catton, *Gettysburg: The Final Fury* (Garden City, New York: Doubleday, 1974), p. 108.

8. FM 100-5, *Operations*, p. 182.

9. "World Wars," *Encyclopaedia Britannica* (Chicago: Encyclopaedia Brittanica, Inc., 1973), Volume 23, p. 710. Another objective of the campaign was to open a supply route to Russia. The primary author of this plan was Sir Winston Churchill, who would attempt to repeat the mistake in World War II by advocating an envelopment of Germany through the "soft underbelly of Europe." As the campaign in Italy proved, Europe had no such thing as a "soft underbelly," though the failing in no way detracts from the reputation earned by this great and good man.

10. Arthur J. Marder, *From Dreadnought to Scarpa Flow* (London: Oxford University Press, 1965), pp. 260–267. The British lost the element of surprise by a sustained but ineffective naval bombardment of the forts and then proceeded to commit an almost endless sequence of blunders. One of these blunders was to publish British military dispositions in various newspapers. The British tendency to this type of error continues and was repeated during the Falkland Islands campaign. See Harry D. Train, II (Admiral, USN, retired), "An Analysis of the Falkland/Malvinas Island Campaign," *Naval War College Review*, Winter 1987, pp. 33–50. The error added to the casualties.

11. "The Soldier's Faith," *Speeches by Oliver Wendell Holmes* (Boston: Little, Brown, 1934), p. 59. In the same essay, Holmes argued, "For high and dangerous action teaches us to believe as right beyond dispute things for which our doubting minds are slow to find words of proof. Out of heroism grows faith in the worth of heroism."

12. Clausewitz, *On War*, pp. 105, 139.

13. T.E. Lawrence, *Seven Pillars of Wisdom* (New York: Doubleday, 1926), p. 1. Some editions of this book do not paginate separately the front material. The quoted passage is from the second paragraph of the first page of the main text.

14. B.H. Liddell Hart, *Strategy*, Second Revised Edition (New York: Praeger, 1967), p. 372.

Chapter 8. The Flawed Perspective of a Good War

1. The key word here is *decisively*. In the Pacific theater, the battle of the Coral Sea (May 3–8, 1942) delayed but did not stop the Japanese advance toward New Guinea.

Similarly, the heroic defense of Bataan and Corregidor only delayed the Japanese conquest of Luzon. And the famed Doolittle air raid on Tokyo was a morale builder, but it inflicted only negligible damage.

2. Vincent J. Esposito, ed., *The West Point Atlas of American Wars, Volume II 1900–1953* (New York: Praeger, 1959), maps 42–45, 53–55. [This book is not paginated; all text is linked to map sequence numbers.] The maximum percentage was calculated by multiplying German army groups by months on the front lines. For the four-year period May 1941–May 1945, the Germans maintained an average of more than four army groups on the eastern front. On the western front, the average was slightly less than two (for 11 months), to which must be added German forces in Italy. The approximate 9-to-1 ratio (in combat man-months) is subject to army group strengths, but the length of the eastern front was on the order of 700 to 1,000 miles, while the western front ranged between 70 and 250 miles (and that for only a fifth of the time). Moreover, Great Britain accounted for roughly one-third of the forces on the western front. Finally, according to B.H. Liddell Hart [*History of the Second World War* (New York: Putnam, 1970), p. 559], the Germans had only 100 tanks and 570 serviceable aircraft to throw at the entire western front spearhead, giving the Allies at least a 10-to-1 ratio in both weapon types.

3. *Ibid.*, maps 113–114, 152–165. The data here are less reliable and in the last year of the war, particularly with the campaign in the Philippines, the U.S. ratio of combat man-months increased through remaining in the minority.

4. U.S. forces operating against the Japanese on the Asian mainland were highly publicized—for example, the 5307th Provisional Unit (Merrill's Maurauders)—but their contribution to the war effort was minor compared to the British. Merrill's unit was largely decimated before it reached its objective, primarily due to disease and the environment. One crusty old sergeant in that unit was reported as yelling out: "Where the hell are the other 5,306 units!" General Stilwell, operating in China, did not have any significant U.S. forces with him.

5. Samuel Eliot Morison, *The Two-Ocean War* (Boston: Little, Brown, 1963), pp. 497, 501–503, 505, 510–511. Japan started the war with 6,000,000 tons of shipping, built 3,300,000 tons more and captured another 800,000 tons, for a total of 10,100,000 tons. In three years she lost 75 percent of this tonnage.

6. Alan S. Milward, *Economy and Society, 1939–1945* (Berkeley, California: University of California Press, 1979), p. 74. By the end of the war, the United States had built 5,424 merchant ships (2,000 in the year 1944 alone) and approximately 71,000 naval vessels of all types, most of them smaller vessels and landing craft but including more than 2,000 capital warships and submarines.

7. Richard M. Leighton, "The American Arsenal Policy in World War II," in Dan R. Beaver, ed., *Some Pathways in Twentieth Century History* (Detroit: Wayne State University Press, 1969), p. 222.

8. Maurice Matloff, "The 90-Division Gamble," in Kent Roberts Greenfield, ed., *Command Decisions* (Washington, D.C.: U.S. Government Printing Office, 1959), pp. 365–382. It was believed that to mobilize more divisions or to mobilize the 90 divisions before the summer of 1944 would have been counterproductive to the economy in the long run.

9. "Berlin," *Encyclopaedia Britannica*, Volume 3, p. 516. It is true that on peak days the tonnage airlifted exceeded, by way of example, that shipped by air to Stalingrad during the eastern front turning point in World War II (December 1942). However, airlifting of supplies in the middle of intense combat is far more difficult than doing so at airports in peacetime.

10. *Memoirs by Harry S Truman*, Volume 2, *Years of Trial and Hope* (Garden

City, New York: Doubleday, 1956), pp. 331–348. Prior to the attack by North Korea, Secretary of State Dean Acheson had stated that Korea was beyond the sphere of American interests. After the attack, Truman changed his mind. As for the continuation of the war into North Korea, MacArthur was given explicit permission to do so but only to crush the North Korean army. Once China entered the war — and there is ample evidence that MacArthur discounted the intelligence reports to this effect — the United States never thought through the consequences. MacArthur was relieved for advocating war with China, *not* to continue fighting the Chinese in North Korea.

11. Dwight D. Eisenhower, *Mandate for Change* (Garden City, New York: Doubleday, 1963), pp. 180–181.

12. "Korean War," *Encyclopaedia Britannica,* Volume 13, pp. 467–471. North Korea's army had 130,000 men (of whom 25,000 were seasoned veterans) but only 150 T-34 tanks, 180 World War II aircraft, and essentially no navy. The U.S.–U.N.–S.K. forces grew to over 200,000 supported by overwhelming numbers of tanks, aircraft and ships. However, the Chinese added at least 400,000 troops to the 100,000 North Korean survivors.

13. Bernard Brodie, *War and Politics* (New York: Macmillan, 1973), p. 89. [MacArthur hearings, part 2, p. 732.] General Bradley, testifying before Congress, said: "Red China is not the powerful nation seeking to dominate the world. In the opinion of the Joint Chiefs of Staff, this strategy [MacArthur's insistence on carrying the war into China] would involve us in the wrong way, at the wrong place, at the wrong time, with the wrong enemy." But when General Matthew B. Ridgway assumed command in Korea, he had to prod the Pentagon into giving him a mission statement. [Maureen Mylander, *The Generals* (New York: Dial, 1974), pp. 188.]

14. Richard M. Leighton, "The Cuban Missile Crisis of 1962," in Eston T. White, ed., *Studies in Defense* (Washington, D.C.: National Defense University, 1983), pp. 153–164. The United States included a *quid pro quo* offer to remove U.S. missiles in Turkey (which the United States had already planned to do).

15. Just what costs should be included in the Vietnam accounting is subject to debate. If the average annual defense budget for the period is taken to be $100,000M (in 1968 dollars) and only one-fourth of it is attributed to Vietnam for the ten-year period, the cost would be $250,000M. However, to this must be added the veteran's administration costs, additional retirement funding for the period 1964–2014, and numerous other costs, all of which would easily increase the dollar figure by 20 percent (to $300,000M). That kind of money could nearly have eliminated the national debt at the time.

16. Harry G. Summers, Jr., *On Strategy: The Vietnam War in Context,* pp. 59–66. Summers suggests that about the only way the United States could have prevailed in South Vietnam, without a decisive war against North Vietnam, would have been to maintain a leak-proof armed barrier around the entire country.

17. Lawrence M. Greenberg, "The US Dominican Intervention: Success Story," *Parameters,* December 1987, pp. 18–29.

18. This issue has not been settled, but a number of factors support the argument that the concern over Soviet escalation was largely a smokescreen. First, the war occurred during the era of detente. Second, Israel settled for equilibrium on the Syrian front in order to concentrate on Egypt. Third, the Soviets had been run out of Egypt a few years earlier. Fourth, the United States had just ended its Vietnam involvement and was not in a position to continue supporting Israel in an extended war against Egypt. Fifth, the Soviet Union would have had a hard time projecting force into Syria and especially Egypt.

19. "The Politics of Blame," *Newsweek,* January 9, 1984, pp. 18–20.

20. See "The Contras' Civil War," *Newsweek,* May 16, 1988, p. 38.

21. The generally accepted figure for United States military fatalities in Vietnam is slightly over 58,000 and in Korea nearly 34,000. However, the exact proportion that were killed in Korea before the initial crossing of the 38th parallel is not certain. Assuming that 4,000 died beforehand, this leaves 30,000, which added to 58,000 is 88,000 plus the casualties in Lebanon. The number of Allied casualties, particularly South Koreans and South Vietnamese, is more difficult to calculate. The records are poor and there is no telling how many would have been killed — perhaps more, perhaps fewer — if the United States had not intervened to the extent she did.

22. James T. Westwood, "The Soviet Union and the Southern Sea Route," *Naval War College Review,* January-February 1982, pp. 54–67. See also the followup article by the same author in the same journal, "Soviet Maritime Strategy and Transportation," November-December 1985, pp. 42–49.

23. For example, see V.D. Sokolovskiy, Marshal of the Soviet Union, "The Role of Strategy in Military Science," in Anthony W. Gray, Jr., and Eston T. White, eds., *Military Strategy* (Washington, D.C.: National Defense University, 1983), pp. 250–252.

24. Paul Kennedy, *The Rise and Fall of the Great Powers,* pp. 416, 521.

Chapter 9. The Rise and Limits of Terrorism

1. In the United States alone, more than 50,000 deaths per year are the result of highway accidents, of which at least 40 percent are attributable to drunk drivers. Ten percent of these 20,000 fatalities is 2,000. The average annual number of fatalities from international terrorism is roughly equal to this number, and in most years only a few of the victims are U.S. citizens. Data on terrorism are computed annually by the *National Travel Report* (because most acts of international terrorism in the victims are in transit). The April 14, 1989, edition of the *Wall Street Journal* (p. A1) reported the 1988 data to be 1,789 casualties, of which 658 were fatalities. The U.S. "share" was 192, most of them fatalities from the blowing up of Pan Am Flight 103 in mid–December 1988. These totals exceeded the 1987 totals by 3 percent. Thus, making allowance for another 10 percent casualties occurring in other than transportation situations, the annual total is roughly 2,000 per year.

2. Sandburg, *Abraham Lincoln: The War Years,* Volume I, p. 33. In *The Prairie Years,* Volume II (p. 192), Sandburg related that on the day John Brown was hanged, Lincoln gave a speech that supported the hanging but used the incident to warn the South that equal violence on their part might prove equally disastrous.

3. Herman Melville, *Moby Dick,* Volume 48, *Great Books of the Western World,* p. 136.

4. "William Bligh," *Encyclopaedia Britannica,* Volume 3, p. 775. The second mutiny occurred when Bligh was the governor of New South Wales. He was sent back to England under arrest, but once there, released. Deputy Governor George Johnson and others were subsequently found guilty of conspiracy.

5. See the preface in Charles Nordhoff and James Normal Hall, *The Bounty Trilogy* (Boston: Little, Brown, 1951), pp. vi–vii. Nordhoff and Hall's research was meticulous, but for obvious reasons the account of the facts depended primarily on the statements of the sole survivor.

6. Mao Tse-tung, *Selected Works,* Volume 2 (1937–1938), pp. 119–156, 222.

7. Robert B. Asprey, *War in the Shadows,* Volume 2 (Garden City, New York: Doubleday, 1975), pp. 781–795.

8. *Facts on File,* May 2, 1980, p. 323.

Chapter 10. *Whys and Wherefores*

1. Bruce Catton, *The Coming Fury* (Garden City, New York: Doubleday, 1961), p. 439. General Scott, of course, was right.

2. *Ibid.,* p. 439.

3. Roy P. Basler, ed., *The Collected Works of Abraham Lincoln* (New Brunswick, New Jersey: Rutgers University Press, 1953), Volume IV, pp. 532.

4. *Ibid.,* Volume 5, pp. 388. Emphasis in the original.

5. *Ibid.,* pp. 433–436. The legal reason was that Lincoln did not have the Constitutional authority to free the slaves in states loyal to, and hence part of, the Union.

6. It would be difficult to prove this point except as can be inferred from Sandburg's biography of Lincoln's war years taken as an entity.

7. Robert B. Asprey, *War in the Shadows,* especially Volume I.

8. Donald E. Nuechterlein, "National Interest and Foreign Policy," *Foreign Service Journal,* Volume 54, July 1977, pp. 6–8, 27.

Chapter 11. *Expanding National Power on a Fixed Globe*

1. See the *Wall Street Journal,* March 18, 1988, p. 23. The report said Japan's per capita GNP reached $19,640 per person as of December 31, 1987, exceeding the per capita GNP of the United States for the first time. With a population of 122,620,000, this means a GNP of 2.4 trillion, higher than the Soviet Union's 1985 figure but not necessarily higher than its 1987 GNP.

2. From the data in Table 2, the GNPs of Algeria ($58,040M), Egypt ($37,700M), Nigeria ($66,210M), and South Africa ($59,910M) add to $221,860M, which is 5.3 percent of that of the United States ($4,221,750M).

3. For example, see "A Victory for Chou—and Moderation," *Time,* February 3, 1975, pp. 22–32.

Chapter 12. *Potential Sources of Disequilibrium*

1. Peter Almond, "Nuclear Material Security Flawed," *The Washington Times,* November 10, 1987, p. A3. Given the lax security, the challenge of developing and emplacing a weapon as suggested would not be too difficult.

2. For example, see "Cracks in the Soviet Facade," *Newsweek,* March 14, 1988, pp. 26–28. But the map included in the article gainsays the concern. The various ethnic groups are highly segregated and spread out over a very large land mass.

3. An interesting account of Tsar Nicholas' indifference and almost childish innocence appears in Robert K. Massie, *Nicholas and Alexandria* (New York: Atheneum, 1967). That account also quotes the assessment of Tsar Nicholas by Winston Churchill written at the time of the revolution, a portrait as sympathetic as Harry Truman was toward Herbert Hoover and the latter's inadequate attempts to deal with the depression from 1929 to 1932.

Chapter 13. *Malaise Versus Maladministration in the Defense Infrastructure*

1. One of the best sources of self-criticism within the defense establishment has been the "View from the Fourth Estate" section in *Parameters,* the Journal of the U.S.

Army War College. Most issues have republished an article from the press critical of the defense establishment. Authors have included Samuel P. Huntington, John Kenneth Galbraith, George Kennan, and Arthur Schlesinger, Jr. Other authors have included less well known military writers if the criticism was particularly biting. For a while, the selection of the articles republished then shifted to authors considered "friends of the court," and even at that, the feature was omitted from some issues. Fortunately, however, it appears that the original practice is being restored.

2. "Jeannette Rankin," *Encyclopaedia Britannica,* Volume 18, page 1163.

3. Richard Harwell, *Washington,* an abridgment of Douglas Southall Freeman, *George Washington* (New York: Scribner, 1968), pp. 594, 667 & 689. John Rutledge was the nominee. He had been one of the original Supreme Court justices but resigned to become Chief Justice of North Carolina.

4. Eston T. White and Val E. Hendrix, *Defense Acquisition and Logistics Management* (Washington, D.C.: National Defense University, 1984), pp. 93–97.

5. This is a matter of public record in the Utilities Account section of the OMA (Operations & Maintenance Army) of the annual defense budget.

6. Two of the prime movers were the late General George Brown (U.S. Air Force), at the time Chairman of the Joint Chiefs of Staff, and General Edward C. Meyer, at the time Army Chief of Staff. See the latter's article "The JCS—How Much Reform Is Needed?" *Armed Forces Journal International,* April 1982, pp. 82–90.

7. Don M. Snider, "DOD Reorganization: Part 1, New Imperatives," *Parameters,* September 1987, pp. 88–100. Like the original Act establishing the Department of Defense in 1947, the necessary clout to manifest all the objectives of this Act was not fully conveyed to the Secretary of Defense, but the groundwork has been laid to do so in later years.

8. The count of defense staffers in the Washington, D.C., area is from the April 1989 Department of Defense telephone directory. When clerical and contract personnel are added (and a considerable slice of defense administration is accomplished by contract), and then that number is factored for all the intermediate headquarters, the total would probably reach 500,000. For the Parkinson reference, see C. Northcote Parkinson, *Parkinson's Law* (New York: Houghton Mifflin, 1957). Parkinson developed a number of related "laws" pertaining to management, many of which addressed the phenomenon of increasing size with decreasing responsibilities. His original example was the British Admiralty between the years 1914 and 1928, when the number of ships decreased from 62 to 20, while the number of Admiralty officials increased from 2,000 to 3,569 and dockyard officials and clerks went from 3,249 to 4,558.

9. Eston T. White and Val E. Hendrix, *Defense Acquisition and Logistics Management,* p. 65.

10. *Ibid.,* p. 59.

11. "Fighting Smart, Not Rich," *Newsweek,* November 14, 1988, pp. 24–25. The current term is "competitive strategy." In addition to the technological edge, this posture entails special tactics to disrupt Soviet control.

12. Gregg Easterbrook, "Big Dumb Rockets," *Newsweek,* August 11, 1987, pp. 46–60.

13. Michael Wines, "Conflict of Interest Rules Ignored, Pentagon Aides Tell House Panel," *New York Times,* June 7, 1988, p. A12. See also "A Big Gun Aims at Defense Companies," *Business Week,* April 25, 1988, pp. 100–103. Robert C. Bonner, U.S. Attorney for the Central District of California, has accumulated 70 convictions against defense contractor fraud with a 98 percent success rate overall.

14. Sandburg, *Abraham Lincoln: The War Years,* Volume 1, pp. 305, 426–435.

15. "Overheard," *Newsweek,* August 24, 1987, p. 11. The story was reported by U.S. Attorney Rudolph Guiliani, following an FBI "sting operation."

16. "It's Hard to Flunk a Weapons Test," *Newsweek,* September 7, 1987, p. 18. On July 20, 1988, a General Accounting Office report concluded that rigged testing of weapons systems had become almost routine.

17. The film was *The Private War of Major Benson.*

18. Bernard Brodie, *War and Politics* (New York: Macmillan, 1973), p. 479.

19. *Ibid.,* p. 89.

20. David H. Hackworth, "Bring Back Blood-and-Guts Patton!" *The Washington Post,* June 7, 1987, p. B2, reprinted in *Parameters,* Sept. 1987, pp. 113–115.

Chapter 14. Parameters and Policy

1. Statistical data extracted and compiled from the *Britannica Book of the Year* (Chicago: Encyclopaedia Britannica, 1988), pp. 860–865. The United States and the Soviet Union account for 55.5 percent of the world total of military exports ($20.4 billion of a total of $36.7 billion). Of the remaining $14.3 billion, France accounts for $4.3 billion, or 26.4 percent.

2. "A World Divided: Free and Not So Free," *U.S. News & World Report,* February 4, 1980, pp. 26–27. The breakdown was 51 "free" nations (37 percent of the world population), 55 nations "partly free" (21.3 percent), 55 "not free" nations (41.7 percent).

3. Hartmann, *International Relations,* pp. 463–465.

4. "The Spy War Is Heating Up," *Newsweek,* August 21, 1989, p. 28.

5. The number of tanks destroyed or disabled was in excess of 2,000, according to U.S. Army Command & General Staff College studies published during the time and used as training material for their courses.

6. "Saudis Denounce Iran Conspiracy," *The New York Times,* August 26, 1987, pp. A1, A6.

7. The comment was published in the instructor notes for the training exercise focusing on a limited war in Israel (code-named *Sadia* at the time).

8. Eston T. White, *Natural and Energy Resources* (Washington, D.C.: National Defense University, 1985), pp. 91–99. The metals at issue are in the platinum group and chromium. Besides the USSR, the United Kingdom supplies some platinum, while the Philippines, Zimbabwe, and Yugoslavia supply some chromium. Most of the manganese used by the U.S. also comes from South Africa, but the alternative suppliers are France, Australia, and Gabon. Strategic reserves further ameliorate the danger of a cutoff.

9. Abul Kasim Mansur (pseudonym), "The Crisis in Iran: Why the US Ignored a Quarter Century of Warning," *Armed Forces Journal International,* January 1979, pp. 26–33.

10. For an analysis of the projected intensity, and insanity, of modern global warfare, see Richard A. Gabriel, *No More Heroes: Madness and Psychiatry in War* (Hill and Wang, 1987).

Chapter 15. Nuclear Defense

1. The reader is referred to the books cited in note 1 for Chapter 4.

2. The announced shift in the Soviet defense policy may or may not be prop-

aganda. When Secretary of Defense Frank Carlucci visited the Soviet Union (August 1, 1988), he stated that he saw no real evidence of the change, basing his conclusion of the disposition of Soviet forces.

3. Daniel Ford, *The Button,* pp. 168–190.

4. In addition to the reasons described here, John Keegan, in *The Mask of Command,* offers another. He suggests that the time between events and possible retaliation has become too short to favor rational decision making, and that SDI would perforce stretch this reaction time sufficient to ameliorate the Dr. Strangelovian hero syndrome.

5. See S. Daggett and R. English, "Assessing Soviet Strategic Defense," *Foreign Policy,* Spring 1988, pp. 129–149.

Chapter 16. *Western Europe, Korea and Japan*

1. As reported in *Newsweek,* October 19, 1987, p. 7, the OJCS conducted a year-long exercise to evaluate the fighting capability of the United States and allies, taking into account the operational problems that the latter would face. But any scenario which presumes a NATO war would not escalate to nuclear war is a little naive. On the positive side, the results of the evaluation suggest the Soviet Union does not have the necessary three-to-one force ratio, either in actual numbers or by dint of extraordinary tactics, to prevail.

2. The literature on this subject is extensive. *Aviation Week,* in particular, tends to publish articles favorable to the process, for example in the March 5, 1984, issue, pp. 60–66. But whenever 16 countries agree to produce armaments on a unified basis, the expense will undoubtedly be enormous and the results meager for the funds invested.

3. The USSR and North Korea share some territorial water near Vladivostok, but it would be difficult to conduct war via the trans–Siberian railroad.

4. Meirion and Susie Harries, *Sheathing the Sword, The Demilitarization of Postwar Japan* (New York: Macmillan, 1987), pp. 307–312.

Chapter 17. *Middle East Flash Points*

1. In the training exercise, which was used for both the resident students and all nonresident students worldwide, Israel was code-named *Sadia,* but all other place names on the maps were actual. Included were several hundred pages on the analysis of the Yom Kippur war of 1973, the thrust of the exercises being to use tactics where outnumbered defenders could reduce the opponent's forces in sufficient measure before decisive conflict, that is (as discussed at length in Chapter 7), to move to the favorable side of the culminating point.

2. Throughout military history disease has claimed more lives than armaments, even in countries noted for relatively healthy conditions. Healthy conditions do not prevail in the Middle East. Foreigners living in this region can take extraordinary precautions in peacetime to reduce the prevalence of disease, but in wartime field operating conditions may not permit these precautions to be taken. The projected ratio of medical to combat casualties resulting from U.S. participation in a Middle East war are in part speculation but ratios as high as nine-to-one have been mentioned.

3. There are many articles on this matter. For example, see "A Questionable Policy; What Are the Administration's Goals in the Gulf?" *Newsweek,* July 1, 1987, p. 20. Even though this commitment put a strain on the defense budget, the

Administration avoided requesting additional funds lest it provide Congress with an opportunity to exercise a de facto legislative veto.

4. "Seven Minutes to Death," *Newsweek,* July 18, 1988, pp. 18–22.

5. Henry Kissinger, "Time to Talk with Iran," *Newsweek,* July 18, 1988, pp. 30–31.

Chapter 18. In the Crescents of Discontent

1. A good example is *Planning U.S. General Purpose Forces: Forces Related to Asia,* Congressional Budget Office, June 1977, SN 052-070-04122.6.

2. Richard W. Leopold, *The Growth of American Foreign Policy* (New York: Alfred A. Knopf, 1962), pp. 44–45.

3. See the *Department of State Bulletin,* May 7, 1978, pp. 52–54.

4. The depravity of events surrounding the Iran-contra scandal was noted in the final Congressional report issued November 18, 1988, in which the conclusions were more harsh than anticipated.

Chapter 19. Defense Against Terrorism

1. "The 'Winds of Death,'" *Newsweek,* pp. 22–25.

2. *Ibid.,* p. 25.

Chapter 20. The Dilemma of Armed Idleness

1. Clausewitz, *On War,* p. 122.

2. Most standard texts in psychiatry and psychology describe the symptoms of depression with consistency, including the several forms and intensities of it. Philosophical discussions of the significance of depression are less consistent, but one of the most insightful is Rollo May's *Power and Innocence* (New York: Norton, 1972). He makes the point that depression and subsequent violence can result from an inability or lack of opportunity to exercise mature power over one's own life. It may be the same for nations after many military failures, such as the United States has encountered since 1945.

3. John F. Lehman, Jr., *Command of the Seas: Building the 600 Ship Navy* (New York: Scribner, 1989), pp. 77–78, 423–424.

4. Richard M. Leighton. "The Cuban Missile Crisis of 1962," in Eston T. White, ed., *Studies in Defense* (Washington, D.C.: National Defense University, 1983), pp. 153–164. The Joint Chiefs of Staff had been unanimous in their recommendation for direct military action, though some wanted an invasion while others would have settled for air attacks to destroy the missiles and sites. To be fair, some civilian aides also recommended military action.

5. *Facts on File,* July 24, 1987, p. 533. Also see *Newsweek,* August 3, 1987, pp. 14–17, and *U.S. News & World Report,* August 3, 1987, p. 18.

6. "Is This Finally It for Meese?" *Newsweek,* April 11, 1988, pp. 34–37. It was.

7. Horace Knowles, ed., *Gentlemen, Scholars and Scoundrels: A Treasury of Harper's Magazine from 1850 to the Present* (New York: Harper & Row, 1959), p. 92.

8. The advertisements in which Mr. Iacocca unflinchingly accepted the blame for the improper automobile testing were run in several national news magazines in the July-August 1987 period.

9. Maureen Mylander, *The Generals,* pp. 188.

10. On November 18, 1988, a panel of the House Armed Services Committee, which had been assessing the senior service colleges for a year, concluded that the National Defense University, especially of the four, should include the economic, political, and diplomatic aspects of war more than it does.

Chapter 21. *Justice as the Moral Equivalent of Peace*

1. Will and Ariel Durant, *The Lessons of History* (New York: Simon and Schuster, 1968), p. 81.

2. "Commencement Address at American University in Washington," *Public Papers of Presidents of the United States John F. Kennedy 1963* (Washington, D.C.: U.S. Government Printing Office, 1964), p. 461.

3. "George Otis Shattuck — Answer to Resolutions of the Bar, Boston, May 29, 1897," *Speeches of Oliver Wendell Holmes,* p. 73.

4. *Schenck versus United States,* 249 U.S. 47 (1919).

5. In international law, the doctrine of justified war dates back to ancient times and was formalized by the Dutch jurist Hugo Grotius in the seventeenth century.

6. For example, see Meirion and Susie Harries, *Sheathing the Sword, The Demilitarization of Postwar Japan,* pp. 170–172ff.

7. Dean Acheson, *Present at the Creation* (New York: Norton, 1969), p. 926.

Appendix A. *Military Technology and Behemoths*

1. Gregg Easterbrook, "Sticker Shock: The Stealth Is a Bomb," *Newsweek,* January 23, 1989, pp. 20–22.

2. *Ibid.,* pp. 21–22.

3. Samuel Eliot Morison,· *The Two-Ocean War* (Boston: Little, Brown, 1963), p. 420ff. Actually, there was a sequence of three photographs, but the same ships appeared in all three.

4. Admiral Harry D. Train, II, "An Analysis of the Falkland/Malvinas Islands Campaign," *Naval War College Review,* Winter, 1987, pp. 33–50. The third-rate Argentine forces sunk 6 and severely damaged 18 other British ships. The losses would have been higher except for the fact the British commander [Rear Admiral John Woodward] was ordered to use tactics that would reduce if not eliminate any further loss of ships.

5. "A Tank in Shinning Armor," *Newsweek,* April 11, 1988, p. 51.

6. For example, see Frank Greve, "Dream Weapon a Nightmare," *The Philadelphia Inquirer,* May 2, 1982, reprinted in *Parameters,* Fall 1982, pp. 76–78.

7. See "A Start on Star Wars," *Newsweek,* February 8, 1988, pp. 30–32.

Appendix B. *Wars, Operations and Tactics*

1. For example, see Philip A. Crowl, "The Strategist's Short Catechism: Six Questions Without Answers," in Gray and White, *Military Strategy,* pp. 94–103.

2. For example, see Ronald Andidora, "The Autumn of 1944: Boldness Is Not Enough," *Parameters,* December 1987, pp. 71–80.

3. Dwight L. Adams and Clayton R. Newell, "Operational Art in the Joint and Combined Arenas," *Parameters,* June 1988, pp. 33–39.

4. A good example of this is Summers' book *On Strategy,* cited earlier. It is an excellent book. The point made here is that if the extension of the principles of war to operations, and even entire wars, is valid, then the principles should be restated in concise terms.

5. *Military Notes* (West Point, New York: U.S. Military Academy, 1954), p. 2.

6. Stephen E. Ambrose, *The Supreme Commander: The War Years of General Dwight D. Eisenhower* (Garden City, New York: Doubleday, 1969), p. 641.

7. Harry G. Summers, Jr., *On Strategy,* p. 1.

Appendix C. Mobilization as an Instrument of Deterrence

1. Jeffrey Record, *Beyond Military Reform: American Defense Dilemmas* (New York: Pergamon-Brassey's, 1988), Chapter 3, as reprinted ["Getting There"] in *Parameters,* June 1988, pp. 89–95.

2. See note 8 in Chapter 8.

3. This statement is based on personal experience of the author while participating in a substantial number of mobilization exercises at the Department of the Army level and in a reserve officer mobilization assignment in the Corps of Engineers. The surge funding requirements estimated during some of these exercises were astronomical, suggesting that a streamlined but centralized adjudication process would be indispensible.

4. The informally stated position of the Corps of Engineers on this matter is that properly funded, they would be willing to take on this responsibility but would do nothing to encourage or discourage it. The invitation to do so must be bona fide and unsolicited. The concept is entirely that of the writer, who discussed it briefly with two COE general officers (one of whom is now the Chief of Engineers). There were no further discussions, and as the writer is now in the retired reserve, there is no possible benefit to be obtained if the proposal were implemented.

Appendix D. Long-Term Defense Programming

1. Congress recently reduced military retired pay after 20 years of service from 50 percent of base pay to 40 percent, though on a linear scale it will still rise to 75 percent with 30 years of service. The provisions did not apply to any individual who had any prior or current military service at the time the legislation was enacted; hence it will be at least 20 years before any impact is felt in the defense budget.

2. See "Horror Stories," *Information WEEK,* November 3, 1986, and "Horror Stories Part II," *Information WEEK,* March 16, 1987.

3. The unfortunate problem with JOPES was that most of the 80 systems were in a state of disrepair or had questionable data or were in a form that made integration of the data bases essentially impossible. See "Know-How Versus Know-When Systems Integration," *Information Strategy,* Winter 1990.

Index

Boldface numbers indicate the first page of a table or figure.

A

Abuse of authority 111, 114
Accidental firing (of missiles) 133
Accuracy 178
Acheson, Dean (quoted) 174
Achilles *(Iliad)* 185
Acquired Immune Deficiency Syndrome (AIDS) 124
Act of war (declared or undeclared) 83, 94, 156–157
Adams, John Quincy 152
Adjudication 174, 192
Administration 112, 167
Admiralty (U.K.) 83
Afghan resistance movement *see* Muja-hedin
Afghanistan 8, **13, 26, 42,** 76; proxy war 124; Soviet invasion of 1, 8, 23, 76, **95,** 129, 210
Africa 5, **6, 13, 18,** 39, **42,** 66, 93–94, 97, 104, 119, 124, 148–150, 152; "horn" 150; nations 37, 86, 97, 106, 149–150; north 70; sub–Saharan 150
Agamemnon *(Iliad)* 185
Aggrandizement 1–2, 4–5, 8, 10–11, 21, 23, 25, 27, 37, **40, 42,** 50, 93, 98–99, 123, 128, 132, 146–147, 172; economic 1, 27, 174
Aggression, aggressors 21–23, 142
Ahab *(Moby Dick)* 82–83
Aides 164
Aircraft **24,** 72, 178, **179,** 181–182
Aircraft carriers 72, 178, 181
Air (fire) support 143–144, 146
Air Force 112, 114, 117, 197; Chief of Staff ix; Department of ix, **168**
Air strikes 163
Air War College vii

Airlift *see* Strategic lift
Airpower 186
Alaskan territories 152
Albania **13, 26, 40**
Alexander (of Macedonia) 25, 185
Algeria **13, 42,** 97
Alliance(s) 1, 4–6, 10, 21, **24,** 28, **40,**57, **68,** 87, 106, 122, 140, 142, 145, 149–151; *see also* ASEAN; NATO; Warsaw Pact
Allied powers (WWII) 66, **68, 71,** 72–74, **73, 95,** 173
Allies 96, 122
America 52, 135, 140–141; *see also* United States
American: commitments, priorities 119, 143; ethos 127; Indian wars 48, **68,** 91; servicemen 77, 112
American Samoa **13, 40**
American University 170
Americans 72, 75, 145, 195
Anaconda Plan (Civil War) 90
Andorra **13, 40**
Angola **13, 26, 42,** 77
Anguilla **13, 40,** 153
Antagonists 127
Antarctica 5, **13,** 23, 92
Anti-air weapons 137–139, 178, **179**
Anti-armor weapons 138–139, 179–180, 182
Antietem 32
Antigua and Barbuda **13, 42**
Antihegemony 99, 103
Antiterrorism 86
ANZUS (Australia, New Zealand, United States) Pact 123
Appropriations (Congressional) 113, 164
Arab sensitivities 143
Arab states 125

O